The Media, Politics and Public Life

GEOFFREY CRAIG

The Media, Politics and Public Life

GEOFFREY CRAIG

ALLEN&UNWIN

First published in 2004 by Allen & Unwin

Allen & Unwin
83 Alexander Street
Crows Nest NSW 2065
Australia
Phone: (61 2) 8425 0100
Fax: (61 2) 9906 2218
Email: info@allenandunwin.com
Web: www.allenandunwin.com

National Library of Australia
Cataloguing-in-Publication entry:

Craig, Geoffrey.
The media, politics and public life.

Bibliography.
Includes index.
ISBN 1 74114 124 9.

1. Mass media – Political aspects. I. Title.

302.23

Set in 10.25 on 13 pt Minion by Midland Typesetters,
Maryborough, Victoria
Printed by South Wind Productions, Singapore

10 9 8 7 6 5 4 3 2 1

Contents

Acknowledgements   vi
Preface   vii

Part One—Introduction
1 The media   3
2 Politics   24
3 The public   47

Part Two—The Media and Politics
4 The print media   69
5 The broadcast media   92
6 Political image and performance   112
7 Political information management   130

Part Three—Mediated Public Life
8 Opinion polls and public opinion   153
9 The nation and national identity   171
10 The governance of everyday life   192

References   208
Index   219

Acknowledgements

Writing is often a lonely activity, but many people have helped me during the production of this book. I also very much appreciate that the book could not have been written without the support of colleagues and friends over many years while I have taught, completed a PhD and been involved in other research projects. Thanks go to all those people, including my colleagues at Murdoch University, who have been so generous with their advice, encouragement, administrative assistance and friendship!

I thank Elizabeth Weiss from Allen & Unwin for her initial proposal of the text and her support throughout the production of the manuscript. I also appreciated the contributions from three readers who provided great encouragement and thorough, helpful advice in their reports on the draft manuscript.

Finally, and most importantly, I thank Wendy Parkins for all her encouragement and inspiration. Her love has supported me throughout the writing of this book and so much more. I thank Madeleine for her understanding that writing a book has placed demands on the time of her father, also for being such a wonderful big sister to Gabriel. Finally, a thank you to Gabriel for being such a good boy and for sleeping through the night!

Preface

The media, politics and public life are such familiar terrain for us: every
day we access news media to see, hear and read about the latest political event and the opinions of public figures. For most of us, exposure
to the news media is a routine activity, a backdrop to our everyday
lives—and yet it is a vital means by which we stay connected to public
life and it is a form of participation in public life, which would not exist
without the everyday involvement of 'the public'. The media, in this
sense, perform the quite extraordinary task of facilitating the public
culture. The media give life to public culture through the ways they
connect public figures to the public, through the ways they give organisations and individuals involvement in public life, through the ways
they provide a domain within which we make and experience the
reason, the values and the pleasures of public life.

While the media, politics and public life are familiar terrain, we
generally know little about how politicians and the news media
interact, we struggle to articulate the nature of the power of the media,
and we are unsure about our own status and roles in public life. Part
of this difficulty resides in the sheer complexity of the field of the
media, politics and public life: power relations occur within and across
institutions and organisations, myriad acts of communication from
voluminous governmental reports through to corridor gossip undergo
complex processes of transformation into news stories and images,
a plethora of divergent individual opinions stand in contrast to the
solidity of 'public opinion'. This book begins to address and explain this
kind of complexity, which I believe warrants greater levels of political

and media literacy. The quality of our public life will be improved by a greater understanding of the communicative work of journalists and politicians.

A central observation in this book is that public life is a mediated phenomenon. While public life is constituted by a great range of individuals, organisations and institutions, the issues, events and discussions of public life are given meaning through media discourse and representations. The media, then, are not 'outside' observers but rather they are now, and always have been, integral components of politics and public life. It follows that we must move beyond a way of thinking that opposes an 'authentic', unmediated politics and public life to an 'inauthentic', mediated politics and public life. This is not to argue that we cannot be critical of journalistic representations, the performances of politicians or the practices of 'spin doctors'.

The media, subsequently, are given a central focus here: I approach both politics and public life through a scrutiny of political and public communication. I examine different types of media, the practices of reporting and their organisational contexts, and the kinds of scrutiny the media provide of politics. I focus mainly on more conventional domains and forms of politics but I also locate the conduct and meanings of politics in the broader cultural contexts of public life. We are interested in politics, then, as part of a communicative exchange whereby politicians and other public figures use the media to gain and enhance their power and legitimacy and win public support.

The public are also an integral part of this communicative exchange. Books on politics and the media often sideline the importance of the public in political communication. If the public are considered at all they are relegated to passive onlookers rather than active participants in political communication. While I will investigate the legitimate concerns about the lack of involvement of the public in contemporary politics and public life, I will also re-establish the public, and their representations, as central components of political communication.

The complexity of public life informs our theoretical understanding of the term. I extend the conventional outline of the 'public sphere' that has informed many discussions about the public significance of the media and employ 'public life' to better capture the multiplicity of public domains and the fluidity of movement across such domains. While important features of the public sphere, such as rational forms of debate, remain central to the discussion, I outline a more heterogeneous public life which acknowledges its performative basis.

The complexity of the terrain of the media, politics and public life further suggests that any singular celebration or denunciation of the subject should be treated with suspicion. Certainly there is widespread social concern about the entanglements of politics and the media, the general performance levels of the news media, and the quality of debate in public life. Media academic scrutiny has been often critical, outlining a range of issues such as the declining levels of 'hard news' stories and investigative journalism with the corresponding rise of 'human-interest' news stories and 'infotainment'. Concern is also raised about the focus on 'image' and 'strategy' in political reportage at the expense of coverage of substantive issues, with the subsequent claim that such trends in reportage serve to further alienate the public from the political process. While there is substance to many of the criticisms about media and political relations and the quality of public debate, this book is informed by the belief that we require a more balanced appraisal of the contribution of the media to the political process and to public life, and that such an appraisal stems from a revised theoretical understanding of the functions of the media and the nature of public life. A promotion of the mediated and performative basis of public life suggests the legitimate importance of political image and of visual forms of communication. The theorisation of public life offered here also emphasises the centrality of the mass media in public formation, in contrast to charges that the media facilitate increased alienation in contemporary society. I argue that a value hierarchy that views tabloid and 'lifestyle' journalism as singularly 'trivial' and 'inconsequential' does not comprehend sufficiently the functions of contemporary media in the production of knowledges and identity formation.

This book analyses contemporary media, politics and public life, but I argue that such an analysis must be located within a historical framework. The media, politics and the structures of public life are historical phenomena that should be understood through an appreciation of processes of continuity and change. The importance of media technologies to public formation, for example, can be explained through reference to historical developments. I further stress that fundamental political concepts such as democracy, citizenship and public opinion are historically based concepts that have changed over time as a result of political struggle, and economic and technological developments. The social impacts of new media forms, and their relationship to existing media forms, can equally be explained through reference to historical developments.

This text is an overview of the important issues relevant to the media, politics and public life, but it also represents my own interests in the topic, my own areas of expertise, and my assessment of the importance of particular media, political practices, organisations and theoretical arguments. The theoretical framework offered here provides a 'media-centric' understanding of politics and public life, and this type of perspective is informed by my own background in mass communication research and teaching. I have focused on mainstream news media throughout, which has meant less attention to alternative media despite their acknowledged importance to the political process. Similarly, while I discuss the importance of the Internet, it is not given the same prominence as print and broadcast media. I acknowledge the considerable and growing importance of the Internet, but I also believe that in the rush to scrutinise the influence of 'new media' we have tended to overlook the persistent power of 'old media' forms.

This text is intended primarily for Australian media and politics students, and the examples used here are subsequently Australian, although I draw on some well-known examples of media and politics from the United States and particularly Britain, where there have been fascinating interactions between the news media and Tony Blair's New Labour. This text is a summary of a broad and complex terrain, drawing on work across many different subject areas and academic disciplines. I hope it will provide a valuable summary for readers: I hope it challenges pre-existing opinions and opens up new ways of thinking, and I hope that it encourages further exploration of the media, politics and public life.

Geoffrey Craig
August 2003

Part 1
Introduction

The media

'Media' is the plural form of 'medium'. Broadly understood, a medium is 'an intermediate agency that enables communication to take place' (O'Sullivan et al. 1994, p. 176). The *communicative* power of the media is a fundamental idea that informs this book. The media are a specific institution in society, informed by particular interests, practices, norms and values; but to highlight the separateness of the media is not to appreciate fully how integral the media are to the meaning-making processes of a society. The functioning of politics, and of public life more generally, is not tainted by the unnecessary and unwelcome intrusions of the media: rather, the media are an indissoluble part of the contexts, the messages and the relationships that create and give shape to politics and public life. We will investigate the *strengths* and *weaknesses* of media contributions to politics and public life, but this will be on the basis that the media are *intrinsic* to the functioning of modern societies.

The media are difficult to capture and define. 'The media' is a catch-all term that includes transnational corporations, communication technologies, policy and regulatory frameworks, the practices of journalists, gossip columns, the nightly television news, blockbuster movies, advertisements, business magazines, music radio, the local newspaper and the Internet. The media are businesses and yet they are also ascribed a special function in the democratic health of a society; the media are the *news* media and function as journalism, but they are also the *entertainment* media and provide escape from the pressures of everyday life.

The phrase 'the media' ascribes a singularity to a diverse range of forms of communication. Newspapers, magazines, radio, television, film and online media generate such an avalanche of information that selecting and navigating through media output has become a valuable skill. Our first inclination in seeking to understand the significance of the media is to break them up into different categories. Before doing that we should note the generalised character of the media. Our everyday lives involve a fluidity of movement between different media forms and content: we read a newspaper for the latest news, we listen to the latest hits on the radio, we flick through a magazine while waiting for an appointment, we access websites during the work day, we watch a quiz show before catching the evening television news and afterwards settle down to watch a video. Any discussion of contemporary political communication must consider these contexts of reception. The meanings of politics are partly determined by the everyday situations in which political issues and debates are interpreted. The communicative forms of the media have blurred divisions between the public and the private, between factual and fictional forms of representation, and have broadened and complicated the field of politics.

Mediated public life

The emphasis on the communicative powers of the media directs us to more than just an acknowledgement that the media are a potent influence on modern life—it points us to an understanding of the *nature* of modern public life itself. The media are not observers on the sidelines, reporting as politics and public life unfold before them. Rather, the media are the sites where politics and public life are played out, the sites where the meanings of public life are generated, debated and evaluated. That is, modern public life is defined as a mediated phenomenon. The public generally do not directly encounter politicians and public issues but rather encounter media images, representations and stories about those politicians and public issues. The phrase 'mediated public life' highlights the kind of social relationships between public figures and the public, and it highlights the textual basis of public life.

We explore this concept of mediated public life throughout this book, but its significance is highlighted here initially because so many judgements about the media's role in modern public life are informed by assumptions that require scrutiny and critique. We need to grasp the significant fact that the public domain in contemporary times is a mediated phenomenon, located in discourse and representation rather than geography. The media have become so pervasive that they *constitute* public life in contemporary societies. This is not to deny that real people conduct significant political and public activity removed from media scrutiny but it is to declare that the actions of people and the meanings of issues assume a generalised public status when they are represented in the media. As John Hartley (1992, p. 1) has noted:

> ... while [the public domain and the public] don't exist as spaces and assemblies, the public realm and the public are still to be found, large as life, in media. Television, popular newspapers, magazines and photography, the popular media of the modern period, are the public domain, the place where and the means by which the public is created and has its being.

The concept of mediated public life may seem plausible at the beginning of the media-saturated 21st century, but the media have always been integral to the creation of the public domain. While our knowledges and understandings of the society in which we live are increasingly the product of television news footage, press stories and talkback radio, the public orientation of the media has been instrumental in the formation of the public since the earliest forms of mass media arose several centuries ago. The rise of a regular, independent and critical press in England in the early part of the 18th century facilitated the development of a reasoning public, which discussed and debated the issues of the day. The rise of the mass market newspapers in the latter part of the 19th century helped bring into being the urban mass publics which have since been such a feature of modern life. The formation of these publics did not occur independently and prior to the rise of the relevant media: it was rather the communicative capacities of these media that enabled people to develop a consciousness that located themselves in broader societal contexts. Benedict Anderson (1991), in his now famous study of the rise of nationalism, details how the print media were integral to the 'imagined communities' of the early nation-states. Although Anderson's work has been criticised for an insufficient scrutiny of communication media (Thompson 1995, pp. 62–3), the phrase 'imagined communities' has had great rhetorical power in capturing the historical process by which individuals became aware they were part of a larger grouping of people whom they would never meet or know but with whom they shared particular knowledges, concerns and identity through their common access of print media.

The relationship between media form and public life is more clearly articulated if we consider how specific types of media have transformed the character of public life throughout modern history (see Thompson 1995 for further discussion). Prior to modern media, public life was linked to a common locale; an event became public when a plurality of people physically congregated to hear and see the communication of a message, whether a band of travelling minstrels or an execution in the town square. Printing ushered in a fundamental reorientation of the nature of public life. No longer was 'publicness' linked to a common locale: rather, it was generated through the process of *publication*. Print media gave rise to a reading public collected together through their common access to printed material, even though the accessing of that information took place in spatial and temporal contexts removed from the production of the message. This represented a revolutionary change to the structure and organisation of public life that still informs contemporary debates on the role of the media.

This production of mediated publicness was further developed with the rise of film and television in the 20th century. Audiovisual media re-established linkages between publicness and visibility that had diminished with the rise of the print media. Television does not represent, however, a return to the traditional publicness of co-presence. While elevating the significance of visibility to the functioning of public life, it remains a mediated form of communication and is available to a much greater range of individuals in different spatial and temporal contexts. The field of vision of television is not limited to one physical site but can represent an extraordinarily wide range of situations from around the world that are removed from the viewer's everyday contexts. As a form of mediated communication, television also limits the possibilities for direct feedback to the producers of the messages. Television provides us with a distinctive communicative context, where the audiovisual presence of the represented subjects is combined at the same time with our spatial and temporal distance from them. Of course, while modern public life is dominated by this kind of televisual form of communication, it remains constituted by other forms of communication, including forms of interpersonal communication. The complexity of modern public life, and the difficulty of comprehending the role of the media in the production of public life, stems from the profusion and interconnectedness of these communicative contexts.

Types of media

The news media are distinguished here against entertainment media, such as fictional film, music radio and advertisements. Entertainment media is not used here as a term to distinguish 'popular' or 'tabloid' news media from other forms of more serious or 'quality' media. Such a distinction was always problematic and is becoming increasingly so with the rise of lifestyle journalism in the 'quality' media. A paradoxical development in recent years has been the convergence of the news agenda in an age of proliferating media forms. Not only are 'quality' media giving us more stories on celebrities and lifestyle and consumer issues, but popular media are giving more emphasis to international events, particularly since the bombing of the World Trade Center towers and the resulting fears about terrorism and national security.

Within the news media we have to distinguish between different types of media. Television, the press, radio and online media have very different textual characteristics and varying kinds of political influence. Television has become the most powerful mass medium in the industrialised world. Television is now a standard feature not only in households but also in public spaces, such as airports, hotels and even public transport. In January 2003 it was announced that 650 buses in Brisbane, Sydney and Melbourne would be fitted with televisions for commuters (Brook 2003, p. 3). In Australia, television penetration has reached 99 per cent of households and many have more than one

7

television. A Productivity Commission report found that Australians spend over 20 hours a week, or 36 per cent of their leisure time, watching television (Productivity Commission 2000, p. 62). Numerous surveys have revealed that a majority of people have television as their primary news source and that they regard television as the most trustworthy type of media. Television is often regarded as trustworthy because of its textual richness: our ability to hear people speak and see people act provides the medium with its high credibility (even though television news footage, like any other news media text, is selected and edited). The textual form of television news and current affairs, however, also provokes criticism of its reportage of politics and public life. The brevity of television news items, the need for good televisual performers or 'talent', and the dependency on good pictures, are offered as textual features that diminish the quality of television's coverage of politics. Of course, contemporary politics is organised increasingly around the successful presentation of an image and the successful management of media events, and these features of modern politics are in no small way prompted by the demands of television. These points will be a subject of discussion throughout this book, and it is sufficient here to note simply how the textual form of television—its process of communication—has fundamentally changed the practice of politics. This gives the lie to any residual support for the argument that the media report objectively, leaving their subject unaffected by the process of media scrutiny; and it highlights the need for us to contemplate the role of the news media in actively shaping how politics is conducted.

Television may have superseded the press as the most popular type of news media, but advocates of the press argue that newspapers retain the mantle of the most politically influential mass medium. They maintain that newspapers, and particularly the 'quality' morning newspapers, set the news agenda for the day and dictate the dominant interpretation of the important news issues. Newspapers have been the traditional forum for public debate—the means by which ideas are disseminated and considered by a society. This has been so, and continues to be so, because of the ability of newspapers to cover a broader range of issues and to cover an individual news story in more depth than other news media. The in-depth coverage of issues is a limited advantage, however, in a world where people do not have the time to thoroughly explore each important news item. Newspaper circulation figures have fallen generally in recent decades: weekly newspaper circulation in Australia fell from 2.5 per head of population in 1951 to 1.2 per head of population in 1997 (Dermott 1998, p. 23). Newspapers, however, retain their political significance because of their readership profile: 'quality' newspaper readers are generally more likely to be professionals and from the more 'elite' strata of society. Tabloid newspapers have suffered the most in recent decades from competition with television, and this has led to the demise of the afternoon tabloid newspaper throughout most of the Western world. Although some tabloid newspapers remain enormously popular and politically influential, the press is defined increasingly by the 'quality' newspapers, including business and financial publications.

Radio is the most underestimated mass medium: it is not attributed the same political influence as television and newspapers yet it is the most pervasive type of mass media in the world, reaching populations with low levels of television penetration and literacy. Radio also remains a politically influential mass medium in the developed world. Radio news and current affairs, particularly those of public broadcasters such as the Australian Broadcasting Corporation (ABC) and the British Broadcasting Corporation (BBC), continue to play a major role in setting the news agenda. Commercial radio stations have cut back on their news services, but considerable political influence is generated through talkback radio. In Australia, politicians have used talkback radio increasingly in recent years because it permits more direct access to the public. Radio, like television, can quickly react to, and continuously update, breaking news stories. Radio, arguably more than any other mass medium, has a ubiquitous presence in everyday life: its aural basis means that it can accompany us while we do household chores, study, and drive in the car.

Newspapers, television and radio outlets now have online versions of their publications and programs. Lists of the most popular websites in Australia regularly include the websites of existing media corporations, such as the ABC (www.abc.net.au) and Kerry Packer's Publishing and Broadcasting Ltd (PBL) (www.ninemsn.com.au). We can now access webcasts of events and listen to web radio. Newspapers have developed a substantial online presence in recent years, enhancing the information and services they provide. Online media, however, are not just sites where existing media texts are relocated. In recent years we have seen the proliferation of online journalism sites, such as www.salon.com and www.drudgereport.com, the site run by Matt Drudge, who broke the famous sex scandal involving former US President Bill Clinton and Monica Lewinsky. Online media represent a distinctly new kind of media, the possibilities of which we are only beginning to comprehend and implement. Online media offer greater potential for interactivity, a feature that can change fundamentally the relations between media producers, public figures and the public. The proliferation of online media has profound potential to fragment the mass public while extending 'the public' beyond national structures into greater global contexts.

Media ownership

Our focus in this book is on the communicative power of the media and its role in public formation, but media ownership remains important because it raises issues about the diversity of voices in a society and the nature of the political culture. We will be focusing on the media in Australia, although I will also be drawing on examples and case studies from the media in Britain and the United States. We cannot provide here a complete listing of media ownership in each of these three countries, but we can give a broad overview of the respective media landscapes. The Australian media landscape is dominated by several large corporations. Rupert Murdoch's News Corp is a global media company with extensive assets around the world, but in Australia it owns capital city daily newspapers which account for about 66 per cent of total circulation. Murdoch newspapers include *The Australian*, *The Daily Telegraph* in Sydney and *The Herald Sun* in Melbourne. News Corp owns the daily newspaper in each monopoly metropolitan market across the country except for Perth and Canberra. News Corp also owns 25 per cent of the pay television operator Foxtel. Telstra owns 50 per cent of Foxtel and Kerry Packer's company, PBL, owns the remaining 25 per cent. Packer owns the Channel Nine television network and controls about 40 per cent of the nation's popular magazine market, with titles such as *The Australian Women's Weekly, The Bulletin, Cleo* and *Ralph*. The John Fairfax company publishes some of the country's most influential newspapers, including *The Australian Financial Review, The Sydney Morning Herald* and *The Age*. The Australian print news media have experienced a long-term trend of fewer titles and fewer owners. In 1923 there were as many as 26 capital city daily newspapers with 21 independent owners, in 1950 there were 15 capital city daily newspapers with 10 independent owners, and now there are 12 metropolitan dailies, including the two national newspapers, *The Australian* and *The Australian Financial Review*, with only four owners.

Further expansion of the Packer and Murdoch media interests in Australia have been limited by the Australian cross-media regulations introduced by the Labor government in 1986–87, which limit large-scale ownership across television, radio and print media (see chapter 2). The Howard government has flagged changes to the media ownership laws but they have not been passed by the Senate and there remains some doubt that these changes will come into effect.

Both Murdoch and Packer have extended their investments into new media, computer and telecommunications companies in recent years, but with mixed success. The collapse of telecommunications company One.Tel had financial ramifications for both Packer and Murdoch. PBL sold out of its share in a customer management group following a credit ratings agency downgrade (Schulze 2002, p. 17). Despite this, traditional media corporations are continuing to look at plans to diversify beyond their traditional media profile.

Radio ownership in Australia is dominated by a few large companies and the number of independent stations continues to fall. There are three major metropolitan networks. Austereo, which includes the Triple M/2Day FM combination, has 10 capital city licences. Australian Radio Network has investments in 12 metropolitan radio stations and Southern Cross Broadcasting has six capital city licences. DMG Radio Australia dominates regional Australia. The company has a total of 64 licences. One consequence of media regulations introduced in 1992 has been the rise of networking. Networking has resulted in the 'national' promotion of major Sydney- or Melbourne-based announcers, there has been increased standardisation of music formats, as well as cuts to newsroom staff with the increasing reliance on syndicated news services (Collingwood 1999, p. 17).

In addition to the commercial media environment, the national public broadcaster, the ABC, carries great political influence throughout the country through its national television network, its national radio networks (which include Radio National and Triple J), its 56 regional and metropolitan radio stations, and its Internet site. The ABC remains a vital part of the Australian media scene with widespread popular support, despite previously receiving savage funding cuts from the Howard coalition government. The Special Broadcasting Service (SBS) provides a valuable contribution to national broadcasting, running a national television service as well as five radio services, broadcasting in 68 languages. Australia also has a community radio sector, which has 154 permanently licensed stations on air. The stations service local communities and various public groupings such as ethnic, indigenous and print-handicapped people. The public has an active role in community radio: an important principle that informs community station licences is the expectation that people from the community concerned will participate in station operations and the selection of program formats and content (Thompson 1999). In Britain the BBC, like other public broadcasters, has had its future role in a multi-channel environment questioned, but it retains both popular support and political influence through its television and radio networks. While the BBC has experienced financial strictures, it has a better and more secure funding basis through the television licence fee system than the ABC with its reliance on direct government funding.

There are more than 1000 newspapers in the UK, although the ten titles that constitute the national daily press account for 69 per cent of total circulation (Sparks 1999, p. 42). The daily press market can be divided into three sections: the 'quality' broadsheets (*The Times*, *The Daily Telegraph*, *The Guardian*, *The Independent* and *The Financial Times*); the mid-market papers (*The Daily Mail* and *The Daily Express*); and the 'popular tabloids' (*The Sun*, *The Daily Mirror*, *The Star*). The newspapers in Britain are quite politically defined, with the conservatism of *The Daily Telegraph*, for example, contrasting with the left-of-centre perspective of *The Guardian*. The variety of 'quality' newspapers, covering a range of political positions, has contributed to the political culture of Britain. The tabloid newspapers have also shaped the political culture of Britain. The endorsement of Labour leader Tony Blair by *The Sun* in the 1997 election was a not insignificant factor in the landslide Labour victory.

The UK television landscape has been less diverse historically, the BBC and ITV being the main two networks until the introduction of Channel 4 in 1982 and Channel 5 as the latest terrestrial service. In recent years the addition of satellite, cable and digital television has boosted the number of channels, most notably through networks such as Rupert Murdoch's BSkyB. In UK radio the BBC dominates, with its five national networks, its three regional services and around 40 local radio stations in England, constituting nearly half of all radio listening. There are four national commercial radio services, seven regional services and 170 local services (www.mediauk.com).

The news media in the United States have always been protected and strengthened by the constitutional guarantees of freedom of speech. The USA has had many world-famous 'quality' newspapers, including *The New York Times, The Washington Post, The Los Angeles Times,* and *The Boston Globe.* As indicated in the titles, these newspapers have been city- and state-specific although they exert tremendous influence over the news agenda for the entire country. The sheer size of the USA (as with Australia) has worked against the development of national newspapers. The two largest-circulation newspapers, and the first truly national newspapers, *The Wall Street Journal* and *USA Today,* built themselves around the new technologies of satellite transmission and remote printing technology (Sparks 1999, p. 45). In television, the networks traditionally have been the central source of power, although their influence in recent decades has been cut by increased cable penetration and regulatory changes that did not require cable television to carry the networks (Barker 1997, p. 47). The US television networks, however, are still enormously powerful and are all part of global media conglomerates. The American Broadcasting Company (ABC) network is owned by the Disney corporation, the National Broadcasting Company (NBC) is owned by General Electric, the Columbia Broadcasting System (CBS) is owned by Viacom, and the Fox network is part of Rupert Murdoch's News Corporation.

Although there are differences in what stories are covered and how they are covered across Australia, Britain, the USA and other Western countries, there is a sameness to the coverage of international stories because of increasing reliance on the output of international news agencies, such as Reuters and Associated Press. Pressures on costs have forced many media outlets to cut back on the number of foreign correspondents in recent years (Utley 1997). The emphasis in this book is on domestic politics but there remains an ease of movement across national boundaries in our consideration of different examples because of the similar values, conventions and practices that inform journalism in the Western world. The issues and dilemmas that we investigate throughout this book are not peculiar to Australia but are more representative of trends informing modern media, politics and public life generally.

Criticisms of media performance

The media are one of the most maligned institutions in modern life. The disquiet about media performance is wide-ranging but it emanates primarily from a sense that the media have an undue influence in politics and public life. Arising from a concern about the nature of mediated public life, there are perceptions that the authenticity and realities of politics and public life are sacrificed increasingly for the demands of the media: politicians construct an image for the media that hides some underlying reality, while celebrations of national culture are staged spectacles divorced from popular sentiment. Criticisms of media performance are also more specific, including fears that growing concentration of media ownership is causing a diminishing diversity of public debate, that the media involve themselves in unnecessary invasions of privacy, and that news values lead to a distorted coverage of public life with an emphasis on scandals and conflict at the expense of a more constructive and reasoned approach.

Many criticisms of media performance derive from unease over the features of mediated public life, and specifically the predominance of visual forms of communication. Television is identified as the main culprit, eroding a print-based culture that was judged to be the ideal form of communication for a critical public sphere. Concern about television's contribution to public life mainly revolves around its representational powers and its communicative contexts. The audiovisual nature of television provides it with a high degree of realism. Opinion polls that place television journalists ahead of print journalists in rankings of trustworthiness and ethical conduct are often attributed to the realist credibility of the medium. While being able to watch and see a politician speak provides us with more information than reading the text of the speech in a newspaper, it is also argued that it limits opportunities for critical engagement. Television, with its audiovisual form and its narrative structures which foreground continuity and flow, has a greater potential to foster believability than print, which, because it is a more abstract form of representation, offers a more detached perspective on the content provided. Concern that contemporary politics relies too much on 'individuals' and 'events' also stems from the representational powers of television and its communicative contexts. Television is extraordinarily adept at capturing and conveying the nuances of personalities and the physical particularities of action. It is argued that such aptitude occurs at the expense of the reportage of more complex issues and policy, which do not lend themselves to easy and dramatic representation.

It is paradoxical that television, which provides such realistic representations of the world and which provides us with such personal portrayals of public figures, has also provoked a crisis over the perceived loss of the real. Contemporary public life is haunted by a desperate clamour for authenticity. A desire for real behaviour and the articulations of some authentic self have informed the popularity of public figures such as Virgin's founder Richard Branson, Princess Diana, and Australian politician Pauline Hanson. Hanson's rise in popularity was partly predicated on her lack of media skill, which was offered as evidence of her authenticity. The authenticity of such individuals, however, not only resides in their performances but is crucially linked to their abilities to establish a special relationship with the public.

The mediated nature of public life causes consternation because it gives the media extraordinary control of information distribution and interpretation and affords the public limited opportunity for direct feedback. The size of media outlets and the costs involved in producing material for public dissemination means there is the generation of a polarity in society between information providers and receivers. Under these circumstances, it is argued that the public feel disconnected from politics and public life; they become spectators of a process in which they have no input apart from the casting of an occasional vote at elections. The media, together with governments and private organisations with well-resourced media offices, have the ability to engage in strategies of knowledge management and ideological control.

While perceptions about the undue influence of the media on politics and public life is widespread, it becomes more difficult to delineate the precise nature of media power. One of the dominant ideas in media studies has been that the media exert an ideological control over society. This argument, which arose when media and cultural studies assumed prominence in the 1970s, is informed by Marxist and neo-Marxist politics, and has come to be understood generally as the process by which the meanings and values generated by the media reproduce and naturalise dominant power relations in society (Hall 1977). Selection of topics and their treatment by the media are said not only to further the direct interests of media owners and other powerful interests in society but more generally to contribute to the production and circulation of commonsense understandings. While it is true that the media do maintain dominant power relations in society, ideological analysis has been criticised for assuming that the preferred media interpretations of issues will be taken up by compliant receivers of the media texts.

More recent media research in the past decade or so has focused less on the production and form of media texts and more on the contexts and processes of the reception of texts (Allen 1992). Such audience research, while not denying the media's tremendous influence, does offer a more tempered account of media power. Other perspectives on media power include the concept of agenda-setting. This idea, which emanates more from mass communication research, is based in the fact that the media determine which issues are salient in the public consciousness but do not determine how those issues are interpreted and understood throughout that society (McCombs 1993).

Perhaps the greatest cause of public unease over the media derives from the power of media barons and the high concentration of media ownership that pervades the Western world. The tremendous power of media owners is not new: in Australia the power of the Packer and

Murdoch families has extended over generations and looks unlikely to diminish. Despite this, concern over high concentration of media ownership has grown in recent years as many already huge media corporations have merged. This process of merging has not been limited to media corporations but is a more general characteristic of global capitalism. Increasing concentration of ownership is a particularly worrying development in media industries, however, because their products are integral to the democratic process and public debate. A vibrant democracy requires a range of forums in which a variety of viewpoints can be expressed. Although the everyday control of media outlets by owners is often overstated, high levels of concentration of media ownership do result in a standardisation of news formats and do not encourage journalists to raise controversial views.

New media technologies may allow the proliferation of media outlets and diminish the power of media barons. The Internet has already influenced the global media landscape, although the emancipatory potential of new media technologies is sometimes overstated. Forms of pay television, for example, may provide a multi-channel environment but they may also entrench the power of existing media owners and not facilitate greater degrees of public debate or a greater variety of media content. While high concentration of media ownership is not desirable, it is possible to overstate its significance as a debilitating factor in the quality of public life. Journalists retain levels of autonomy in their normal practice and the viewers, readers and listeners of media texts exercise their agency through the active and critical interpretation of the information they receive. Despite the power of media owners, social change does occur and often the media are integral to that change. Media owners must also abide by popular demand. As Brian McNair states: '. . . even where there is identifiably excessive concentration of ownership in a particular media sector, the workings of the information marketplace may militate against the straightforward translation of proprietorial influence into editorial bias' (1998, p. 109).

One consequence of mediated public life is the breakdown of the distinction between the public sphere and the private sphere. The media increasingly render public issues that were previously free from public scrutiny. Media invasions of the privacy of public figures, and media forays into the private lives of individuals thrown into the public spotlight because of exceptional circumstances, are another cause of public concern over media performance. Privacy laws, and journalistic treatments of the privacy of public figures, vary greatly across nations. In the United States, the diminished right to privacy of public figures is enshrined in legislation, and journalists have been very active in exposing the private activities of public figures. This is different from Australia, where privacy laws place great restrictions on media activity and journalists historically have abided by an unwritten law not to report such matters as politicians' extramarital affairs. It is difficult to provide a definitive judgement of the media treatment of privacy. Public figures have a right to privacy, but it could be argued that they lose that right when their public pronouncements are at odds with their private practice. Some media, such as television current affairs shows, have made invasion of privacy through the use of surveillance cameras a standard feature of their programs. This often amounts to simple voyeurism and serves no public good. Media attention to the private sphere can have tremendous social benefits, however—as witnessed by the greater coverage of domestic violence in recent years.

The contemporary media are also criticised for their overly negative and sensationalist accounts of public life. It has been argued that such an approach is a major cause of growing public cynicism about politics. The adversarial nature of much journalistic reportage results in an undue focus on negativity, mistakes, gaffes and crises. Contrary to popular perception, this does not occur because journalists are malicious by nature but rather results from the news values that inform journalistic practice. These news values are not applied systemically but instead structure how journalists perceive an issue or event. The preponderance of news stories about political scandals highlights the functioning of the contemporary news media. As Rodney Tiffen (1999, p. 252) has declared:

> The increasing political role of scandals is consonant with a political communication system where disclosure rather than argument and analysis is the main activity. The news media are relatively weak and erratic conveyors of policy debates and performance, but are powerful narrators of concrete events and effective portrayers of the drama of conflict . . .

Scandals are newsworthy because they have the human interest value of high-profile individuals, they are unusual events that rupture regular political process, they have a high degree of clarity and are unambiguous, and they are negative events that foster conflict and drama. While news media scrutiny ensures a degree of political accountability, the random nature of scandals, their unpredictable narratives (where they can be quickly discarded from the news pages and forgotten), and the journalistic focus on the downfall of individuals rather than the viability of political structures, all contribute to the declining public confidence in both media and political performance.

Merits of media performance

The merits of media performance are rarely proclaimed. Rarely do we stop and consider how much the media contribute to the constitution and quality of our public life. It seems that a wave of discontent swells whenever public discourse occurs on the performance of the media. Individual journalists, newspapers, television and radio programs may engender esteem, even affection, but that does not extend to a general media appreciation. This lack of appreciation stems partly from a deficient understanding about forms of media communication and the nature of public life in contemporary times.

The merits of media performance reside in the ongoing scrutiny of public life. The media, while often working to reproduce dominant understandings of issues and events, nonetheless enact a process of questioning and critique that animates the democratic health of a society. This idea has been captured in titles given to the media, such as 'watchdog of society', or 'fourth estate' for their scrutiny of other institutional domains (see Boyce 1978 and Schultz 1998 on the fourth estate). This watchdog function of the media only grows in importance as the distance between the governors and the governed grows.

The media are, however, not just observers of the democratic process, providing notification when it goes awry. The media are, and always have been, profoundly integral to democratic process. The media, and specifically journalism, *problematise* society. Contemporary political and institutional power, for all its careful management, is always rendered fragile because the public realm is grounded in a logic that questions manifestations of power and critiques expressions of 'reason'. For all the smooth delivery of soundbites, for all the prescheduled media events, the practice of politics is always fraught with potential danger because the mediated nature of the public realm opens up such political behaviour to scrutiny, and there is no guarantee about the control of disseminated information. As Thompson states, 'the visibility created by the media' becomes a 'source of a new and distinctive kind of *fragility*' (1995, p. 141, author's emphasis). He notes how the source of political trouble often emanates from gaffes, scandals, leaks and other failures to successfully manage a public image (pp. 140–8). It is not possible for politicians to attempt to escape their potential fate: in the contemporary democratic process, politicians must submit themselves to this type of public scrutiny.

This process of the journalistic problematisation of society has a historical basis. After the French Revolution there were no more ultimate guarantors of truth: sovereignty had been relocated in the people, and authority became diffused throughout the social body. Journalism was the means by which a collective political consciousness was established, and ideas of popular sovereignty burgeoned. Hartley argues, following the work of Ernesto Laclau and Chantal Mouffe (1985), that journalism was '*the* necessary mechanism' for articulating and communicating a logic of equivalence (Hartley 1996, p. 109, author's emphasis). Journalism enabled the spread of equality and liberty throughout the populace, and the indeterminacy of democracy also meant that society became problematised—subject to continual struggle. The 'ungraspable, uncontrollable society' (Lefort 1986, p. 303) initiated by democracy meant that an unending process of questioning and critique was unleashed on society, and journalism was the central forum through which such scrutiny occurred. The subversive power of the imposition of the democratic principles of liberty and equality spread throughout the social domain and continues to inform political struggles, such as those for women's and gay rights.

The merits of the media are also contained in the way they facilitate the performative basis of public life. The media provide the setting or stage on which public life is enacted. The news itself, as a cultural form, enables performance. The value hierarchy of our culture is such that we associate this phenemenon with ideas of artificiality and manipulation: events are 'stage-managed' and political performances hide some underlying reality or identity. While this is so sometimes, such judgements deny the reality that a vocabulary of drama and performance is integral to understanding the production of meaning and the forging of collective identities in mediated public life. We see the importance of the performative basis of public life in the protest actions of environmental groups such as Greenpeace. These groups make spectacles of themselves in order to attract media attention and trigger debate on the promoted issues. Such acts are not limited to large, 'media-savvy' organisations such as Greenpeace: many resident groups successfully protest about local issues, generating media coverage and forcing action from governments. The general public can also show public opinion through performance: the walks for reconciliation between Aboriginal and non-Aboriginal Australians in 2000, where hundreds of thousands of people took to the streets, was a powerful performance of public opinion. The performative basis of public life is explicitly highlighted in the actions of the public and protest groups but is also integral to the everyday production and maintenance of power by political leaders. The authority of political leaders stems partly from the performance of that authority through their interactions with other people, whether world leaders or ordinary people, and the witnessing of the performance of authority by others.

It follows from assertions about the performative basis of public life that another merit of media performance resides in the ability to provide visual representations of public life. Such a declaration may seem unusual because, as already noted, these features are often the basis for criticism of the media. Contemporary public life is saturated with visual images, and the ubiquity of images informs the rhythms, spaces and meanings of public life. General social unease about this media environment, which foregrounds visual forms of communication, stems mainly from the perceived manipulative basis of these forms of communication and their commercial basis. Visual media have been implicated in critiques of the growing consumerism of modern life and the manipulative powers of mass culture. There is a complex history to ideas of mass culture as social decay (Brantlinger

1983), but fears about cultural decline through the deployment of visual media gained prominence in the earlier parts of the 20th century when propaganda techniques were used prominently by totalitarian regimes, most notably by the Nazi party in Germany.

Such criticisms stem from the already identified general unease about mediated life, part of which is informed by a value hierarchy between written and visual forms of communication. While visual forms of modern media are obviously implicated in commercial contexts, we need to develop a more subtle and complex understanding of the visual media that also articulates their fundamental role in the sociality of modern public life. This understanding would posit visual media and forms of media drama and spectacle as neither intrinsically negative or positive, and it would be cognisant of the grammar of visual images and the visual literacy of the public. We need to challenge the distinctions that often arise from the verbal/visual opposition, where writing is encoded as 'rational' while the visual is encoded as 'non-rational'—as 'mere appearance'.

Conclusion

The media encompass a diverse range of communicative forms, including television, newspapers, the Internet, radio and magazines. Any appraisal of the social importance of the media as an institution could consider such matters as ownership, policy and regulation, as well as new technologies. Our focus here has been on the communicative powers of the media and the fundamental role they play in the functioning of politics and public life. Modern public life is a mediated phenomenon: opinions, debates and protests assume a generalised public status when they are aired on television or reported in the newspapers or on radio. Successful political strategies are increasingly dependent on the management of the media. But the media have been criticised for a variety of reasons: they are said to focus too much on conflict and personalities, they are involved in unnecessary intrusions of privacy, they exacerbate the distance between the public and those who govern them, and they do not facilitate a great diversity of viewpoints. The media, however, contribute also in positive ways to the functioning of politics and public life. The media provide the setting or stage on which public life is played out, and they continue to provide the scrutiny and critique of the players in public life that is central to the democratic process. It is important that we critique modern media methods that alienate the public and hinder the democratic health of a society, but we must do this within a context that locates the media as a legitimate and central communicative mechanism in modern societies that validates the performative basis of public life.

2
Politics

Politics is difficult to define, because its influence extends into public life and it also structures the values and practices of the private sphere. Politics can be conceptualised as a specific sphere of society incorporating the workings of formal institutions and their legal relationships. Politics in this sense is limited to 'the state', to the realm of parliaments and their constitutional basis, cabinet, political parties, the public service, and associated political actors such as unions and employer associations. Alternatively, politics can be broadened so that it incorporates the struggle over the values that inform all social relations. Understood this way, politics is part of general social and psychological behaviour and arises out of our relationship to basic material needs and desires. Politics is practised at various levels in society: from the neighbourhood to the regional and state levels, through to the national and international arenas.

The study of politics has long been the subject of scrutiny: Aristotle (1981) wrote on the subject over 2000 years ago, calling politics the ruling discipline and labelling man a 'political animal'. As Graham Maddox notes, Aristotle did not mean to label humans as devious and power-hungry—rather to say that humans are social animals who work towards the common good and the 'good life': 'Aristotle's argument was that the human is a creature born to live in complex organisation with his or her fellow creatures, in community and harmony, through compromise, but united through a common purpose, which is to live a shared life' (Maddox 1996, p. 5).

Politics is, however, also about the expressions and management of conflict, and it is centrally concerned with the concept of power. As one political theorist has put it: 'A political system is any persistent pattern of human relationships that involves, to a significant extent, power, rule or authority' (Dahl 1970, p. 6). Power is one of those fundamental terms that can be variously conceptualised, and its definition is open to much dispute (Barnes 1988; Hindess 1996; Lukes 1986; Wrong 1979). Power has several common understandings: it can refer to a particular kind of energy, or it can refer to the skills, talents or 'faculties' of a person. In one definition, power is 'the capacity of some persons to produce intended and foreseen effects on others' (Wrong 1979, p. 2). Power is not only about the ability to force effects or change on others against their will; it often carries a sense of legitimacy and occurs with the consent of the ruled. The distribution of power throughout society has been variously theorised, from an emphasis on the pluralism of power to a focus on the power of elites in society (Maddox 1996; Hindess 1996). Power can operate not only at the level of the individual but also at a 'macro' level, through workplaces, institutions and social structures. There are, of course, many different types of power—political and military power, economic power, and types of social power, manifested in institutions and relationships. Wrong identifies four different forms of power: force, manipulation, persuasion, and authority (1979, p. 24).

Power is sometimes understood as being distinct from more general forms of social control, where individuals internalise group norms and undergo processes of socialisation, but we also need to consider whether more pervasive social effects can be attributed to it. Power is also expressed through the processes of subject formation, in the reproduction of dominant social values, in the general regulation of forms of behaviour. Much political, social and media theory has emphasised a view in which the victims of power do not realise that such power is being exercised and that it works against their interests. Steven Lukes, for example, identifies how power is exercised through 'socially structured and culturally patterned behaviour' (Lukes 1974, p. 22). Antonio Gramsci's (1971) theory of hegemony has been influential in media studies over several decades. Gramsci's theory explores how the domination of the bourgeois ruling class in capitalist societies is exercised through the ways ideas and representations are presented in order to naturalise ruling-class ideology, rendering it as 'common sense' and subsequently 'winning the consent' of the populace. While such theories examine the diffuse distribution of power in society, they nonetheless posit a singular or dominant concept of power. In contrast, Michel Foucault sees 'power' as a more plural entity, not informed by a single source or 'ideology'. Foucault's theorisation of power is complex and broad-ranging but, while he acknowledges that power operates at the level of a government and that explicit domination of others does occur, he is more interested in how power is exercised through the practices and rationalities by which people regulate their own behaviour. For Foucault (1995, p. 27), power needs to be understood through its relationship with knowledge:

> We should admit that power produces knowledge . . . that power and knowledge directly imply one another; that there is no power relation without the correlative constitution of a field of knowledge, nor any knowledge that does not presuppose and constitute at the same time power relations.

Politics is popularly perceived as dealing with conflict, disagreements and 'grubby' uses of power, but we also need to remember that consensus is central to politics, whether it be over the 'rules' of the political system or a common recognition of values that occur in a society. An overview of political philosophy and political science is beyond the scope of this project. We can simply note that approaches to politics incorporate the study of institutions and social structures, norms, values and behaviour. One possible summary of politics (Ponton & Gill 1993, pp. 5–6) states that it is:

> . . . the way in which we understand and order our social affairs. This applies especially to the allocation of scarce resources, and its underlying principles. It also involves the means by which some people or groups acquire and maintain a greater control over a situation than others. Thus politics is above all an activity—concerned with people's social and material relationships, expressed in various ways in different places and continually changing through time.

I focus here on the more traditional domain of politics: the case studies and discussion will circulate around the conduct of politicians, the media management strategies of political parties and the more traditional issues associated with politics. But we are also interested in how the political domain is increasingly problematic, how a greater range of practices and issues are considered to be 'political', how politics is influenced increasingly by a greater range of media, how an increasingly diverse range of political actors employ new political strategies in order to communicate their message and bring about change.

My focus is more specifically on the issue of political *communication*. Political communication occurs primarily through the media, and the nexus between politics and the media plays a fundamental role in the practice of politics. Political communication includes not only forms of communication undertaken by politicians and other political actors but also forms of public communication undertaken by media personnel and citizens that might be addressed to politicians and political actors or even a more general contribution to public debate. Political communication, then, does not have to be addressed to a specific receiver but includes broadly all public discourse about politics. Its forms are broad-ranging and include not only conventional forms of text and speech but more 'aesthetic' and 'bodily focused' forms of communication, including marches, hunger-strikes, forms of 'culture-jamming' and even the throwing of custard tarts! Our emphasis here is on *public* forms of political communication, which exclude private and interpersonal forms of political communication such as internal party discussions and the correspondence of a politician with a constituent.

Any overall discussion of the relationship between politics, the media and public life must encompass a broad territory, from issues of political theory to everyday relations between politicians and journalists. The relationship between politics and the media is complex because it involves so many different types of power at different levels, from the power of prime ministers and media moguls through to the way journalists interpret an event in the construction of their news story. The relationship between politics and the media is also complex because of the way the exercise of power works in conjunction with the 'freedoms' of debate. As we see in chapter 3, this is not to 'separate'

27

power from the functioning of the public sphere, but neither is it to discount the importance of public discussion and evaluation of political events and individuals.

Democracy and citizenship

Ideas about democracy and citizenship have existed as long as people have speculated about politics, and they have an equally complex history (Green 1993; Maddox 1996; Weale 1999; Andrews 1991; Heater 1990). But how are democracy and citizenship practised in contemporary times, and how do the media contribute to expressions of democracy and citizenship? The contribution of the media to politics, and to political communication more generally, is a constitutive feature of politics: democracies are founded on discussion and the communicative actions of politicians, and all citizens define and assign value to themselves, others and the community. It is also necessary, however, to ground our understandings of democracy and citizenship and the role of the media in a historical context. Democracy and citizenship are not just *categories* of political system and identity but are *historically based concepts*, which have changed dramatically over time as a result of political struggle and which remain open to further development.

The etymology of 'democracy' suggests that it refers to 'rule by the people', but beyond that there is much debate, conjecture and political struggle over the meaning of the term: many very different political systems around the world profess to being democracies. Many of the ideals of democracy spring from its earliest manifestation in ancient Greece, although the contemporary practice of democracy bears little resemblance to its ancient origins: modern mass societies employ forms of representative democracy, in contrast to the forms of direct democracy of the smaller city-states of ancient Greece. Democracy has a distinguished history but was once a term of derision, understood as a kind of 'mob rule'. Democracy did not automatically present itself as a desirable political system: its legitimacy was the result of hard-fought political battle, as was the extension of the franchise to working-class men, women, indigenous peoples and other racial groups. It is also important to note that modern forms of democracy did not arise as a 'pure' political system but grew out of the bourgeois critique of autocracy in early modern Europe. The emergence of the early capitalist classes required greater individual political freedom and freedom of thought as a corollary of their economic freedoms and entrepreneurial skills.

Despite its contested nature and the historical changes of democracy, it is possible to offer definitions of the term. Democracy generally refers to a society where equal rights for all are upheld, rather than a system based on hereditary or class distinctions, and it is a system with tolerance for minority views. Albert Weale offers the following definition: 'in a democracy important public decisions on questions of law and policy depend, directly or indirectly, upon public opinion formally expressed by citizens of the community, the vast bulk of whom have equal political rights' (1999, p. 14). Democracy often refers to a particular political system and form of government, but it also extends more broadly to the nature of the society. Maddox summarises five features of a democratic polity: constitutionalism, where the power of a government is limited by a constitutional order; responsible government, which has power to effect change but which is limited in the reaches of its power and limited to a particular term of office; an opposition that scrutinises and questions the actions of the government; democratic ideals, such as justice, liberty and equality, which should animate all political institutions such as the legislature, the courts and the public sector; and a free and pluralistic society which maintains a strong sense of community and group life (Maddox 1996, pp. 113–14).

Democracy, then, can be encapsulated as a form of government by the people, exercised directly by either the people or their representatives, but democratic principles inform public life more broadly, through a range of institutions, organisations, workplaces and family structures. There are certain principles that generally inform democratic theory, such as: everyone has an equal right to express their interests; each individual opinion is to be considered on the basis of its merit, regardless of the social rank of the opinion-holder; and majority decision making should determine most political issues. The communicative processes of a society and the media are therefore central to the democratic health of a society, and issues to be monitored include the kinds and rates of participation in decision making, the nature of dialogue, the exercise of reason and rhetoric. We consider later how the media contribute to the democratic health of society, but we need to note here that the legacy of more direct forms of democracy sometimes diverts us from a complex assessment of the contribution of the media to democratic health in *mediated* public life.

The status or position of a citizen can be defined as an inhabitant of a nation or other state possessing particular civic rights and participating in the public life of that society. The ancient origins of citizenship are located in membership of city-states but our contemporary understandings of citizenship are very much informed through the historical development of modernity. Citizenship assumed an importance with the rise of nation-states based on processes of secularisation and a process of law indifferent to the social status of legal subjects. Primarily, citizenship was defined by the notion of an individual's right to exercise their conscience and rationally pursue their idea of the common good in an overall context of freedom and non-coercion. The French Revolution was a critical event in the development of modern citizenship: it linked the idea of citizenship to ideas of equality and community, it established a relationship between citizenship and nationality, and subsequently it connected citizenship to the desire for political liberation.

The individual's rights as a citizen have developed significantly over several centuries. The historical basis of modern citizenship has been detailed most famously in the work of T.H. Marshall, who divided citizenship into three parts: civil, political, and social citizenship, arguing that each rose to significance in specific historical circumstances. For Marshall the formative periods of civil, political and social citizenship were the 18th, 19th and 20th centuries respectively, with each of these types of citizenship not supplanting each other but extending the concept of citizenship. Civil citizenship is composed of 'the rights necessary for political freedom' (Marshall 1964, p. 71), which include the right of an individual to own property, to receive justice and to exercise freedom of speech. Political citizenship refers to 'the right to participate in the exercise of political power, as a member of a body invested with political authority or as an elector of the members of such a body', while the social element of citizenship is manifested in the rights of an individual to access welfare and education and to 'share to the full in the social heritage and to live the life of a civilised being according to the standards prevailing in the society' (Marshall 1964, p. 72). Marshall's work has met with some criticism (Turner 1993), and some have suggested extensions to his historical narrative (Hartley 1999), but his categorisations of citizenship do point to its complex identity in contemporary times (Dahlgren 1995, p. 136):

> Citizenship is a more complicated and contested matter than may at first be apparent. It has to do with belonging, with inclusion; to be a citizen is to be a member of something we (metaphorically) call a community. It also has to do with participation in that community, while community as such has become a highly problematic notion in the contemporary world . . . To be a citizen means to be included civically and socially, not just politically. This in turn points to issues of the material foundations of that inclusion, the economic prerequisites for participation. Moreover, citizenship touches on the allocation of cultural as well as material resources.

Such simple summaries of democracy and citizenship, however, beg many important questions which are tackled by a variety of theoretical understandings. Put very broadly, democracy and citizenship can be understood from the point of view of liberalism, communitarianism, deliberative democracy, the agonistic pluralism perspective and the governmental perspective, all of which we now briefly consider.

Liberalism emphasises the rights of the individual over and above any conception of the common good (Gray 1995; Heywood 1998). It maintains that democracy is the political expression of an autonomous civil society and it understands citizenship as the capacity of each individual to rationally pursue their own conception of the good. Liberalism posits 'negative' freedoms: it is concerned with the rights that protect the individual from the excesses of the state, as long as individuals abide by the law.

The communitarians criticise liberalism for providing an atomistic view of democracy and citizenship (Tam 1998). They argue that democracy is much more than the accumulated views of individuals and is more centrally concerned with political participation and politics concerned with community creation. The communitarian position emphasises the relational aspects of citizenship, declaring that the common good has higher priority than individual desires and interests. In this sense the communitarian position posits 'positive' freedoms: it emphasises one's possibilities and rights to participate as citizens in the democracy.

Advocates of deliberative democracy object that both liberalism and communitarianism, for all their differences, focus too much on a view of society as centred in the state (Elster 1998). The deliberative democracy position offers a more decentred view of society: it is concerned less with the centrality of the state or the political system and more with the processes and procedures by which citizens, in a variety of social contexts, exercise public reason. Deliberative democracy, then, focuses less on democracy as a form of government and more on the nature of the debates and dialogue citizens hold on the problems, actions and goals of a society. The advocates of deliberative democracy often emphasise social unity as the goal of the democratic process, unlike the advocates of the 'agonistic pluralism' position. This understanding of democracy and citizenship is generally categorised by its anti-foundationalism, its belief in the inescapability of conflict, and its recognition and acclamation of the fact that democratic life is always heterogeneous and indeterminate. Advocates of an agonistic model of democratic politics do not seek to realise an ideal of democratic deliberation that would produce social unity, instead arguing that democratic struggles are always informed by the specificity of local circumstances and the exigencies of political contestation and rejecting the erasure of difference that occurs in the constitution of any form of social unity.

The agonistic pluralism position incorporates principles from both the positions of liberalism and communitarianism, as we see in Chantal Mouffe's understanding of citizenship. While Mouffe believes that the communitarian perspective on citizenship offers a richer account of our status as citizens, she argues that what citizens share in a democratic regime is not an idea of a common good but a set of liberal political principles based on notions of freedom and equality. These principles help constitute 'a "grammar" of political conduct' (Mouffe 1993, p. 65), or the 'respublica' (1993, p. 67), which are the rules or norms that must be subscribed and adhered to in political conduct. These rules, however, are not unchanging but are the site of political struggle. Mouffe, then, argues that liberalism relegates citizenship to a mere legal status, protecting the rights of individuals against the state; but it is important to retain the idea of individual liberties articulated in liberalism, not through any privileging of 'the individual' but through an understanding that complex modern democracies are marked by a radical indeterminacy that precludes any articulation of a comprehensive common good.

The final position on democracy and citizenship here is the governmental position, which is informed by the Foucauldian theories of governmentality and technologies of the self. Michel Foucault's historically specific account of governmentality details how the practice became prominent in the 18th century with the demographic expansion and the subsequent identification of a means of managing those populations. While Foucault notes that governmentality was 'first discovered in the eighteenth century' and was concerned with the management of populations, he does not posit it in the context of the democratic revolution. The governmental position, then, is distinguished from democratic theory but it is interested in citizenship, not as the embodiment of individual political will but as a means of educating individuals into appropriate value systems and forms of behaviour. Governmentality concerns 'the conduct of conduct' (Gordon 1991, p. 3)—that is, a type of activity that establishes the behaviour of individuals across the sweep of the private and social realms, from interpersonal relations through to relations with the state itself. Foucault locates the power of governmentality not within the centralised domain of the state but in its more diffuse distribution throughout a range of 'political' and other institutions, apparatuses and practices. As Foucault (1991, p. 95) states:

> Government is defined as a right manner of disposing things so as to lead not to the form of the common good, as the jurists' texts would have said, but to an end which is 'convenient' for each of the things that are to be governed. This implies a plurality of specific aims: for instance, government will have to ensure that the greatest possible quantity of wealth is produced, that the people are provided with

sufficient means of subsistence, that the population is enabled to multiply, etc. There is a whole series of specific finalities, then, which become the objective of government as such.

Political organisations

Within the conventional sphere of politics there are a number of political organisations that contribute to the political process. These political organisations are usually formally structured and seek political change through institutional means. They include political parties and pressure groups such as trade unions and consumer groups. As we have already noted, politics is also practised by a broader range of political actors, who either directly engage public attention through media coverage or challenge the authority of institutions and the political process more generally. These political actors include a spectrum of agents, from social movements through to terrorist organisations. These kinds of divisions are not clearcut or unchanging: the Green movement, for example, is both a social movement and a political party with a parliamentary presence throughout Australia and Europe.

Political parties constitute the most prominent form of political organisation. Political parties are united around particular ideological positions but they often represent a range of interests within a society. Major political parties represent a coalition of interests in order to attract a significant proportion of the electorate in mass societies, and the fact that voter choice in many complex societies, is limited to two main political parties is testament to the degree of aggregation of political interests. Political parties are an important means by which citizens engage in political activity, and they facilitate the formation of governments and the implementation of government policy. On gaining government, a political party exercises power at an executive level and through the parliamentary assemblies. For all their ideological differences, political parties abide by constitutional arrangements which enable and limit their powers, including having to win public support at elections and subsequently to convince the public of the virtues of government policy. This suggests the centrality of political communication to the successful functioning of political parties. A political party will engage in a variety of forms of political communication such as press conferences, party conferences and the daily management of media opinion through the lobbying of journalists or the use of media 'spin'.

The political landscape features a range of political organisations and actors other than political parties. These pressure groups bring about political change through their associations with political parties, their lobbying of parties and their contributions to public debate. The trade unions and business councils or chambers of commerce often share ideological interests with political parties and have organisational links. The Australian Council of Trade Unions (ACTU), for example, has majority representation at Australian Labor Party (ALP) state conferences, although this is under review. Other pressure groups are structured around professional memberships, such as the Australian Medical Association (AMA), or specific interests of the general population, such as consumer groups. Sometimes distinctions are made between such pressure groups and social movements, which usually have less of an institutional basis and come to prominence only when a single issue assumes salience. Groups opposing nuclear energy in the 1980s and contemporary groups opposing genetically modified foods would be examples of social movements (see Chapter 7).

The final kind of political organisation stands outside and challenges the bounds of political legitimacy. Such groups are difficult to collect into a single category but they are often oppositional groups that do not recognise the authority of the state, do not follow conventional forms of political behaviour and communication, and often use violence to promote their cause. Terrorist organisations, for example, do not abide by constitutional process and use violence in an attempt to further their interests. Of course, governments themselves often use violence in military action and in the exercise of the death penalty, but that violence is state sanctioned. The violence of terrorist organisations is a particular kind of political communication: these groups, without any institutional authority, depend on media coverage of their actions to highlight issues, challenge political values and institutions, and place political pressure on their opponents. While groups that use violence, against property or people, are almost always criticised in contemporary media coverage, violence has been, and continues to be, a part of political action: the suffragettes in England in the early part of the 20th century used violence against property to gain voting rights for women; violence was used in South Africa to overthrow the apartheid regime; and (as we see in chapter 6) violence is used in contemporary protests against the unchecked growth of global capitalism.

While the public may not qualify as a political *organisation*, it remains a significant political actor. The acts of political communication by parties, professional associations, pressure groups and terrorist groups may be oriented towards other political organisations but they are usually designed ultimately to achieve public acceptance. We investigate the public in greater detail in chapter 3, but it is useful to state here that the public are not just the passive recipients of communication from political organisations: they themselves exert considerable influence over the political process. This influence might be exerted through direct action, as when large numbers of people participate in demonstrations or sign petitions. The public can also exert political influence through more indirect means, when perceptions of public opinion, measured in opinion polling, lead to changes in policy and strategy by political parties and other organisations.

As we have already seen, the media are significant political organisations, which exert great influence over the political process. Mainstream media are big business and, as part of the corporate world, they have and promote particular ideological and corporate interests. The media do not simply transmit the messages of political organisations and actors but are themselves active contributors to political debate. Despite journalistic conventions of objectivity and balance, the media contribute to the political process in a variety of ways (as in the selection of news topics and the priority assigned to stories). The media also contribute directly to political debate, through editorials and 'commentary' journalism. Sometimes a media outlet will take an explicit stand on an important issue, as with *The Australian* newspaper's strong support for a republic during the republic referendum campaign.

The media are vital political organisations, not only because they themselves are important institutions in society but because they are the sites that produce social meaning. The media are not only the forums in which the range of political organisations congregate to take part in public debate, but they assign value and meaning to the pronouncements and interactions of political organisations. As we saw in chapter 1, there is debate over the ideological power of the media, but regardless of the extent of media power it is undeniable that the media do play an integral role in the reproduction of power relations between different political organisations. The media provide explanatory frameworks for issues and are important means by which social consensus is produced. These value constructions are made possible because of the organisational features of the media. Different political organisations will experience tremendous differences in access to the media and will have their point of view subject to greater or lesser degrees of interpretation. A Prime Minister, for example, normally will have less trouble gaining access to a media outlet to voice an opinion than the spokesperson of a terrorist organisation and, while the Prime Minister's views may be subject to scrutiny, the foundational values informing the views are more likely to be assented to than the values of the terrorist spokesperson.

Media regulatory frameworks

In chapter 1 we discussed the concept of mediated public life, noting how the media constitute politics and public life. We also need to note that the media arise out of, and are located within, particular political systems. The media are a consequence of a democratic political system that promotes freedom of speech and the principle of informed citizens participating in public life. The structure and the practices of the media are also informed by the political system. On a general level, the media, like other businesses, are affected by structures ranging from the taxation system to copyright law. The political system also puts in place a regulatory framework more specifically oriented to the media, which includes such matters as ownership structures and content provisions.

Media policy in Australia is the complex result of actions and debates by a broad range of groups, and the significance of media policy has been interpreted in different ways by media academics. Mark Considine (1994) describes a policy system 'as a way of understanding the intersection between the administrative and procedural routines of policy development and the wider political, historical, economic and ideological frameworks in which they are developed' (Cunningham & Flew 2002, p. 51). Media policy is not simply implemented by government but is a process whereby corporations, trade unions, thinktanks, public-interest advocacy groups, international regulatory bodies and many other groups engage in public debate and lobbying in order to bring about change. In media studies, issues of policy have been often interpreted from a neo-Marxist political economy 'oppositional' perspective that seeks to demonstrate how dominant media corporate interests are furthered through linkages with government and regulatory bodies. More recently, cultural policy studies, defined by a more 'centrist' political position, has emphasised the importance of working within the policy frameworks of liberal-capitalist societies. As Stuart Cunningham and Terry Flew note, the cultural policy advocates believe that 'an ability to influence the more "mundane" technical, administrative and organisational aspects of policy formation can make a significant political difference' (Cunningham & Flew 2002, p. 49).

In Australia, the press and broadcasting media are subject to different regulatory regimes. Broadcasting media are subject to the Broadcasting Services Act of 1992. This Act represented a substantial change in media regulation, moving from a system of external regulation by the Australian Broadcasting Tribunal (ABT) to a system involving greater degrees of media self-regulation, which featured co-regulatory arrangements between the ABT and the media industries as well as industry administration of codes of practice. The Act renamed the ABT the Australian Broadcasting Authority (ABA) while it reworked the body's responsibilities. The regulatory changes were based partly on a belief that the future media environment, characterised by the rise of new media technologies, would facilitate a greater abundance of media and diminish the need for governmental regulation. As Flew has noted, the industry approved of such regulatory changes because it simplified administration and provided a more direct link between broadcasters and viewers and listeners; others declared that the regulatory changes shut out public-interest and advocacy groups from the regulatory process (Flew 2002, p. 179).

The ABA has the general tasks of allocating and reviewing licences, monitoring media ownership laws and investigating complaints about the broadcasting industries. The ABA's public profile was elevated in 1999 and 2000 during the so-called 'Cash for Comment' crisis. Following a report by the ABC's *Media Watch* program, the ABA conducted an inquiry into the conduct of talkback radio hosts John Laws and Alan Jones as well as other broadcasters. The inquiry investigated the allegation that the broadcasters were receiving money to make positive editorial comments and that they had failed to disclose their commercial agreements. One of the allegations was that the Australian Bankers Association paid Laws to present a favourable image of banks, which he had previously criticised. The ABA found that there had been breaches of the industry code, and it imposed new conditions on radio station 2UE's licence requiring differentiation between advertising and program content and the disclosure of any commercial agreements with presenters. The ABA also imposed a new set of 'standards', requiring other commercial radio licensees to follow similar rules (Gordon-Smith 2002).

While the trend in media regulation is towards less governmental influence and greater self-regulation by media outlets, it remains the case that important democratic principles inform the media regulatory framework. Much may be made of a new multi-channel media environment enabled by new digital media technologies, but the airwaves, which are used by existing radio and television licence-holders, remain a national resource and the licensees have significant obligations to the community to use that resource in a productive and socially beneficial manner. Media regulation is informed by beliefs that the community should be provided with adequate levels of news and information, that there should be adequate levels of Australian content, and that 'community standards' should be maintained in matters such as the representation of sex and violence. The ongoing need for media regulation is also prompted by the economics of the media industry. While the Internet and new media technologies do promise a new media environment characterised by greater plurality of ownership, the huge start-up costs and the comparatively small size of the Australian market has made it difficult for new players to enter traditional media markets. Media regulations are needed to address concentrations of media ownership, because for a democracy to work well there has to be a free flow of information, and allowance for the expression of a wide range of views, including unpopular and minority views. It is something of a paradox that governments are required to regulate the media to ensure the freedom of speech and healthy media environment that can subsequently become the source of critique of government. As John Henningham (1995, p. 277) states:

> Governments try to influence media because of the power news-papers and other media have to influence public opinion about governments. As in other western democracies, Australian news media have a significant role, not only in reporting upon and evaluating government activities, but also acting independently to scrutinise politicians and government employees .

The Australian print media remain outside the regulatory net of the government, but they were effectively captured by the cross-media ownership laws announced in late 1986. As suggested briefly in chapter 1, the cross-media ownership legislation prevents media owners from assuming dominance across a range of media in particular markets. As former Labor Prime Minister Paul Keating put it, cross-media ownership laws allow you to be either a 'prince of print' or a 'queen of screen' but not both. Under these laws, a television proprietor is limited to a 15 per cent stake in a print media outlet in the same market, and vice versa. Overseas investors cannot own more than 25 per cent of a newspaper and 15 per cent of a television station. A Productivity Commission inquiry in 2000 recommended that the cross-media ownership laws be abolished, although it added that broadcast and print group mergers should be based on public interest, as defined by the Australian Competition and Consumer Commission (Conley 2002, p. 198). The legislation remains in place, even though a number of media owners have lobbied for change and the Howard government has moved to change the legislation. The print media are regulated by the Trade Practices Act, which is a general law preventing market domination by particular companies. The print media are also subject to laws of defamation and contempt. The Australian Press Council, started in 1976, is a private organisation without any legislative or legal power to discipline the press. The Council does, however, has as its charter the job of maintaining journalistic standards and press freedom and commenting on matters such as ownership and control. Its main function is to hear and judge complaints from the public about unethical and inappropriate journalistic behaviour. The Press Council, however, has often been criticised as a powerless body (Conley 1997, p. 264). Individual journalists are also accountable through their union, the journalists' section of the Media, Entertainment and Arts Alliance, and its code of ethics.

In Britain, the state has always had a central role in structuring and regulating the media system. Until 1955, broadcasting in Britain was a state monopoly conducted through the BBC, a public body that remains the largest single broadcaster of television and radio. When commercial radio and television were permitted, companies still had to obtain a licence fee from the state and were subject to control by the then state-sanctioned regulator, the Independent Broadcasting Authority (IBA). In May 2002, the British government announced plans to change the media ownership laws (Department of Culture, Media and Sport 2002). Under the proposed changes, a single powerful regulator would be established—the Office for Communications (Ofcom). Despite this, the proposed media ownership changes would liberalise the market further. Some of the rules that are set to be scrapped include those preventing the single ownership of the ITV television network, those limiting ownership of more than one national radio licence, and those preventing large newspaper groups from buying the television broadcaster Channel 5, a move that is said to allow Rupert Murdoch to acquire a terrestrial broadcaster to complement his satellite television operations ('Murdoch gets his way' 2002) although this is being strongly challenged by a House of Lords committee. The government has said that it would retain some key limits on cross-media ownership, including the rule that any newspaper group with over 20 per cent of the national market would not be able to have a substantial stake in ITV, as well as a scheme that would ensure at least three local commercial voices in addition to the BBC in almost every community.

In the United States the state has played a less significant role in the structuring and regulation of the media. The US political system has always been opposed to the involvement of the state in the media. The USA does not have an equivalent public broadcaster to the ABC or the

BBC, and broadcasting has always been overwhelmingly commercial. As with the other political systems, however, the apparent existence of a 'free' media requires qualification. All broadcasters in the USA require a licence from the state and must abide by media regulations. In 2003 US media regulations were further liberalised. Broadcast networks are now able to reach 45 per cent of the national audience, rather than 35 per cent.

Political and media relations

The political system exerts a less formal kind of control over the media landscape, through the personal influence of politicians and political actors on media owners and journalists. While the common concern is related to the political influence of powerful media owners, we should not forget that politicians also possess considerable power in their dealings with the media. Politicians have the power to enact legislative changes, and they can bring considerable public pressure to bear on media organisations. Apart from legislative and regulatory changes, politicians can shape media organisations through staff appointments. In Australia, the appointments of the chairperson, the managing director and the board of the ABC have provoked much controversy and accusations of political interference. As we saw in chapter 1, media owners do exert influence over politicians, but their power is not automatic and their influence depends on a number of context-specific circumstances such as personality and the prevailing economic and political health of the political system.

The influence of political actors over journalists on an everyday basis is more readily observed and realised. Politicians and their staff know that the journalists are dependent on a supply of information, and considerable political power is exercised through decisions about what information to release and the timing of its release. The close relationship between political actors and journalists is compounded by their physical working environments. Unlike many journalistic 'rounds', where the journalists work in separate physical locations from their sources, political journalists often work in the parliamentary building. This facilitates intense relationships between the two parties which can work for and against the journalist. On the one hand, the journalists have close scrutiny of the political actors, which provides them with a greater opportunity to discover the true state of affairs; on the other, the closeness of their relationship with sources can mean they do not have sufficient critical distance from the information they receive.

Political management of the media is further exercised through a range of specific forms of political communication, from the elaborate spectacles of party conferences and US Presidential conventions through to the humble press release. They include 'media events', news conferences, photo opportunities, media interviews, and the activities of 'spin doctors'. These forms of political communication are discussed in greater detail in chapter 7, but they are introduced here because they are the predominant ways in which politics interacts with the media and they are the public face of politics. Politics, of course, is constituted through a wide range of actions and behaviour, much of which remains hidden from the general public gaze, but the *public significance* of politics is revealed through these forms of political communication.

One important form of political communication is political advertising. It is distinguished from the other forms because it is not 'free media', which are those forms of political communication where the political actors are subject to scrutiny and gain publicity without having to pay media organisations. Political parties have control over the content and meanings of political advertising, but the public is also aware that the message emanates from a single, uncontested source. This factor limits the effectiveness of political advertising, compared to other forms of news media-based political communication, where a degree of scutiny of the information enhances its political efficacy. We are more likely to believe the political message of the Prime Minister if his communication of the facts occurs through questioning by a journalist than if the message had been directly conveyed through a political advertisement. The use of 'free media' by political actors is, however, not without its costs. The scrutiny afforded to a politician in an interview or at a news conference means that the message can be seriously challenged and undermined. The most carefully organised party conference or the most deferential political interview can result in unexpected outcomes, either through the actions of the interrogator or through a mistake made by the political actor. There are also some forms of political communication that are not mediated by journalists or classified as political advertising. A Prime Minister's address to the nation, for example, is a direct address to the public which, on the one hand, diminishes its political believability; on the other hand, the genre of the 'address to the nation' carries with it a prestige and social value that tends to enhance the significance of the information imparted.

The increasing importance of political communication has seen a rapid growth in political personnel working in the area. Politicians, particularly those at ministerial level, are likely to have a number of staff in media-related areas in addition to their media relations officer or press secretary. Media relations officers are not public servants but are political appointees. Usually, the media relations officer has worked previously as a journalist, and so has an intimate knowledge of the needs and strategies of journalists. The functions of the media relations officer include the issuing of press releases and the organisation of news conferences, handling inquiries from journalists and following up on information released to the media, and organising media access to their politician. The media relations officer will advise their politician on media strategy and work on the politician's media presentation skills, including voice and style training. The media relations officer may also oversee the work of other staff members, such as researchers, and liase with other party staff.

Another important feature of contemporary political communication is government media offices. These offices are not aligned with a particular politician but work more generally to distribute information and promote the work of the government of the day. At a federal level in Australia, the Fraser government in 1978 established the Government Information Unit, with an initial staff of six journalists; when the Hawke government came to power it established the National Media Liason Service (otherwise known as aNiMLS), with a staff of 22 (Ward 1995, p. 170). The government media offices have attracted attention in recent decades because they have become increasingly politicised, instead of keeping to their supposedly more neutral public service role of supplying information relevant to government activities and functions. In keeping with this more politicised role, government media offices also engage in media surveillance. In this sense they play an active role in controlling the news agenda by attempting to minimise media investigation, advising government of media strategy, and monitoring and countering Opposition statements.

In recent years politicians and their media-related staff have developed a more sophisticated understanding of the needs and functions of the media. They have learnt to tailor the various forms of political communication to maximise the communication of their message and to minimise media scrutiny and editorial 'interference'. Such strategies range from minimising dissent on the floor at party conferences to timing the release of information shortly before media deadlines, to deflecting interview questions towards the content the interviewee wishes to discuss. Some political observers believe this increased sophistication has shifted the balance of power in political communication too much in favour of the politicians. It is believed that the media have become too dependent on the information supplied by political actors and not sufficiently critical and detached from the information sources. Growing public cynicism about politics is said to be a consequence of this process. While there is merit in these views, it also needs to be noted that growing political sophistication in media management has resulted in the public developing a greater media literacy. We are increasingly aware of the strategies of politicians in media interviews and are able to decode the political intent behind the visual images used in a policy launch. This view, in turn, is countered by the argument that the emphasis on media management has resulted in media coverage and public reaction focusing unduly on political strategy and the process of communication, and not sufficiently on the relevant issues and matters of substance.

Conclusion

Politics is a difficult term to delineate because, while it relates to a specific sphere of society with recognisable institutions, organisations and actors, it can also refer to the struggles to assign value to a broad range of social relations and practices. As we saw in chapter 1, the media have a similar definitional complexity: they have specific democratic and informational functions, but they are also involved in meaning-making processes that encompass social and everyday life. Effective political communication between the governors and the governed is necessary for the democratic health of a society and for the promotion of an active citizenry. How democracy and citizenship should function in a society is difficult to evaluate, and it is difficult to describe the effects of political and media relations in modern public life. A range of value positions on the importance of the 'individual' and the 'community', 'unity' and 'conflict' inform theoretical understandings of liberalism, communitarianism, deliberative democracy, agonistic pluralism and governmentality. Politics plays an important role in structuring the media environment through formal mechanisms such as regulatory laws, the work of government media offices and political staffers, as well as through more informal and personal networks. Politicians and other political actors are adept at manipulating the media to further their interests, but this sophisticated use of the media needs to balanced with an appreciation of the ongoing scrutiny of political performances by the media. It is clear, however, that any understanding of contemporary politics needs to consider its entanglement with the media.

The public — 3

The public is both a body of people within a society and a domain within which debate about that society occurs. The concept of 'publicness' permeates much of our discourse, from the most esteemed civic activity through to the local toilets. Publicness is defined partly through spaces that may be accessed by all members of the community, such as public parks and galleries. Publicness is also defined partly through visibility: an activity or event is public if it is open to general scrutiny. Publicness can be defined through an association with the state: hospitals, universities and broadcasters are public because they are owned and funded by government. Publicness carries with it particular values: to be 'public-spirited' is to be motivated by a desire to promote the common good. It follows that, while publicness is usually conceptualised as both a domain and a body of people, it also encapsulates a kind of subjectivity. The condition of publicness fosters a particular ethico-political orientation towards others. As outlined in chapter 1, the public in contemporary times is constituted through media discourse: we experience public life chiefly through our common consumption of the media rather than experiences of physical co-presence. 'Public' generates meaning through its opposition to 'private'. To make this point is to highlight that the public and the private are not *a priori* categories but are defined through political struggle and public debate.

'Public' has a broad range of applications but carries with it very particular connotations. 'The public' is distinguished against 'the social' through the foregrounding of civic functions and duties; it carries with it connotations of rationality and concern with the political realm. In this sense, the public domain is part of the broader domain of the social which incorporates a wider range of activities and events featuring individuals interacting with others. The distinction between the public and the social has been the subject of much theoretical scrutiny. Hannah Arendt (1958), for example, argued that the rise of the social in modern times has been at the expense of a particular understanding of the public realm. The work of Jürgen Habermas has also mobilised particular values of publicness in its account of the public sphere. While these kinds of distinctions are important, they can hinder our understandings of the contemporary public domain. As John Durham Peters reminds us, the translation of the original German term *Öffentlichkeit* as 'public sphere', while emphasising the political and institutional framework in which the body of the public can find expression, has to some extent also created the new concept of 'the public sphere' and obscured other, broader senses of the term (1993, pp. 543–4). *Öffentlichkeit* also literally means *publicness*, incorporating senses of the citizens, readers and viewers who constitute the public as well as the condition of being rendered public, as in openness or publicity. It is this broader understanding of publicness that provides us with a better understanding of the function of the media in public life. The media renders public that which it discusses—whether it be the parliamentary system, the financial markets or the latest gay beat (McKee 1997). It is this condition of publicness—which includes all kinds of traditional private concerns, such as finance, sexuality and the consumption of consumer goods, as well as traditionally public concerns—that constitutes public life.

'The public' is a strange entity because it is both an object and a subject, and its existence arises through the dialogue between these different statuses. The public is rendered an object by the ubiquitous discourses about the public and public opinion. Opinion polls, commentators, marketing surveys and politicians all construct the public as an object while they seek knowledge about the public so they can speak for the public. It is, of course, necessary to make such 'readings' of the public because the mass public as a whole is amorphous— 'unknowable' in any singular sense—yet so many decisions in public life are based on and granted legitimacy because they are judged to be supported by public opinion. The public is also a subject, and people come together as a public in modern times when they engage in the consumption of media, when they all engage in readings of the events, the stories, the debates that circulate in that society. It is important to stress that the public does not have some pre-existing existence: it is rather the media, among other institutions, that bring people together as a public through their common access to and consumption of media content. This process of public formation facilitates the organisation of consent, as well as expressions of difference. Public formation involves a dialogical process, where the reading public appraise the representations of public opinion offered to them by the readings of the public in the various polls, surveys and commentaries.

The public sphere and public life

'The public sphere' is a difficult concept to delineate, but it often encompasses the former grandeur of ancient Greece and 18th-century English coffee houses as well as a negative orientation towards the contemporary industrialised and commercialised world in which we live. As Terry Eagleton has stated, 'The "public sphere" is a notion difficult to rid of nostalgic, idealising connotations; like the "organic society", it sometimes seems to have been disintegrating since its inception' (1985, p. 8). Despite this, the concept persists, largely because it describes a social terrain and communicative process which is seen, however problematically, as the basis for democratic politics. The concept persists today precisely because the public sphere has become a more complex phenomenon: traditional democratic process meshes with identity politics and the ubiquity of the mass media.

The starting point for much of this debate is Habermas' *The Structural Transformation of the Public Sphere*. Although Habermas' work has been criticised for vacillating between normative analysis and descriptive account, his conception of the public sphere has been influential and is acknowledged 'both as a standard of evaluation and as an empirical concept' (Hallin 1994, p. 3). Habermas argues that from roughly the mid-17th century to the 18th century the public sphere arose as a realm that existed between the state and civil society.

Civil society was composed of both the expanding domain of economic relations and the intimate sphere of personal relations. The new sphere of 'the public' was a bourgeois public sphere, which consisted of private individuals who came together to debate among themselves the regulation of civil society and the conduct of the state. The public sphere was physically located in the coffee houses, the public libraries and reading societies that began to spring up during this time. The idea of the public sphere was also largely facilitated by the rise of a press that for the first time was relatively free from state control and regulation.

Habermas maintains that this bourgeois public sphere of the 18th century was the nearest historical approximation we have ever had of the ideal of the public sphere. The rest of Habermas' history charts a decline of the bourgeois public sphere, through the industrialisation of the 19th century and on into the 20th century. He notes a number of features that contributed to the decline of the bourgeois public sphere: the growing relationship between increased state interventionism and organised capital; the blurring of the distinctions between public and private; and the transformation of the family into consumer units. The rise of the popular press and the general commercialisation of the media also contributed to the decline of the public sphere. Habermas argues that: 'The public sphere in the world of letters was replaced by the pseudo-public or sham-private world of culture consumption' (1989, p. 160). James Curran (1991, p.83) summarises Habermas' position on the modern mass media, stating that:

> The media ceased to be an agency of empowerment and rationality, and became a further means by which the public was sidelined. Instead of providing a conduit for rational-critical debate, the media manipulated mass opinion.

Habermas is less interested in accounting for the historical change he describes than in deriving from those circumstances a normative formulation of the public sphere. That is, while the public sphere might be described simply as the forum within which public opinion is circulated and formed, Habermas is more interested in how public opinion *ought* to be formed. From Habermas' work such a model of the public sphere can be articulated—a neutral arena where information about issues affecting 'the public good' is available, regardless of individual rank and free from the domination of the state. The private opinions of individuals assume a public character when they are subject to rational debate, a process facilitated by the media. Crucially, public opinion and agreement on society's direction and values are determined not simply by accessing existing opinions but by the deliberation of all citizens.

Habermas' conceptualisation of the public sphere, however, has equally attracted considerable criticism, much of which Habermas himself has subsequently acknowledged (1992). Critiques of the bourgeois public sphere have focused on the way significant numbers of people were excluded from the domain and the manner in which the specific interests of the bourgeoisie were able to be represented as universal interests. The patriarchal character of the bourgeois public sphere has been noted in a number of studies (Fraser 1989; Landes 1988), which have demonstrated that the exclusion of women was not simply an unfortunate historical byproduct of the domain but a constitutive factor of the bourgeois public sphere. It has been argued that Habermas' singular focus on the bourgeois public sphere meant that he did not consider other groupings and the general fragmentary nature of the public realm. It is necessary to conceive of the public realm as consisting of a plurality of public spheres. Nancy Fraser takes up this point, arguing that 'in stratified societies, arrangements that accommodate contestation among a plurality of competing publics better promote the ideal of participatory parity than does a single, comprehensive, overarching public' (1989, p. 122). Perhaps the major point informing the critiques of Habermas' work is that Habermas does not consider the necessarily *conflictual* nature of the public sphere, and he does not explore the relationship between reason and power. Some people have maintained that because of Habermas' concern with the 'free space' of society there is little discussion of the role of the state per se. They argue that ultimately Habermas' conceptualisation is limited because it does not fully consider the political and ideological struggle between different interests that occurred in order to represent the bourgeois public sphere as the singular forum of reason. Rather, according to Eley (1992, p. 306):

... the public sphere makes more sense as the structured setting where cultural and ideological contest or negotiation among a variety of publics takes place, rather than as the spontaneous and class-specific achievement of the bourgeoisie in some sufficient sense.

Habermas' work is also the focal point of a tradition (discussed at the end of chapter 1) in which criticisms of modern media underestimate the significance of visual forms of representation and the performative basis of public life. Habermas contrasts the early bourgeois public sphere with the form of representative publicity of the king in the feudal society of the High Middle Ages, where the publicness of the king 'was not constituted as a social realm, that is, as a public sphere; rather it was something like a status attribute' (Habermas 1989, p. 7). That is, representative publicity was embodied in the spectacle of the king himself—in his personal attributes, such as his dress and demeanor and the visual displays of his court. Habermas argues that modern forms of mass media have initiated a 'refeudalization of the public sphere' (Habermas 1989, p. 195), where visual forms of communication and personal spectacle are said to be only objects of display, hindering critical debate. In this sense, Habermas is suspicious of representation in both the political and semiotic meanings of the term. He is suspicious of the political form of representation, where the people are symbolically embodied in the form of an individual representative, such as the type of representative publicity found in the High Middle Ages. But Habermas is also suspicious of aesthetic representation. As Peters (1993, p. 562) states:

> Habermas prizes conversation, reading and plain speech as worthy forms of discourse for a democratic culture and is frankly hostile to theatre, courtly forms, ceremony, the visual, and to rhetoric more generally. The brief flowering of the bourgeois public sphere is sandwiched, in STPS's [*Structural Transformation of the Public Sphere*] narrative, between two moments of 'representation': feudal pomp and modern PR. 'Show' and 'manipulation' always go together in STPS.

Such discussion highlights both the difficulty and the importance of constructing a specific and comprehensive understanding of public life that encompasses the intersections between the public sphere and the vicissitudes of social experience. Habermas himself acknowledges at the start of his study that the historical and contemporary understandings of the term 'fuse into a clouded amalgam' (1989, p. 1). Oskar Negt and Alexander Kluge also note that the public sphere 'as a frame of reference fluctuates confusingly' (1993, p. 1), denoting specific institutions, agencies and practices while at the same time representing 'a general social horizon of experience in which everything that is actually or ostensibly relevant for all members of society is integrated' (1993, p. 2). More recent accounts of the public sphere have explicitly addressed the political and cultural dimensions of public life. Peter Dahlgren, for example, while noting that he emphasises 'the political public sphere' rather than 'the more broad cultural public sphere' (1995, p. 7), argues that the public sphere can be seen not just as 'a "marketplace of ideas" or an "information exchange depot", but also [as] a major societal mechanism for the production and circulation of culture, which frames and gives meaning to our identities' (Dahlgren 1995, p. 23).

Such discussion highlights the difficulty of delineating the public arena, but it also provides some pointers as to how it will be conceptualised throughout the rest of this book. First, I will use the term 'public life' rather than 'public sphere' in order to signal a broader conceptualisation of the public domain than is encapsulated in ideas of the public sphere. The use of the broader term 'public life' is also motivated by a belief that we cannot, nor should we, circumscribe boundaries for a public sphere where particular kinds of political and civic activities occur. Even though our major interest in this book is the territory of politics and the role of the media in public debate and deliberation on civic matters, I maintain that these subjects can be analysed effectively only by understanding their immersion in broader cultural contexts. The issues and debates of the 'political public sphere' can derive meaning and value only from their understanding in the contexts of 'the more broad cultural public sphere'. To promote such a conceptualisation of public life is not to render redundant the idea of a public sphere where 'politics' is conducted, but it is to maintain that such a site cannot be isolated in order to function 'properly' because such a site is always informed by, and in constant dialogue with, more comprehensive societal figurations which together constitute public life.

This notion of public life, then, foregrounds the multiplicity of public domains and the porousness between these domains. We live in a world where the financial markets and business, a 'private' realm traditionally dissociated from the public sphere, have tremendous influence on politics and the organisation and values of public life. We live in a world in which celebrities and sporting stars, such as Australian Aboriginal athlete Cathy Freeman, have real political influence through their actions and comments. We live in a world of proliferation of 'alternative' or 'counter-publics', such as the anti-globalisation activists who use the Internet to organise themselves and develop media strategies to engage with the broader public domain. We live in a world in which a US Presidential campaign is determined not only by fiscal and social welfare policies but also by the publicity surrounding a passionate embrace. Public life is the complex product of the intersections, alliances and clashes between the political public sphere, other publics, the state, the mechanisms of the market, and areas of life, issues and types of activity traditionally delineated as 'private'. The difficulty of delineating what constitutes public life resides in its very ubiquity: the interplay between semiotic and institutional manifestations of publicness; the complex coexistence of traditionally 'public' forms of life with the public orientation of more traditionally 'private' forms of life; the dialogue between 'political', 'financial' and 'popular' realms; and the proliferation of forms of representation of public life.

The conceptualisation of public life outlined here offers a critique of any attempt to insulate the public sphere from other areas of public life, but it also embraces a broader range of human behaviour, activities and values, and more fully acknowledges the role of power in the formation of any public domain. Habermas' conceptualisation of the public sphere foregrounds the use of reason in public deliberations with the ultimate goal of social unity. This focus can be seen even more clearly in his later work on communicative action (Habermas 1984). There, Habermas distinguishes between 'strategic' or 'instrumental' rationality, which is informed by principles of technical effectivity, and 'communicative' rationality, which has 'connotations based ultimately on the central experience of the unconstrained, unifying, consensus-bringing force of argumentative speech' (Habermas 1984, p. 10). While such work is valuable, and the exercise of rational debate is integral to the functioning of the public domain, it has also been criticised for positing a too limited portrayal of public life. An exclusive focus on the 'rationality' of public life and a suspicion of other forms of expression and communication only prevents us from understanding how public life functions. We need to establish a more heterogeneous public life, where expressions of difference are not subsumed by expressions of unity, where desires, emotions and bodily aspects of communication are granted legitimacy and their centrality to communication in public life is fully recognised (Young 1987).

Finally, any theorisation of contemporary public life needs to incorporate more fully questions of power, given that public life is constituted through multiple forms of publicity that engender discursive contestation among diverse constituencies. Our understanding of contemporary public life argues that public life is constructed through the recognition of mutual interests and the establishment of networks of association. This does not discount the importance of principles of free association, equal and undifferentiated access to the public realm and rational deliberation, but it emphasises and grants legitimacy to the concrete needs of particular constituencies, expressions of protest, conflict and power. In this sense, the *hegemonic* basis of public life is emphasised. To maintain the hegemonic basis of public life is not to reassert views about ideological control by powerful interests but to maintain that public life is the product of social struggle and that it is shaped through its confrontation of the role of power in the formulation of situated alliances, which are always open to contestation.

The mediated public and public subjectivity

In the concept of mediated public life introduced in chapter 1, we focused on the role of the media in the constitution of public life. We noted how the public domain in contemporary times can be found in media discourse rather than a physical location. Here, we need to focus on the nature of the public in mediated public life. There are a variety of forms of public subjectivity in the mediated public. Public figures, such as politicians and celebrities, stand out from the general public but, for all their unique qualities, their status is necessarily bound up with their relationship to the broader public. The individual person also becomes a public subject through their orientation to a mass public. This is most traditionally found in the category of the citizen (discussed in chapter 2), but it incorporates other types of subject positions in contemporary public life, such as that of consumer or fan.

In any democratic society, the public has enormous power and a pervasive influence in everyday life. The public, in effect, 'rules' through its representatives—those elected to govern. The perceived wishes of the public also inform implicitly every debate covered in the daily media. Whether the price of petrol, whether Australia should become a republic, or the size of the budget surplus, each issue is driven not only by those individuals who have an interest in the issue but also by their attempts to mobilise public opinion behind their judgement. Of course, while we speak of the public as a single entity, it is in reality an extraordinarily diverse, complex and fractious collection of people who hold an equally bewildering array of ideas, values and attitudes. The public is also not just a collection of individuals but is constituted by a range of organisations and groups, which formulate and promote particular interests. But we speak of 'the public' as a singular and generally unified entity, and we believe we can 'know' public opinion. This, of course, highlights the fact that 'the public' we know is a product of discourse; the public we know are representations, surveys and polls of the public and public opinion. Only at the time of a general election do we have a snapshot of the entire public, although this could only be said of countries (such as Australia) that have compulsory voting. We also need to note that the general election result is still a representation of public opinion, formulated through a particular kind of voting system.

The mediated public is populated by a broad range of individuals and types who assume a particular kind of subjectivity through their functioning in the public arena. The mediated public is littered with a range of public figures, including politicians, actors, journalists and broadcasters, businesspeople, senior unionists and public servants, sports stars, supermodels and a host of other celebrities. Public figures are not just individuals who become well known while remaining essentially the same person: rather, the process of becoming a public figure involves the creation of a new subjectivity, which is the product of a struggle between that person and their media representations. People undergo an extraordinary transformation when they become public figures, as they are subjected to successive readings by journalists and the public, and inserted into the complex media, economic, promotional and political networks that constitute public life. We, the public, have a peculiar relationship with public figures, knowing their charms and flaws intimately while not knowing the people personally. We have seen the fundamentally different orientations subjects have to themselves as they become subjects of publicity and take on the burden of public expectations, as in the frequent invocations of 'role model'. We have seen this process played out through a range of public figures, including British business tycoon and Virgin founder Richard Branson, Australian tennis star Lleyton Hewitt, and actor Russell Crowe. In each of these cases, with varying degrees of success, people have had to learn to manage and cultivate their public persona through their engagements with the media and the public.

The 'public relations' that are fostered between public figures and the general public are highlighted in the figure of the celebrity. The concept of celebrity is slippery, and it increasingly permeates all domains of public life. As Turner, Bonner and Marshall have noted, there is a 'syllogistic logic lurking behind discussions of celebrity' (2000, p. 9): the meaning of the term has become so broad that anyone who attracts public interest is deemed a celebrity. One way to try to limit the meaning of celebrity is to note that the term is conventionally reserved for those who are not elected to public office, those who have special talents in the realm of entertainment, the media and sport, and those who consciously seek and cultivate a public profile while having their private lives subject to public scrutiny. For celebrities, power resides in the ability to maintain a bond with the public at the same time as promoting their unique status. That is, the power of celebrity derives from the negotiation of an extraordinary/ordinary binary. In attempting to characterise the appeal of celebrities, some scholars have drawn on the notion of 'charisma' (Brunt 1992; Chaney 1993). This notion focuses on that special quality that *distinguishes* the celebrity from the ordinary person rather than emphasising the *connections* between celebrated and prosaic souls. Increasingly, however, the reporting of the lives of celebrities works not to promote a fantasy world but to highlight the exigencies of everyday life. While celebrities are marked by their difference from the ordinary person through their status and the domain in which they circulate, it is surprising the extent to which stories about celebrities deal with everyday problems, such as the juggling of career and family, and the management of personal relationships and personal finances. In this way celebrities provide a vocabulary of values and style; they function more to embody social typifications than unique, special qualities. As David Chaney (1993, p. 144) has argued:

> . . . it seems more appropriate to suggest that the nature of the appeal of contemporary celebrity status is to forms of re-communalisation— ways in which individuals can feel themselves to be a member of a collectivity with recognisable norms, order and existential validity . . .

Public subjectivity incorporates not only the privileged, highly visible bodies that circulate in public life. The individual becomes a public subject through their orientation to mass public. All of us adopt positions of public subjectivity through our identities as citizens, fans and even consumers. The identity of fan and consumer, dealing with activities conventionally associated with the private sphere, is traditionally differentiated from the more traditional public subject position of citizen; fans and consumers are considered here as forms of public subjectivity because of their general public orientation. Our acting out of roles such as citizen, fan and consumer involves our negotiating a relationship between our personal life and those public subject positions. All of those roles involve our taking on a set of values and assuming a certain relationship vis-à-vis the mass public or a particular constituency. We have to negotiate the contradictory subject positions of contemporary public life when the self-interest of the consumer clashes with the public-spiritedness of the citizen. As people have a fundamentally different orientation to themselves when they become public figures, so too does an individual person have a different orientation to themselves when they consider themselves part of 'the public'. That is, it is necessary to undergo a process of self-abstraction—we need to be blind to our particular features and to expressions of difference—when we include ourselves as part of the mass public.

One of the dominant tensions in contemporary public life arises from the conflict between the proliferation of the representations of bodily difference and the tradition of the public sphere, where the particularities of bodily difference are bracketed theoretically to allow a rational, objective consideration of an issue. That is, the principles of openness and universality that were integral to the rhetoric of the bourgeois public sphere, meant that the merits of a person's argument were judged independently of who they were; features of a subject's 'status-life' were theoretically not relevant to the public judgement of their views. Now, while there remains significant residue of the rhetoric of abstract disembodiment circulating in the contemporary public sphere, it competes with a very different kind of publicity, where public contemplation dwells on a plethora of bodies for a variety of purposes. Public figures act to embody the previously 'disembodied' public: 'Public figures increasingly take on the function of concretising that fantasmatic body image, or in other words, of actualising the otherwise indeterminate image of the people' (Warner 1992, p. 388). As a result, the mass public sphere has had 'to develop genres of collective identification' to satisfy conflicting mass desires—to abstract oneself into a 'privileged public disembodiment' and to actually embody that public through a variety of discursive and promotional strategies (Warner 1992, p. 392).

Publics and audiences

Publics are also defined through their differentiation from and relationship to audiences. The boundaries between our understanding of 'publics' and 'audiences' have become increasingly blurred in mediated public life, where the public is constituted through its accessing of mass media. When we watch the television nightly news we are addressed simultaneously as members of the public and as members of an audience.

Mass communication researcher Denis McQuail discusses the audience as a group or public when it 'is a collectivity that has an independent existence prior to its identification as an audience' (1997, p. 26). He says that the clearest examples of the audience as public are likely to be either historical or small-scale. The readership of a local newspaper or the audience of a community radio station share a physical location and a range of social activities and networks that exist independently of the media. This definition, though, privileges the public's pre-existing physical status, and it is difficult to consider how the modern media audience could also be considered a public. McQuail notes that 'the early television audience, despite its size and heterogeneity, could possibly have qualified as a certain kind of public in the sense meant here, since it was distinctively *national* and content provision was also national' (McQuail 1997, p. 28, author's emphasis). This is, however, still the case, despite the contemporary multi-channel environment in which we live. The contemporary public is a more flexible and elusive category, and while it is still linked to conditions such as geographical proximity, it is also variously formed through the accessing of a range of mass media.

Despite their close association, differences remain between the two concepts of audiences and publics. To say that we are a member of an audience is to highlight our status as an 'individual' in our audience participation. While we share some association with others who are also members of the audience, our identity as part of an audience is determined less by our relationship to other audience members and more through our common accessing of the same text. An audience is defined as a grouping where processes of commercialisation and commodification are highlighted. This conceptualisation of the audience as market is from the perspective primarily of the media producer, and we have to be careful not to ignore the communicative relationship that occurs with audiences through their negotiations of texts and through their interactions with other audience members.

A public is conceptualised more as a political or civic identity, distinguished from the commercial forces that inform an audience. Membership of a public downplays our status as individuals and more fundamentally foregrounds our relations to others. As I have already suggested, to consider yourself a member of the public involves a process of self-abstraction, where you are indifferent to individual defining characteristics. Of course, an audience can be abstracted through ratings figures and market segments, but even then individual defining characteristics such as age and income levels are usually relevant. Membership of a public emphasises interactivity, as in debates about issues and activities such as voting. This raises McQuail's point about a public's extratextual existence, but we need to be cognisant of the interactivity that occurs through the public's accessing of media texts. The interactivity of the public also suggests that publics perform an active role in their self-formation, direction and normative regulation. While we accept structured positions as members of an audience, membership of a public commonly suggests more of a sense of *agency*, where we as members of the public decide such matters as which government to elect, which values inform our identity, and how we should punish wrongdoers.

The national public

'The public' is not defined by any particular geographical boundaries or limited to a specific size: it may be designated as the residents of a country town meeting on a planned highway bypass or it may be designated as the national population voting on a referendum. As implicit in these examples, membership of the public is not just an identity that can be assumed passively but carries with it ideas of activity and engagement with issues of general concern. The degree of activity and engagement can vary, of course: in a mediated society we actively engage with public matters every day through our consumption of mass media. Membership of the public is generally aligned with citizenship, but people can be members of the public without being citizens. Membership of the public often foregrounds civic rights and duties but it also extends to our general association with others, such as when we attend the Test cricket or a concert. 'The public' is therefore a category of identity which, while often relating to the political and civic realm, more generally extends to a shared association with others.

'The public' is chiefly conceptualised, however, as a national public. The national public has both political and cultural orientations, which are inextricably linked. The debate about an Australian republic, for example, mobilised the political views of the national public as a citizenry and mobilised discussion about the national identity and the ordinary Australian way of life (see Craig 2000a and chapter 9, for further discussion). As with other expressions of the public, the national public is a mediated phenomenon. The national public is captured in the representations and narratives of the nation; it is exhibited and given life through the portrayals of the national identity and nationalism. While representations of the national public and expressions of nationalism are often criticised because they highlight conservative and commercial features of national identity, the concept of nationalism is not in itself coloured with any political hue but is rather a site of struggle. As Stuart Hall (1993, p. 355) has written:

> Nationalism . . . isn't *necessarily* either a reactionary or a progressive force, politically . . . It is capable of being inflected to very different political positions, at different historical moments and its character depends very much on the other traditions, discourses and forces with which it is articulated. [Author's emphasis.]

The national public is also realised through the functioning of national public broadcasters, such as the BBC and the ABC. Public broadcasters were conceptualised to serve a national public in both its unity and diversity. Recent perceived crises in the logic of public broadcasters have occurred at a time when the unity of the national public has become increasingly problematic (Craig 2000b; Hawkins 1997).

The national public, then, is not a singular or easily containable entity, and is characterised less by its unity than its management of difference. In Australia there are many 'faultlines' that are continually negotiated, such as the division between the city and the bush. Although national structures, institutions and traditions may give the national public a sense of permanence and certainty, the national public is characterised more by its ongoing making of itself through processes of debate. In recent years the Australian national public has been produced through the political struggles over the republic referendum, the Sydney 2000 Olympic Games and the treatment of refugees.

Subaltern publics and the global public

We tend to think of 'the public' as having a singular and permanent status. Politicians and other public figures may come and go but 'the public' is that constant participant that animates public life. 'The public' also has a solidity to it: 'public opinion' is the bedrock on which common sense and norms in a particular society are based. Habermas' ideal public sphere, while a site of ongoing vigorous debate, is informed by a vision of ultimate social consensus and unity. Membership of a public, however, can also cut across different kinds of groupings with a less stable basis and informed by less conventional values. Every day we move effortlessly between our identifications as members of the local public, the state public, the national public and the global public. Membership of a public is not limited to a geographical identification but can be motivated by other kinds of associations. In this sense we can talk about a plurality of 'publics', which together constitute public life.

The plurality of publics that inform the broader public domain have been noted by a number of scholars. In her discussion of the public sphere, Fraser examines 'interpublic relations' (1989, p. 66) and identifies what she calls 'subaltern counterpublics' (1989, p. 67), which are arenas where subordinated groups can establish identities and arguments, arenas from which action against the wider public can be launched. She gives the example of the feminist subaltern counter-public in the late 20th century, where a range of publishing companies, journals, bookstores, festivals and local meeting places enabled women to reformulate their needs and identities and establish a perspective on language that was used subsequently in political actions in the wider society.

Distinctive groups in society assume a character as a public: young people, for example, together constitute a youth public. The youth public is formed through people of a certain age bracket recognis-ing shared interests and values, but they are constituted as a public because those interests and values are subject to public debate and change, and 'membership' of that public is open to all youths in the society. The youth public not only engages in discussion and debate among themselves through particular media forums such as Triple J— it also engages with the broader public on the issues and values of interest to youths.

The public can even extend globally. The rise of global movements around environmental issues such as global warming prompts responses from people all over the world, and anti-globalisation rallies at the meetings of international financial organisations such as the

International Monetary Fund and World Economic Forum have triggered responses from a global public. The global public is formed through people's recognition of their common association and common interests as inhabitants of the planet. Global publics do not form spontaneously and independently but, as with all manifestations of a public, are linked to the wider organisation of public life. Global publics arise as business and capital assume a more global orientation, as global media become more of a reality, and as transnational political institutions take on greater authority. Global publics, as with all publics, are not only organised around overtly political developments but arise also in response to emotional events and changes. The destruction of the World Trade Center towers, for example, focused the attention of people all over the world, uniting them through their grief and generating global discussion about the state of global society (Buck-Morss 2002). The global public is realised increasingly through the Internet, which generates a global consciousness generally and prompts public responses to specific issues.

Conclusion

The condition of 'publicness' is under much stress as the quality of public debate is criticised and as public institutions struggle against the onslaughts of privatisation. 'The public' is sometimes said to have lost its way because there is less social unity and an erosion of traditional values, while politicians are often presented as invoking the wisdom of the public merely in an attempt to align opinion to their own designs. Alternatively, public opinion retains a potent force, which sometimes sweeps the most powerful politicians out of office and which can be mobilised to great effect to fight for embattled public institutions such as hospitals, schools and broadcasters. These factors prompt us to reconsider the activities and duties of we individuals who together constitute 'the public', as well as the values and functions that should inform and structure public life. These factors direct us to dwell on the historical development of the public domain in order for us to comprehend the possible future manifestations of public life. Habermas' theorisation of the public sphere gives us valuable insight into its historical constitution and foundational values, but I have also suggested that the communicative basis of public life needs to be conceptualised more broadly and that the fragmentary and contested natures of the public domain are desirable characteristics. While we may commonly perceive the public as a national public, the public is not limited to a particular geographic identity and can encapsulate a variety of networks of association, providing that there is open access and debate within those networks of association. The public is also populated by a range of public figures who increasingly traverse traditional boundaries of politics, culture and business. The mediated basis of public life means that particular forms of subjectivity are produced through celebrities and other public figures, and I have noted how such public figures serve an important function of embodying values and 'problems' for a society. The public has become a difficult concept to delineate in mediated public life, not least because of the blurred distinctions between publics and audiences. Such a distinction, however, also helps us to focus on the civic identity of publics and our activities and relations with others through membership of a public.

Part 2
The Media and Politics

The print media

4

The future of the print media at the beginning of this century is at its most uncertain since Gutenberg's invention of the printing press in the middle of the 15th century. For many centuries, print media were the pre-eminent means of public communication. Only in the 20th century, with the rise of the cinema, radio, television and ultimately the Internet, was the dominance of newspapers challenged. Even in this context the print media retained the mantle as arguably the most influential type of media in political communication. At the start of the 21st century the media landscape is in a state of flux, with the development of the Internet, new television technologies and greater convergence of media forms. The future of the printed word in newspapers and magazines and the future mode of delivery of the written word is the subject of much conjecture. While we are entering a new media age which will bring about fundamental changes in political practice and public formation, the written word in some form will certainly remain integral to that media age, and it even seems more than likely that for some time yet we will continue to pick up the morning newspaper off the front lawn.

In this chapter my focus is on the print *news* media and newspapers, but our discussion will also consider the growing importance of magazines and Internet news media. The Internet is a particular type of media, with its own conventions of textual organisation and communicative dynamics; it is not the simple electronic posting of written text. Web-based 'newspapers' are considered here because they have not as yet assumed the importance of more conventional types of news media and still derive much from traditional print news. This is changing rapidly, and web-based news services will increasingly realise their potential as audio and video become a more substantial component of online news services.

Besides major mainstream newspapers and magazines, the print media encompass many other kinds of publications. Apart from the metropolitan and national press, there are a large number of community newspapers serving local areas. Suburban newspapers and local publications have burgeoned in recent years due to suburban population growth, demand for local news and information, and advances in desktop publishing (Conley 2002, p. 229). Any search of a newsagent's shelves shows the tremendous number of specialist magazines in circulation, and this does not take into account many more trade publications. In the financial domain there also has been an explosion of corporate newsletters and pamphlets in recent decades, offering general business news and investment advice. All news media use the written word: a press photograph will carry a caption and, while television news may be driven by the need for dramatic pictures, television journalists still need to craft the written word to construct a powerful story. The centrality of print to all news media cautions us from making easy and clearcut divisions between the various forms of media. Similarly, print is a form of visual communication, a point not lost on the layout editor but often 'overlooked' by the rest of us.

Newspaper history

The newspaper seems an old form of media in the current media environment but the modern mass-market newspaper is a relatively recent invention, rising to prominence only in the second half of the 19th century. Arguably the earliest popular mass-market newspaper was the *New York Sun*, which started in 1833. The *New York Sun* contained human-interest stories, crime stories and local news (DeFleur & Ball-Rokeach 1989, p. 52). The growth of the mass-market newspaper throughout the second half of the 19th century occurred as a result of a number of factors, including the cutting of stamp taxes, great advances in printing technology and a reduction in the cost of newsprint. During this time literacy levels also rose, aided by the establishment of the first statewide public school system in the USA during the 1830s and by the introduction of the 1870 Elementary Education Act in Britain, which enshrined state responsibility for educating the populace.

The growth in literacy and a more informed population did more than enhance processes of public formation and democracy. The growth of the mass-market newspaper was integral to capitalist expansion: not only a more educated populace but a large market of consumers was created. This facilitated a massive expansion of advertising, including the development of display advertising, which, in turn, helped promote processes of commodification and the first brand name marketing. People started to buy brand names, not the products themselves: they didn't just buy tea but *Tetley*'s tea; they didn't just buy soap but *Pears* soap.

We also need to do more than merely acknowledge the historical economic contexts of the print media: we need to see the print media as a constitutive feature of the burgeoning capitalist system. The earliest journalistic publications were composed of economic information. The development of commercial and financial newspapers actually predated the arrival of the political press (Parsons 1989, p. 12). The rise of news was linked to the flow of information along the early trade routes. The greater flow of commercial and political information, distributed along increasingly integrated communication networks, resulted in regularly produced journalistic publications. As Jürgen Habermas notes, the 'traffic in news developed alongside the traffic in commodities' (1989, p. 16). The formation of early journalistic publications was also prompted by the recognition of the commodity status of the news itself. Journalism assumed an embryonic form when the contents of private correspondence detailing the news of distant wars, harvests, transportation routes and trade were deemed to have more general significance.

The print media have never been simple recorders of society but have always been active agents in political change, economic development and social formation. Newspapers have always struggled against forms of state control and in turn facilitated political change. A regular and relatively independent press occurred in Britain only around the start of the 18th century, after the lifting of the Licensing Act in 1695 (Curran 1977). While there had been pamphlets and newspapers in Britain prior to 1695 (Harris 1987, p. 8), it was only then that what we might recognise as modern journalism began. *The Daily Courant*, which is usually credited as the first daily newspaper, started in 1702. Habermas notes specifically that with the publication of *The Craftsman* in 1726 'the press was for the first time established as a genuinely critical organ of a public engaged in critical political debate' (1989, p. 60).

In England during the 1830s there was the rise of a very successful radical or working-class press. The radical papers, which were often published 'underground' to avoid heavy state taxes and duties, became so popular that their collected gross readership exceeded that of the 'respectable' press of the day. Newspapers were read aloud in social settings such as pubs or they were shared between friends, and that sort of social interaction and discussion helped forge a class identity during the times of the Chartist and early socialist movements. The radical papers also played an important role in the creation and rise of trade unions and other working-class organisations (Curran 1977).

The very form and content of the modern newspaper facilitated the historical development of a particular kind of urban subject and orientation towards the world. The regularity of the daily newspaper, its easy transportability and its presentation of everyday, secular matters shaped the knowledges and values of public life and its temporal and spatial organisation. Indeed, Denis McQuail (1994, p. 14) goes so far as to suggest that:

> In a sense the newspaper was more of an innovation than the printed book—the invention of a new literary, social and cultural form—even if it might not have been so perceived at the time. Its distinctiveness, compared to other forms of cultural communication, lies in its individualism, reality-orientation, utility, secularity and suitability for the needs of a new class: town-based business and professional people. Its novelty consists not in its technology or manner of distribution, but in its functions for a distinct class in a changing and more liberal social-political climate.

'Quality' and 'tabloid' print news media

The newspaper landscape in most countries contains a range of newspapers, but how are those newspapers different and what criteria are used to distinguish between newspapers? The tag of 'quality' on the broadsheets implicitly suggests that tabloid newspapers are 'without' quality, but is this true? Alternatively, does the tag of 'popular' media imply that broadsheet newspapers are without popular support? The task of delineating the newspaper landscape is made more difficult by the simple binary classification system that casts newspapers into either the 'quality' or 'tabloid' basket. Such a system is unreasonably restrictive, but it does raise the thorny issue of judging 'quality' in newspapers. Of course, at a simple level, 'broadsheet' and 'tabloid' refer to the different page sizes of the newspapers, but there are 'quality' newspapers of tabloid format, such as *The Australian Financial Review*.

Part of the difficulty in judging 'quality' across forms of mass media and across the spectrum of the print media stems from the different uses of the term. Sometimes, 'quality' revolves around *aesthetic* judgements and is used as a marker of *taste*. Here, a complex mix of criteria that distinguish 'high culture' from 'popular culture' are mobilised. These criteria include: a hierarchy of artistic form or genre (a television drama might be marked as quality cultural product because of its literary origins); the non-commercial nature of the cultural product (quality product is said to be more assured if commercial pressures are diminished); appropriate choice of subject; and appropriate *treatment* of content (a feature story about a marriage break-up would be restrained in its descriptions of the sexual conduct in an affair). Such criteria of 'quality' have been used as *class* distinctions, and while such judgements no longer carry the cultural weight they once did, they still circulate and have resonance in media debates. In contemporary times, 'quality' is more likely to be judged in terms of *content* and *professionalism*. As with the comparison between print and broadcast media, and with judgements about broadsheet newspapers, 'quality' is assessed in the news media on the more comprehensive treatment of a range of serious issues. The mix of news in 'quality' newspapers has a greater emphasis on political, business and serious social issues. The 'quality' of broadsheet newspapers also resides in the *reporting* of such issues. The quality of journalistic professionalism means such issues will be reported with fairness, balance, and a concern for accuracy over and above the dramatic or sensational aspects of a story.

The tabloid media carry with them a range of cultural and journalistic values that extend well beyond the simple definition of the format of the media. Traditionally, 'tabloid' was associated with newspapers, but recently the term has been used to describe a range of media, including current affairs and reality television programs as well as lifestyle and other entertainment-based magazines. In Australia tabloid newspapers have a more 'respectable' image, but in Britain some of the tabloid newspapers, while part of the mainstream press, have a quite controversial image. Attempts to define such an amorphous kind of journalism inevitably raises difficulties, but its content typically focuses on entertainment news and issues traditionally associated with the private sphere. Traditional tabloid or popular journalism content is marked by an emphasis on: bizarre, extranormal happenings; crime stories, particularly with 'ordinary' people as victims; and stories on celebrities. John Fiske (1992, p. 48) has stated that:

> Tabloid journalism's economic success is beyond question, but its popularity has hardly been investigated and its defining characteristics are remarkably hard to pin down with any precision. Its subject matter is generally that produced at the intersection between public and private life: its style is sensational, sometimes sceptical, sometimes moralistically earnest; its tone is populist; its modality fluidly denies any stylistic difference between fiction and documentary, between news and entertainment.

Considerable struggle has occurred over the merits of tabloid media. It has been something of a conventional wisdom to criticise tabloid newspapers and other popular media for their distraction of readers from the traditional news concerns such as parliamentary politics, policy issues and foreign affairs. It has been argued that the tabloid media quest for the largest possible audience has resulted in a trivialisation of the news and contributed to an impoverishment of public life (Franklin 1997). Colin Sparks, for example, has distinguished popular journalism from the 'quality' press by stating that it is through the former that 'the "personal" obliterates the "political" as an explanatory factor for human behaviour' (1992, p. 40); that 'the structure of "the popular" in modern journalism is ... one which is massively and systematically "depoliticised"' (1992, p. 39). Others have promoted the positive contributions of the tabloid media. Fiske, for example, has argued that popular journalism, with its sensationalism, contradictions and its delight in blurring fact and fiction distinctions, generates a sceptical, active reader, unlike the more passive, believing subject of the more 'respectable' forms of news (Fiske 1992). On another topic, tabloid journalism has been criticised rightly for its voyeuristic treatments of women, but it has also highlighted issues that have not been covered traditionally by the 'quality' newspapers: important social problems relating to the private sphere, such as domestic violence, teenage anorexia and sexual harassment, have been given special emphasis in the tabloid media and have subsequently influenced coverage by other media outlets (Lumby 1999).

Newspaper readerships

The political influence of the broadsheet newspapers stems not only from their focus on more substantial news issues and their interpretive powers but also from the nature of their readerships. The 'quality' press may attract a smaller proportion of audience share than the 'popular' media, but the broadsheet newspaper readership comes generally from the more 'elite' sections of society. The readership of the broadsheet newspapers will draw on a proportionally larger share of professionals and other people who have an interest in, and influence on, matters of public policy and social change. Such distinctions regarding news media readership are, however, harder to make in the contemporary media environment, particularly in Australia. The spectrum of newspaper readership is less clearly defined than in previous decades, when class divisions played a substantial role in distinguishing print media readership profiles. The greater levels of media generally available, easier access to media and higher numbers of tertiary-educated people has rendered distinctions between the readerships of 'quality' and 'popular' news media more complex than in previous times. This does not invalidate such distinctions: the broadsheet newspapers still exert a particular political influence, and they are still adept at capturing a particular kind of reader.

The overall readership of newspapers is generally becoming more class-based because broadsheet newspapers, while often contending with falling circulations, are retaining a solid core of professional-class readers, while the tabloid newspapers have suffered a number of closures in the past decade and a loss of readers to television news. The Australian newspapers that actually recorded circulation rises in the decade to 1996 were the 'quality' newspapers, *The Australian Financial Review* and *The Australian*. Both newspapers target upmarket, business-oriented A and B demographic readers (Brewster 1996). A and B refer to the upper end of a spectrum used by market researchers to distinguish media audiences. A/B readers are often in managerial or professional occupations on higher-level incomes with interests in areas such as real estate, travel, wine and cars. Such readers are attractive to advertisers, who will pay higher advertising rates to capture such a readership; readers at the other end of the spectrum are less attractive. Advertising revenue is a much more substantial component of overall newspaper revenue than the income raised through the cover price of the newspaper. The purchasing power of A/B readers explains why smaller-circulation broadsheet newspapers can be highly profitable and why larger-circulation tabloid newspapers can be closed down.

The readerships of tabloid newspapers may not encompass the professional and managerial strata of society but the 'popular' press remains politically influential because of the sheer size of its readership. The circulations of some tabloid newspapers are many times larger than those of their broadsheet competitors. *The Sun* in Britain, for example, has a circulation of 3.4 million, compared to the circulation of *The Times* at 710 302 (Audit Bureau of Circulations 2002). Politicians know that they ignore the popular press at their peril, particularly if many of the popular newspaper readers are swinging voters. The tabloid newspapers have had a chequered record over the past few decades, with the most substantial change being the closure of many afternoon newspapers. This has been due to a number of factors, such as the increasing use of the car as transport to work instead of forms of public transport (enabling the popularity of 'drive-time' radio), the rise of early evening television news, and the decline in advertising revenue due to the class-based nature of the tabloid readership.

The remaining tabloid newspapers are very strong in circulation and political influence. The political power of tabloid newspapers is most graphically illustrated in the example of *The Sun* in Britain, whose editorial blessing is now a vital part of political success in that nation. In Australia, fewer newspaper titles in specific markets mean that the tabloid newspapers retain considerable political influence, but these are more mainstream in their tone and content. In the larger markets of Sydney and Melbourne, the tabloid newspapers *The Daily Telegraph* and *The Herald-Sun* are pitted against their respective broadsheet competitors, *The Sydney Morning Herald* and *The Age*.

Newspapers do more than supply information to a particular kind of readership. The press enable—and are involved in—a complex communicative process, which involves the readers, the subjects of the news (whether politicians or other public figures), and the newspaper itself. All of these entities are participants in the process of political communication. The newspaper itself can be a site where debate between these participants occur. The letters-to-the-editor page and the commentary or opinion ('op-ed') pages contain often vigorous debates between the public, politicians and other public figures. The newspaper is also a participant in the political process through the promotion of certain causes, and this sometimes results directly in provoking political action. One example is Prime Minister John Howard's personal intervention in the petrol-sniffing crisis afflicting Aboriginal communities, which was raised by *The Australian* (Toohey 2001).

One way the news media have attempted to forge stronger links between themselves and the community is through forms of 'public journalism'. Public journalism re-emphasises the civic dimension of journalism (Rosen 1996; Lloyd & Hippocrates 1997). The redundancy in the name public journalism highlights the extent to which conventional journalistic practice has been judged to have sidelined the public and contributed to a desiccation of political life. Instead, public journalism seeks to break down the barriers between the news, political and bureaucratic professionals, and citizens. It argues for a more active contribution from the citizenry in the setting of the news agenda and a greater degree of activism from journalists. Public journalism, which is more prevalent in the United States than Australia, is manifested in various ways but generally involves a project where a journalistic outlet promotes over time a particular issue of community concern, organises events and meetings for public discussion, facilitates further research and data collection, and regularly reports on this process. Public journalism may seek to raise public awareness of a problem in order to manage community divisions, and it may result in policy changes or particular actions, such as the opening of a needle-exchange centre in an area in which illegal drugs are commonly used. Public journalism has the laudable goals of promoting a greater sense of participatory democracy and facilitating closer links between journalists and the public, but it has been subject to a number of criticisms. These criticisms include the charge that the public journalism project can be used primarily as a promotional strategy for the news organisation—also that public journalism runs counter to conventional journalistic standards, where journalists report the news instead of making it.

Newspapers are also criticised for their perceived remoteness from the concerns of their readers and the population more generally, particularly in the area of the reportage of politics. It is argued that political reporting is overly negative, focusing on 'catching out' politicians rather than facilitating genuine public debate. Politics is seen to be reduced to a 'game' between politicians and the news media—a game that limits readers to the position of spectators. In a bid to overcome this remoteness, newspapers have been trying to more directly target the needs and interests of their readers. Broadsheet newspapers have given more emphasis to 'lifestyle' issues and included more liftouts on subjects such as computers, wine and travel. They have even introduced format changes in response to the ever more frantic lifestyles of their readers, such as *The Sydney Morning Herald*'s '10-minute-Herald', which provides a one-page summary of the newspaper's content.

Such criticisms of the performance of the press are part of a more general critical perspective on the political process and the quality of public debate. The divide running through a number of political issues in Australia in recent years has prompted accusations that politicians are not 'listening' to the public. The general decline of the rural sector and rural communities, and specific issues such as the privatisation of Telstra, have exacerbated public feelings of dislocation from their representatives. Increased volatility in the electorate is said to be a consequence of this perceived inability to 'connect' with the concerns of the public. The remoteness of politicians from the public has grown to such an extent that management of the communication process is now an integral part of everyday politics. Politicians are constantly stressing the need to 'listen to' and 'hear' the opinions of their constituents, and political schedules and media events are increasingly organised to 'show' politicians meeting the public.

This highlights a paradox of modern political and public communication. On the one hand, the news media are central to the constitution of the public in contemporary mediated public life. The pages of newspapers, television current affairs stories and talkback chatter are sites where the beliefs, fears and values of 'the public' find their expression as 'public opinion'. On the other hand, the news media are criticised for their remoteness from the real concerns of their audiences and targeted as one of the causes of public feelings of alienation from politicians and the political process. This paradox is, however, not so much a problem that needs to be 'resolved' as the very nature of mediated public life which must be negotiated. Former US President Bill Clinton, for all his self-imposed difficulties, was successful because he was both a good media performer as well as having the 'common touch' with the people he personally encountered. News media outlets, through their presenters and journalists, also struggle with this negotiation of the 'mediated' and 'personal' realities of modern public life.

Setting the news agenda

The press exert political influence through their roles in setting the news agenda each day for other media. Newspapers may be suffering increased competition from television news and newer media sources such as the Internet, but the front-page stories of the morning newspapers will still usually inform morning radio news bulletins, talkback sessions, and television news stories that evening. This is the dominant rhythm of the daily news cycle, but it does not preclude other forms of influence: the morning newspaper may include a more comprehensive treatment of a story that broke on the previous evening's television news. The establishment of the daily news agenda is also not limited to the *press*, of course, but includes other media, most notably the ABC morning radio news and current affairs. This also highlights the unity of the news agenda across the many different media outlets and the different types of media. The news agenda is generally not autonomously generated by media outlets in their interactions with the public and newsworthy institutions and people but is generated largely through their interactions with other media.

The news agenda is, however, sometimes set by investigative reporting, where one news outlet discloses a major issue that is subsequently reported by other news media. Investigative reporting mobilises many romantic connotations about journalism, but the reality is that investigative reporting has been under much pressure, particularly in Australia. Investigative reporting arguably reached a high during the late 1980s when a number of newspapers and broadcasters, such as the ABC's *Four Corners* program, helped bring about several royal commissions. Since then, the amount of investigative reporting has been cut—due to the high costs of devoting a team of reporters to a long-term project and due to Australia's restrictive defamation laws, which can limit the disclosure of sensitive information. Despite this, some newspapers in recent years have revived investigative or 'in-depth' reporting teams (Conley 2002, p. 28).

The press retain great influence, not only in establishing *which* news stories are to be covered but in determining *how* those stories are to be presented and interpreted. The interpretation of the journalist occurs both in the framing of the news story and in forms of more subjective reportage, such as columns, editorials and opinion pieces. A growing feature of newspapers in recent years has been the proliferation of opinion pieces on news pages other than the traditional 'op-ed' pages. There will now be a conjunction of a major news story and an opinion piece on that issue, often written by the same journalist. The press has the highest proportion of what Nimmo and Combs refer to as journalist-pundits. The journalist-pundit is accepted as an authority on political affairs, has good access to political circles, and is 'a source of opinion-formation and opinion-articulation, agenda-setting and agenda-evaluation' (Nimmo & Combs 1992, p. 8). The journalist-pundit or political commentator is able to express opinions through a regular column in the newspaper. The column allows the journalist to express a subjective point of view, assess arguments and provide direct advice to participants, give background details gleaned from political connections, and even appeal for some kind of action. As Nimmo and Combs declare, the 'column is a stylistic dramatisation not only of the subject or issue at hand but also of the pundit's rightful status to speak on it authoritatively' (Nimmo & Combs 1992, p. 12).

Another form of 'opinion journalism' occurs in the editorials of newspapers. The editorial is the public 'voice' of the newspaper, and it often also professes to be the collective voice of its readers. The authority of the newspaper editorial stems from the tradition of the press's partisan political positioning. Editorials, usually written by the editor or a senior editorial staff member, do not have the political import they once had and tend to attract most attention at election time, when the newspaper advocates a particular vote. The editorial can, however, signpost the promotion of a particular issue by the newspaper and articulate why the newspaper has initiated the reporting project.

Our discussion of the interpretive powers of the newspaper journalist highlights the general journalistic functions of selection, framing and interpretation. Despite the professional discourses of objectivity and balance, journalists are always active agents in the manufacture of the news. Events are not intrinsically newsworthy but events, issues and sayings become news if they fit certain news values—values that are informed by cultural ideas about the way the world works and by the way journalists process the news. Journalists have a series of 'frames' through which the chaos of the events of the day can be organised and interpreted. These news frames, which help to establish the routine nature of news production, arise out of the need to efficiently produce a newspaper each day from a multitude of events and a deluge of information. They are employed throughout the process of constructing a news story, from a reporter's assessment of whether an event or issue is worth covering to the subeditor's rewriting of the opening paragraph to enhance the story's newsworthiness.

The journalistic set of news values is informed by and, in turn, reinforces, ideological values in a society. In order to 'make sense' of news stories, journalists must draw on and reproduce 'commonsense' understandings, and they must mobilise notions of hierarchy and dissent. In the most famous study to date of news values, Galtung and Ruge compiled a list of news values such as negativity, reference to elite nations and persons, personalisation, the clarity of an event, the composition of a news agenda, and unexpectedness (Galtung & Ruge 1981). How such news values work ideologically can be demonstrated through a discussion of personalisation. While it may seem 'obvious' to focus on individuals relevant to a particular issue, personalisation highlights a view of people as independent, free agents who are able to bring about change and downplays the social forces shaping the circumstances of that issue.

Galtung and Ruge's study highlights those newsworthy features of the *content* of news stories, but the news value of a story is determined also by the processes of news production and other institutional and economic factors. A story is more likely to be published, for example, if there is a high degree of prefabrication, in the form of a press release or some other kind of text. The value of a news story is further dictated by the perceived audience of the newspaper. Competition is another important factor in news judgement: a story is deemed to be more newsworthy if it is exclusive (Tiffen 1989).

Parliamentary reporting

An important domain of political reporting is parliamentary reporting. While public confidence in politicians may have subsided and the public esteem of parliament has declined, parliament remains the central source of political power and the main object of political scrutiny. The media coverage of parliament is crucial to the democratic health of a society: it is the primary source of communication between the governors and the governed. Despite the obvious importance of a media presence in parliament, journalists have historically had to struggle to find a permanent seat in the building. It was not until 1803 that the British parliament gave its first official recognition of the press, when a speech by Pitt on the war with Napoleon went unreported and the speaker of the parliament subsequently ordered that a bench be set aside for reporters (Lloyd 1988, p. 14). The parliamentary round for journalists is now the most prestigious area of reporting: parliamentary reporting provides journalists with a high public profile and a close relationship to the political leaders of the country or state. Increasingly, however, the parliamentary round does not involve the reporting of parliament. Instead, there is a focus on the activities of the Executive and leading members of the Opposition, with the activity of parliament functioning as a kind of theatrical backdrop. Occasionally, activities such as parliamentary committee hearings provide important news stories, and occasionally backbenchers will raise important points, but generally the focus is on the Prime Minister and the Cabinet.

The reporting of parliament now has a visible presence in the building and considerable influence on the political process. There are 141 reporters in the federal parliamentary press gallery in Canberra (Steketee 2001, p. 7). The job of parliamentary reporting is influenced by the physical working environment of Parliament House. Unlike on most other reporting rounds, journalists reside in the same building as their major sources. While journalists are not so close to politicians and political staff in the new Parliament House as they were in the old House, the physical working environment still engenders a 'hothouse' atmosphere and an active rumour mill. Journalists are deluged with information: documents and press releases are constantly deposited in the press gallery boxes. Journalists estimate they can spend 80–90 per cent of their working day within the building (Tiffen 1989, p. 34). The self-contained physical working environment also means that gallery journalists find their primary social support from among their own ranks and from political staff.

Press gallery journalists are not only ensconced with politicians and political staffers in Parliament House—they are also isolated on a daily basis from their editors in the newsroom and other journalistic colleagues. This semi-autonomous nature of press gallery journalism, together with the pressured working environment, produces a particular type of journalist. Press gallery journalists are often described as extremely hard workers and professional, but also as more cynical and colder (Payne 1999, p. 30).

The gallery is organised along hierarchical lines. Margaret Simons details three levels: the 'Young and the Restless' junior reporters; the 'heavy-hitters' in their 30s or 40s who hold senior jobs, such as bureau chief; and the gallery leaders, such as Laurie Oakes from the Nine television network and *The Bulletin* magazine, and Glenn Milne from the Seven television network, who also writes for *The Australian* (Simons 1999, p. 23). The gallery leaders, or 'God correspondents', have tremendous political influence and good political contacts; they often break the major news stories, although their power is said to be in decline (Simons 1999).

The gallery journalists and politicians share a symbiotic relationship, which is nonetheless complex and fragile. Politicians need to develop links with journalists to communicate policy and opinion to the public, while reporters need the information and insight that the parliamentarians can supply. The journalist–politician relationship (explored further in chapter 7) is fraught with difficulties. Apart from special cases of leaks, politicians and political staffers must decide on an everyday basis how much and what level of information can be disclosed, well aware that their point of view may not be promoted in a news story and that journalists are speaking to a range of people. As Trish Payne notes, a successful relationship, informed by such difficult circumstances, requires a degree of honesty about mutual exploitation and a good dose of realism: 'The balance between successful use of each other, while accepting and respecting that at times there must be conflicting agendas, requires a certain level of trust—an ability to balance the relationship of user and used' (1999, p. 35).

One of the dominant criticisms of the press gallery, as of others in Parliament House, is that they are too insular, elitist, and disconnected from the concerns of the general populace. Such criticisms maintain the media focus on political machinations in Canberra blind journalists to the impacts policy has on society. Perhaps the most famous example of this in recent years was the inability of the news media to identify and explain the Hanson phenomenon (Kingston 1999). The political importance of Pauline Hanson was often dismissed by journalists because she was not a political insider and did not abide by political conventions, but her political naivety and her manner of 'plain speaking' made strong connections with sections of the

Australian public. Some journalists counter these criticisms by declaring they have the specific task of reporting power machinations and policy debates (Payne 1999, p. 41). Others maintain that a close relationship with politicians is a necessary feature of a press gallery that is performing its democratic function: 'The whole rationale for having a press gallery is to allow journalists to get close to politicians; to form alliances, to push and blur the lines between public and private; to swap confidences and find out what is going on . . .' (Simons 1999, p. 6).

Another criticism of the press gallery is that it adopts a 'herd mentality' in its reportage of parliamentary politics. Although the press gallery works in a highly competitive environment, where journalists seek to obtain news stories before their competitors, it also exists in an environment where there is a dominant understanding of the political process that is difficult to challenge. As discussed above, all journalism employs particular news frames to select and interpret information, and this is particularly relevant for political reporters. It is argued that parliamentary reporters continually reproduce and reinforce a portrayal of politics that emphasises strategy and 'point-scoring' at the expense of a scrutiny of policy design and outcomes. However, this 'herd mentality' is a strategy that can be used to good journalistic effect: the sheer number of press gallery journalists gives them a critical mass which makes it hard for politicians to ignore or easily appease them.

Magazines

Magazines are an important part of the print media industry, and the variety of titles cover a broad range of modern life. Magazine consumption is a part of the lives of most Australians: $1.36 billion was spent on magazines in 2000, 70 per cent more than a decade earlier, although total circulation was 328 million, up only 10 per cent on ten years earlier (Bita 2001, p. 6). The situation is similar in Britain, where magazine circulation grew by 13 per cent between 1990 and 1999 (McKay 2000, p. 204). This period has seen a great proliferation of titles, which has cut into the circulation figures of established magazines as well as fragmenting the market while publishers have chased more focused niche readerships. The main companies in the

Australian magazine market include: Kerry Packer's ACP Publishing, with 65 titles including *The Australian Women's Weekly*, *The Bulletin*, *Cleo* and *Ralph*; and Pacific Publications, owned by the Kerry Stokes-controlled Seven network, which has 13 titles including *New Idea*, *B* and *Home Beautiful*.

In Australia, magazine content is primarily concerned with entertainment and lifestyle. News magazines, such as *The Bulletin* and *Time*, constitute a small section of the overall Australian market, although in the larger markets of the United States and Britain there remains a greater diversity of mainstream news and issues-based magazines. The proliferation and popularity of entertainment and lifestyle magazines may signal greater degrees of 'depoliticisation' as readers turn towards matters of home furnishings and personal finance management. While there is some merit in such a judgement, it overlooks how much such magazines are part of a fundamental reorientation of the public domain, captured in John Hartley's category of the 'postmodern public sphere' (1996, p. 155). Hartley distinguishes the postmodern public sphere from the traditional public sphere, arguing that the latter obfuscates the important functions that the contemporary popular media perform in the production of knowledges, virtues and pleasures. Hartley's postmodern public sphere highlights that which is not privileged in the traditional public sphere of Habermas: it is 'a newly privatized, feminized, suburban, consumerized public sphere' (1996, p. 156). In such contexts, the boundaries between the public and the private are increasingly blurred and become a site of contestation. We see this, for example, in the reportage of the rise and fall of former Australian Democrats leader Cheryl Kernot. Her political ascension was accompanied by the use of the media to cultivate a public image, and her downfall involved issues of gender, sex, family and media publicity. Distinctions between the public and the private are still important but such factors as sex and gender are legitimate matters for public debate, particularly in the example of a public figure who has actively courted the media for their own benefit. It was interesting to note, however, that when the story about the affair between Kernot and former leading Labor politician Gareth Evans broke there was considerable media debate about whether reportage of the affair was appropriate and relevant. Part of this concern stemmed from the fact that both Kernot and Evans no longer held public office, but the discussion also demonstrated that the subject matter and boundaries of the 'public sphere' remain subject to debate.

More so than any other form of mass media, gender is a dividing factor in magazines. The majority of the most popular magazines cater to a female readership: magazines such as *The Australian Women's Weekly*, *New Idea* and *Woman's Day* have a long history. Age has become another important distinction, as the greater number of titles has meant magazines having to target readers in very particular age brackets. While the most popular magazines have targeted older female readers, there are a great number of magazines that target female teenagers, such as *Dolly* and *Girlfriend*. Women's magazines focus on stories about celebrities and 'personal' issues relating to the body, health and relationships. Such content cannot be dismissed as trivial, and it performs important functions in identity formation and the management of the self. As Catharine Lumby (1999, p. 8) has written:

> These magazines place strong emphasis on reader surveys, letters pages, 'share a secret' pages, competitions, reader make-overs and advice columns. They act as a forum for adolescents and twenty-somethings to negotiate their identities. The fact that many of the articles in these magazines focus on the body, the personality, sexuality and relationships isn't an automatic sign that the magazines trade in trivial issues at the expense of real politics. Feminism has long recognised that the private sphere . . . is an inherently political arena which can't be neatly annexed from the world of work or public life.

In accord with conventional gender divisions, men's magazines have been limited traditionally to news and business publications, as well as more private interests such as cars, sport and pornography. In recent years more generalist or lifestyle magazines such as *Ralph* and *FHM* have become popular. As Tony Schirato and Susan Yell have noted, there are several reasons for the appearance and popularity of these so-called 'laddish' magazines. First, the rise of the 'men's movement' has created a public discourse through which men can discuss masculinity. Second, there has been an increased recognition of men as 'consumer subjects', and advertisers have demanded print outlets where they can market to men more broadly. Third, the rise of the feminist movement has problematised ideas of gender identity: 'Feminist discourses now speak and are spoken with increased authority within both the public and private spheres, and this means that masculinist and sexist discourses must to some extent define and contest their position against these discourses (particularly across certain cultural fields and demographics)' (Schirato & Yell 1999, pp. 83–4).

Internet news media

The Internet continues to initiate a cultural revolution in many ways, including faster and more comprehensive forms of personal correspondence, an explosion in the amount of information and types of information available, and new forms of shopping, financial trading and the supply of services. This cultural revolution is based generally on the provision and distribution of information, and it is not surprising when the revolution extends to changes in news media. Virtually all print news outlets now have an online presence, where some of the newspaper content is available free. While many newspaper companies have set up an online division to exploit the Internet potential, some are having difficulty making such divisions financially viable. Fairfax, for example, was losing about $40 million on its F2 Internet site in 1999 and by 2001 the losses were rising to nearly $50 million per year (Conley 2002, p. 311). The *Wall Street Journal* has been one newspaper that has charged subscription rates to the online version of its publication. The Wall Street Journal Online is the largest subscription news site on the Internet, with over 600 000 subscribers (Dow Jones 2002).

While existing newspapers are developing an online presence, some fear that traditional print news will disappear altogether, or at least be seriously marginalised by their online or electronic 'forms'. Internet news media have the great advantage of being able to provide almost instantaneous coverage of events, unlike the day-old response of newspapers. The Internet news media can not only provide information faster but are better equipped to provide more comprehensive background information. Newspapers have always offered better context in news stories than broadcast media, but the Internet news media can tap into databases that supply much more extensive contextual information. A story on elections in Croatia, for example, can be linked to a database on the history of the Balkans. Journalists are generally using the Internet more in the form of computer-assisted reporting (CAR), which can involve everything from simple search tools and the use of discussion lists through to the merging of databases. Perhaps the greatest advantage of electronic 'newspapers' is that they can be genuine multi-media texts, employing video and audio to complement the written word. Such multi-media newspapers are not only more entertaining and visually attractive but are able to provide more comprehensive communication, including a greater degree of realism.

It remains to be seen how the potential of electronic newspapers will be exploited, but some have argued that online news media can improve the quality of the modern democratic process. The proliferation of electronic newspapers makes the control of the news agenda by multinational news corporations more difficult, although such a challenge can be overstated. Nonetheless, the Internet and web-based news services do allow a greater and more chaotic flow of information, which makes the task of political management of news and information more arduous and challenges the conventional journalistic treatment of issues. (In Australia, the Internet site <www.crikey.com.au>, operated by Stephen Mayne, has played a role in several leading news stories through the disclosure of sensitive information.) Some have argued that the Internet will revolutionise the contemporary public sphere, ironically reinstating the 'coffee-house culture' of the 18th century, supposing that the proliferation of sources of news over a wider range of individuals than professional journalists, and the heightened accessibility and interactivity of the Internet will enable more vigorous and lively public debate (Sampson 1996).

Arguments about the inevitability of the success of web-based news services and the subsequent death of the newspaper are being seriously challenged. Currently at least, the communicative potential of many Internet 'newspapers' is not being realised, and many simply replicate the content and design of established newspapers. Access to an electronic newspaper is also much more difficult than to conventional newspapers. Although computer access and literacy is growing, electronic newspapers still require a considerable investment of time and money in computer hardware and software, computer literacy, telephone usage and subscription to Internet Service Providers. Conventional newspapers, conversely, are cheap and portable, not susceptible to power blackouts, computer crashes and busy Internet lines, and serve many alternative everyday uses, such as pulling errant dogs into line!

The ability of the Internet to provide much more comprehensive information from a greater range of sources may even work against the medium. Such features of the Internet may contribute to feelings of 'information overload', and conventional forms of mass media that distil and evaluate information will perhaps be more appreciated given the greater pace and pressure of modern living. The argument that the rise of the Internet will lead to the death of the conventional news-paper also ignores the history of mass communication and previous evidence about media innovation. The introduction of a new medium does not result in the death of older media: rather, the older media adapt to the new media environment. The introduction of television did not kill radio, and home video has not destroyed the cinema market. It is likely that the conventional newspaper will undergo changes in a web-based culture, but it is equally likely that it will persist as an influential form of communication.

Conclusion

The print news media are being buffeted by a number of different factors—the growth of the Internet, competition from television, the decline in interest in politics and the busier lifestyles of their readers. Despite this, print remains a dominant form of news media and stub-bornly persists as a politically influential medium. The print news media perform a central role in setting the news agenda and providing in-depth coverage of issues and events. Despite their long history, it is important to note that newspapers and magazines are not a static type of media, limited to bravely persisting in the face of changes in other media. The print news media are constantly experiencing change as they manage their place in the new media environment. In Melbourne recently, for example, News Corp and Fairfax started free commuter newspapers. Fairfax's *Melbourne Express* has since been closed but News Corp's *MX* continues. Such newspapers are aimed at a younger readership, in the 18–39-year range, and the news stories are usually of a shorter length. It remains to be seen whether this new type of newspaper, which targets the traditional strength of the newspaper's commuter readership, will be successful in attracting a new generation of readers, although such giveaways have already been successful in Europe, the USA, South America and South Africa. Whether these kinds of innovation are successful or not, the newspaper will, for some time yet, not only survive but remain a mass medium of tremendous political influence.

5

The broadcast media

The broadcast media are politically influential not just because an increasing number of people use radio or television as their main news source. The broadcast news media are politically influential because they have changed the very practice of politics. The packaging of political stories on television news, the cut and thrust of current affairs interviews, and the dynamics of talkback radio, have had a tremendous impact on how politicians and public figures communicate with the public. Here we investigate both television and radio. While both types are often lumped together as 'broadcast media', there are important differences that inform our discussion, such as the obvious differences in their forms (the visual dominance in television, the aural dominance in radio) and their varying orientations towards the general public.

The reportage of politics by the broadcast media is quite different from the reportage of politics by newspapers because news and current affairs in broadcast media constitute a much smaller proportion of total output than they do in newspapers. While newspapers are commercial products which carry advertising and a variety of non-journalistic information, they are more so vehicles for news and current affairs than broadcast media, where news and current affairs are but one genre of programming among many, including music, drama, comedy and quiz shows. Broadcast news and current affairs programs are discrete entities, but the programming contexts in which they are aired does influence their production and reception. Charges that the news media are threatened by the increasing prevalence of 'infotainment', or 'softer' news stories with an undue emphasis on 'entertainment', are most commonly sheeted home to *broadcast* news media. While there is some concern regarding the broadcast news media coverage of politics, we need to be cognisant of the specific communicative form of each medium and equally critical of the assumptions that inform criticisms of broadcast news media performance.

Characteristics of television

It is axiomatic that television has profoundly influenced the content and structure of everyday and public life. The patterns and rhythms of our lives are routinely influenced by television, whether through organising dinner around our viewing habits or spending time with friends viewing music videos or the football. Our conversations and gossip are littered with references to television programs and television celebrities. The influence of television on public life stems from the medium's problematisation of traditional boundaries between the public and the private realms. While 'the box' increasingly invades public spaces, television—more so than radio—is defined by its domestic consumption. The 'publicness' of politics is transformed by the private consumption of television images. As we note in chapter 1, television implements an unusual communicative context, where the audiovisual presence of politicians occurs in conjunction with our spatial and temporal distance from them.

For some, television is the prime culprit for a pervasive social malaise. Concern about the effects of television has been manifested in a range of 'panics' about matters such as the prevalence of televisual representations of violence and sex, the influence of advertising and the excessive promotion of commodities, as well as the breakdown of family and social structures and regimes of authority. Such concern is not without some validity, but, as the brilliant satire of *The Simpsons* reveals, direct deleterious effects are often attributed to television quite simplistically.

Modern society is, nonetheless, profoundly shaped by the medium of television. The complexity of television stems from its 'centripetal' and 'centrifugal' relationship to society and politics more specifically

(Corner 1995, p. 5). On the one hand, television draws to itself the content and character of politics and culture; it becomes a stage or setting for public life. Alternatively, the texts, narratives and images of television are projected out onto, and influence, the character of public life. Such a categorisation delineates the nature of mediated public life and underlines the importance of the relationship between the television form and the sociocultural environment.

Television is a swirling mix of fictional and factual genres. We are informed each day by news, current affairs and documentaries and we are diverted by dramas, comedies and soap operas. Part of the difficulty in unravelling the significance of television and its representation of politics lies in television's social ubiquity: so much of everyday culture and popular consciousness is informed by the texts and rhythms of television. Frustrations arise when the distinctiveness of politics seems to be lost in such generalised cultural contexts. Television is, however, highly generic, and we do make distinctions between 'factual' and 'fictional' kinds of programs. Another difficulty in analysing television's representations of politics resides in both retaining these distinctions as empirically valid while problematising many of the assumptions that inform such distinctions. It is not possible, given the semiotic environment of television, nor desirable to try to distil the public meanings of politics by establishing some false separation between 'information' and 'entertainment'.

Television news is now widely acknowledged as the main source of news for most people. Unlike commercial radio, television promotes news coverage as being of central importance, even though there have been some cutbacks in the production of news. Television news has been criticised because the newsworthiness of stories is unduly affected by the presence of strong images, also because of its trend towards shorter stories and soundbites. The average length of a soundbite on US television news dropped from 43.1 seconds in 1968 to 8.9 seconds in 1988 (Hallin 1994, p. 134). Current affairs television covers a broad spectrum, from tabloid-style programs such as *A Current Affair* through to such programs as the ABC's *Lateline*. The representation of politics on television is not limited to traditional news and current affairs programs. Talk shows have been a part of the television landscape for many years, and they retain a political influence: an important feature of the 2000 US Presidential election was the appearances of candidates Bush and Gore on the daytime talk show *Oprah*, hosted by Oprah Winfrey. In Australia, there are popular chat programs such as *The Panel* that provide a laid-back, comic analysis of the week's news and gossip and include the canvassing of current political issues.

The debate about the relative merits of television's influence on politics is broad-ranging and complex. John Corner provides a neat inventory of both negative and positive features of television's development of democratic politics which can help inform our discussion (1995, pp. 43–5). On the negative side he raises three points. First, he declares that 'television has become . . . a sphere of intensive and sophisticated *knowledge management*' (1995, p. 43, author's emphasis). Television produces an imbalance of sources and reproduces the interpretive frameworks of public relations agencies and other organisations that are able to fund and manage media activities. Second, 'television has turned the sphere of politics into one which is dominated by *strategic personalisation*' (1995, p. 44, author's emphasis). This well-known argument refers to the ability of television to present politics within a theatrical framework, where the personality and personal qualities of individuals assumes prominence. Finally, 'television represents the world through visual and aural conventions which work to invoke *realist credibility* rather than critical engagement' (1995, p. 44, author's emphasis). Here, Corner refers to the claim that the realism of television, through its visual and aural representation, together with its editing technique which emphasises continuity and flow, is ideally suited to ideological communication and less suited to expository evaluations of arguments.

On the other side of the ledger, Corner details three positive points pertaining to television's enhancement of the democratic process. First, he proposes that television, and broadcast news media more generally, has 'massively increased the proportion of the population who have regular political information which they are able to place within a broad framework of national, and international, political understanding' (1995, p. 45). This greater rate of access of public knowledge occurs because the audiovisual means of communication of television is more accessible than print. Second, despite the proliferation of public relations activity and spin doctors, television journalism has helped intensify the degree of scrutiny of politicians and public figures. This greater degree of political accountability has most notably occurred through political interviews on television. Third, the speed and diversity of messages that flow through the global media 'makes it harder for a national government to "manage" its media output with any sustained tightness' (1995, p. 45).

Visual representations in television

Television's visual nature is, of course, a defining feature of the medium. The visual representations of television are strikingly characterised by their degree of realism. As Corner has reminded us, realism is a highly complex concept, drawing on matters of both representation and epistemology (Corner 1992). In Corner's inventory, television is often criticised because the realism of its images is said to enhance 'credibility' at the expense of 'critical engagement'. Before we contemplate such a charge, we should not glide too easily over an acknowledgement of the representative powers of the televisual image. Television has radically changed the public realm because of its high degree of realism and also because of the extensive scope of television's coverage of the public domain. The audiovisual image can graphically capture in close detail the dramatic narratives of public life, including demonstrations, political 'coups', accidents, sporting triumphs, criminal convictions and artistic performances. Television provides us with images of a tremendous range of individuals, from powerful business people through to ordinary folk on the street, from politicians of a distant regime through to local activists.

The power and scope of the televisual image is also, however, the basis for common criticisms of the medium. Newsworthiness in television news and current affairs is influenced by the presence or absence of good 'visuals'. Television demands pictures and is not adept at covering stories that are not easily visualised. This is a serious problem in the reporting of politics, where important matters of policy are distilled in 'unvisual' documents and reports and considered in such forums such as parliamentary committees. It is also argued that the representational powers of the televisual image sometimes paradoxically hinders communication rather than provoking engagement. Extensive footage of perennial news stories, such as the suffering of famine victims, is often cited as contributing to people's declining levels of interest in the issue. Television's ability to 'desensitise' is not limited to terrible suffering in distant locales but applies also to issues and events more relevant to the everyday lives of the television audience. Along the lines of the adage that 'familiarity breeds contempt', it could be argued that declining interest in politics is fuelled by the prominent but repetitive nightly parade of politicians and public figures.

The realism of televisual images and other types of news media images, such as press photographs, has been used to support journalistic claims to objectivity. The mechanical reproductive powers of the camera are said to 'guarantee' the transparent reproduction of the real world. Television news images do provide a high degree of realism, but such images are always constructed 're-presentations' of reality. The subjectivity of the images arises from the way certain images are selected over others, the way individual shots are framed, the way footage is organised into a narrative among other things. News images, in this way, can serve ideological functions. As Stuart Hall (1981, pp. 241–2) has declared with reference to press photographs:

> News photos have a specific way of passing themselves off as aspects of 'nature' . . . But by appearing literally to reproduce the event as it *really* happened, news photos suppress their selective/interpretive/ideological function. They seek a warrant in that ever pre-given, neutral structure, which is beyond question, beyond interpretation: the 'real world'. At this level, news photos not only support the credibility of the newspaper as an accurate medium. They also guarantee and underwrite its *objectivity* (that is, they neutralize its ideological function). [Author's emphasis.]

News media visual images, then, generate 'credibility', but they are also used to validate particular ways of making sense of the world. However, definitive judgements about the value of news images are complicated (as we note in chapter 1 with respect to the overall power of the news media). On the one hand, the powers of realism contained in television images do serve ideological functions by invoking notions of credibility. On the other, to argue that images work against critical engagement tends to downplay such factors as the activity of the viewer, meta-coverage by journalists, and the literacy involved in reading images.

Criticisms of the undue power of visual images are often informed by assumptions about the seductive power of images that run contrary to the notion of an active viewer. Television journalists may produce stories with increasingly powerful and authoritative images, and political sources may provide ever more dramatic media events, but this has not necessarily corresponded with an increasingly manipulated or gullible public. Rather, the 'visual turn' in political communication has engendered an increasingly sceptical public. This scepticism is a problem when it results in a generalised distrust of politicians and the political process, but it is also evidence of an engaged and critical public. This feature of the public's response to the prevalence of visual representations of politics is assisted by the journalistic coverage of politics. As Brian McNair notes, media coverage of political events increasingly includes not only an account of the event itself but also a critique or 'meta-coverage' (McNair 1999, p. 137) of its status as a 'media' event and its coverage by other media.

More fundamentally, the powers of transparency of television and other news media images have overshadowed the visual grammar we use to read images. Conventionally in texts that use both written language and images, the words are described as fixing or 'anchoring' the meaning of the image. A caption for a newspaper photograph identifies participants, describes action and directs us to a particular reading of the photograph. While we do not deny that images and text work together in such ways to generate meaning, such a perspective overlooks the fact that visual images are independently organised and contain their own form of grammar (Craig 1993; Kress & van Leeuwen 1990).

Television political interviews

Television interviews are a prominent form of contemporary political communication. Television political interviews are defined not only by the often lively dynamics between interviewer and interviewee but also by the implicit involvement of the public in the interview. Political interviews on television tend to follow a ritualised pattern, with both participants adept at deploying the conventions of the interview to their own advantage. Despite this, the genre of the interview is considered the most truthful mode of address in public communication. In an age of increasingly 'manufactured' media texts, it is not surprising that this form of 'personal' communication is valorised. Interviews are privileged because they give the appearance of a lack of artifice: they apparently allow people to speak 'spontaneously' and 'directly'. Interviews are ubiquitous and we consider them a 'natural' part of contemporary political communication, but they were not hailed as a worthwhile innovation when they appeared in the press of the 19th century (Bell & van Leeuwen 1994, p. 28). Critics saw interviews as an invasion of privacy and a trivial form of communication in contrast with formal speeches.

The interview is, of course, a form of communication not limited to the mass media. Many other professions, such as psychiatry and social work, employ interviews to generate information, and there are the types of interviews used in tests and interrogations (Bell & van Leeuwen 1994, pp. 1–27). The media interview is defined by its public orientation: media interviews 'give the public a perspective on the *social actors interviewed* and/or the field of their expertise or experience' (Bell & van Leeuwen 1994, p. 22, authors' emphasis). The media interview is used by all journalists, but it assumes special significance in broadcast journalism because there the interview is more explicitly part of the media text. The meaning of the media text is influenced by the fact that we can hear the politician speak—we can see the politician sweating under the studio lights. In broadcast interviews, and particularly television interviews, the interpersonal meanings generated by the interaction are arguably just as important as the meanings generated by the content of the interview. This point highlights the embodied nature of television political interviews. That is, television political interviews are not just an institutionalised form of interpersonal communication where politicians 'have their say': they are also, importantly, a form of drama—a form of visualised communication.

Television political interviews contain a clear division of labour between interviewers and interviewees. Interviews are informed by a set of implicit rules that structure particular roles for participants which, in turn, govern their verbal and physical behaviour. Although the interviewee may have much greater social authority, the interviewer is in control of the mechanics of the interview: they start it, have the right to ask questions and even interrupt answers, and have the right to end the interview when they wish. The interviewee is free to give answers that are non-supportive of the posed propositions but must initially accede to the interviewer's authority: a politician can shift the focus of discussion but cannot completely ignore a posed question. The interviewer's authority is manifested in the language and the visual presentation of the interview. A question is also a command to answer (albeit a polite and implicit command) and a 'statement' because, however 'open' a question may be, it offers information and frames an issue. The interviewer can sharpen the challenge to an interviewee by not asking an open 'wh' question (where, when, what, why) but asking a 'polar' question, where the scope of the reply is theoretically limited to a yes or no. Questions can also be put with a negative or positive orientation, making it difficult to answer against the orientation. The media interviewer has considerable power, as the interview is usually seen from their perspective through conventions such as introductory narratives and the camera framing of interviewees.

Interviews are presented in the guise of an open and equal exchange where the interviewee is given the chance to have their say. The relationship is, however, by no means equal, and the extent to which the interviewee's 'say' is entirely their own is problematic. But, an interview is open to oppositional viewpoints. The interviewee may be confronted by a set agenda and have to acquiesce to the interviewer's authority, but they can inflect the question to their own advantage. In this sense, the interview is an ongoing struggle over the site of meaning.

Many television political interviewers are themselves public figures, and their fame (or notoriety) is based on their interviewing 'style'. Richard Carleton from *60 Minutes* is well known for his sceptical interviewing manner. Other interviewers, such as Jana Wendt, Laurie Oakes from Channel Nine and *The Bulletin*, and the ABC's Kerry O'Brien, are public figures with an impact on the political landscape. These political journalists have a political impact through their decisions to run news stories and through their personal, but public, interactions with politicians. (Oakes, for example, decided to disclose information about the relationship between former Foreign Affairs Minister Gareth Evans and former Australian Democrats leader and Labor politician Cheryl Kernot.) Nonetheless, the authority of such interviewers stems not from any celebrity status but from the assumption that they are adopting the role of the public's representative. In a mediated society, the interviewer becomes the means by which 'our' concerns are posed to public figures, particularly those elected public figures. The watching public, then, are not insignificant observers but are central to the authority of the interviewer and the overall meanings generated by the interview. Of course, what is deemed to be in the 'public interest' will vary widely across different programs and different interviewers. It is not so much one particular public that is invoked through questioning but more the public's right to know.

The interviewer's role as the public's representative allows journalists to be critical and subjective without seeming to contradict their need to be objective and free from bias. The interviewer has been described as an 'honest broker' of opinion (Kumar 1977). Interviewers do not side with any particular position but they have a 'value site' from which the merits of arguments can be scrutinised and evaluated. As Bell and van Leeuwen (1994, p. 134) write:

> . . . 'honest brokers' remain *neutral* in that they allow equal access to the plurality of views that exist in modern society, but they are *partial* in that they take the side of the viewers, the 'ordinary people', the 'voters', the 'consumers', the 'citizens', and in doing so they take up a more active, more investigative and more interrogative role. This is done on behalf of the audience, for their interventions will always be legitimated by an appeal to the interests of the public, as mediated by opinion polls or justified by their own and other media professionals' . . . knowledge of what the public thinks, needs and wants. [Author's emphasis.]

The problem with the honest broker role for the political interviewer is that it often structures a limited political arena, and it can also depoliticise the public. The interviewer may not take sides in a debate but does circumscribe an acceptable arena within which debate can occur. The journalist as the neutral intermediary reproduces a particular model of society in which two (or more) points of view are tested against a 'middle ground', which is portrayed as the truth or desirable norm. This structure reinforces a perception that the truth lies not with the 'Liberal person' or with the 'Labor person' but somewhere in between. This 'other' position is represented as 'common sense', as 'not political', and it is occupied not only by the media professional but also by the 'general public'. The form of the political interview, then, can work to position 'the public' as a depoliticised and unified entity, rather than as the fragmented and agonistic entity that is the very site of politics.

Characteristics of radio

The influence of radio is often overshadowed by the power and presence of television, but radio has proven itself a remarkably resilient medium and retains a political significance not fully appreciated by many. For most people, though, radio is an entertainment medium, accessed for music. Many commercial radio stations advertise that they play 'more music', implicitly and explicitly offering less of everything else, including chatter, advertisements and news. Despite this, radio is also a medium dominated by talk. The personality and verbal skills of the announcer are always integral to the success of a radio program. 'Talkback' radio is one of the most popular types of radio programming, and the likes of John Laws and Alan Jones have over many years amassed a cult-like following. Arguably, the greatest source of political influence emanating from the radio these days is offered by talkback. In this context, radio news and current affairs reporting have struggled to retain a prominent profile.

Radio has a ubiquitous presence in our lives and reaches out to almost every person in society. Nine out of ten people listen to the radio every week, and 78 per cent listen to commercial radio. There are almost 37 million radios in Australia, with almost 60 per cent of homes having five or more radios (Pink 2000, p. 5). Radio is an influential medium because of its insertion into almost every spatial and temporal context of everyday life. We use the radio to rouse us in the morning, we listen to the radio at home, while driving and also at work. Radio helps reproduce the rhythms of the day: from the chirpy breakfast crews to the calmer, laid-back tone of evening programs. Radio is a very immediate form of mass media: we can get updates on breaking news stories, and we listen for changes in the weather forecast and the latest road traffic reports while driving home.

Radio makes a particular contribution to the structure of modern public life and public subjectivity due to its process of communication. Radio is a much more intimate, personal medium than either print or television (Adams & Burton 1997, p. 17):

> Film and television presuppose a mass audience. Newspapers and magazines conjure cinematic images of racing presses spewing editions. But radio is simply a voice in your ear. It can be as intimate, as conspiratorial, as a whisper.

The medium of radio engenders a close relationship with the listening public because radio discourse is so conversational. As journalism students know, radio news is written to be spoken and is less formal than print news writing. This close relationship with the listening public is not only generated through radio's greater ability to enable feedback, as in talkback radio. The nature of radio discourse, with its aural focus and the dominant single voice of an announcer, works to forge close personal bonds with the listener. More so than in television, for all its celebrities, the identity of a radio program is embodied in the identity of the announcer.

These properties of radio enable the medium to be successful in its interpellation of us as members of 'the public'. The process of interpellation refers to the way we are ushered into our identities as public subjects through our acceptance of the mode of address of the media. The particular properties of radio facilitate certain public subject positions for us: radio can work to foreground more emotional and 'personal' subject positions as members of the public. Radio interpellates us as members of the public but the greater diversity of radio outlets, compared to other forms of mass media, also mean that the radio-listening public is more fragmented: it is harder to assume a generalised audience than with the address of a television program or the readership of a newspaper, particularly in a 'one-paper' city. Nonetheless, many radio programs do represent the particular views and values of their listenership as representative of the general public: the opinions of an older and more conservative listenership of a talk-back program, for example, may be represented as the 'real Australia' and the source of 'common sense'. Such a portrayal needs to be understood not so much as a deliberate misrepresentation but more as part of the general struggle over the meanings of 'public opinion'. The 'real' opinion of the public does not have some singular pre-existence but is produced every day through media discourse. This production always involves the contestation of competing opinions and values, as they are expressed across a radio spectrum from the youth-oriented discourse of Triple J to the conservative views expressed through the John Laws program.

Talkback radio

Radio is the most interactive mass medium, and nowhere is this more evident than in talkback radio programming. Other types of mass media have comparatively few mechanisms for direct public feedback, apart from the letters-to-the-editor pages in newspapers. Talkback radio is the most open and participatory mass media forum. Unlike most forms of mass media, where experts and authoritative sources predominate, or at least a strict hierarchy of sources exists, talkback radio allows the 'average' person to express their views on almost any topic.

Talkback radio emerged as a popular format during the 1980s. In the United States, the so-called 'shock jocks' of 'talk radio' also arose as a phenomenon. Announcers such as Rush Limbaugh, Gordon Liddy and Oliver North attracted public attention for their articulation of extreme conservative opinions. In Australia, talkback radio is most popular in the mornings, when discussion topics are usually assembled from other media, most notably the morning newspapers. A great variety of radio programs employ talkback, but the term 'talkback radio' is usually reserved for those programs in which talkback is the dominant part of the program, where there is a high-profile announcer, and where a particular range of topics are often discussed. Talkback radio is much more than the simple expression of the views of listeners. Sometimes the focal point for talkback is provided by studio guests. More generally, talkback programs are a complex mix of talkback, editorial comment from announcers, advertisements, music, gossip, regular segments, and the usual updates on weather and financial markets.

The participatory nature of talkback radio also requires qualification. Presenters have considerable power in selecting topics for discussion and foregrounding preferred interpretations. While callers can challenge such interpretations they must be prepared to undergo aggressive questioning and tolerate ridicule, interruption and other verbal gestures of disagreement. Presenters also have access to the 'dump button' and can cut off callers at any time. Before callers even get to air they are screened by producers to ascertain what issue they want to raise and what they intend to say. This information is then forwarded to the announcer, who can choose from the list of waiting callers and be prepared for each individual caller.

Talkback radio may facilitate the democratic process through the expression of the views of the 'average' person, but radio stations have a more basic motivation to run talkback programs. The predominance of live talk on talkback programs creates a more conducive environment for advertisements, as articulated in the following comments from a radio station promotional document (in Mickler 1998, p. 62):

> Logic says that a commercial in a talk environment will be heard—
> there is not the turn-off factor such as there may be when music is
> interrupted by a commercial break.
>
> The power of a live read is even greater. The listener is attuned to
> talk and to a particular voice and then is subject to a commercial from
> that voice. Talk radio is foregrounded, it cannot be ignored!

Talkback presenters have assumed tremendous political influence due to their high public profile, the popularity of their programs and the nature of the talkback audience. As former Prime Minister Paul Keating once declared: 'Forget the Press Gallery in Canberra. If you educate John Laws, you educate Australia' (in Adams & Burton 1997, p. 2). Talkback presenters do not cover the latest news and current affairs in any conventional journalistic sense, where notions of objectivity and balance govern reportage, but in a more robustly subjective manner, more akin to the work of newspaper columnists. Announcers such as John Laws and Alan Jones are themselves celebrities and have often achieved status as public figures in other fields: Jones was the coach of the Australian Rugby Union team, and Laws a recording artist and 'poet'. The celebrity status of talkback announcers gives them a special status as political commentators, highlighting their individuality. Their non-journalistic identity makes their discussion of issues seemingly more sincere and genuine. As discussed in chapter 3, their celebrity status paradoxically works to 'humanise' the announcers and helps to establish and strengthen the bonds they have with their listeners.

Talkback radio is very much concerned with politics. Gillian Appleton's study of John Laws' program confirmed that a significant amount of airtime is given to politicians and party politics (Appleton 1999, p. 88). Interestingly, while Laws made many references to party political news, relatively few listeners commented on party political issues, even when Laws specifically invited a response. But talkback announcers do wield great political power. The power of the announcers over the listeners is not monolithic, and to some extent simply reinforces existing viewpoints, but power resides in the selection of topics, their treatment, and the production of a site where the rhetoric of 'common sense' is generated and sustained.

The power of the talkback announcers is most evident in their ability to regularly draw on major political figures as studio guests. Politicians such as Australian Prime Minister John Howard and New South Wales Premier Bob Carr, realise the popularity of the talkback announcers and have actively courted them. Politicians use talkback radio as a media strategy because a 'chat' on talkback radio is usually less gruelling than a conventional political interview; it also gives them more immediate access to the large talkback audience. Although every interview and talkback session can provoke mistakes and poor performances from politicians, talkback remains a valuable form of political communication because it provides the politicians with an opportunity to present themselves as more 'human' and allows them to engage in direct conversation with members of an electorate that usually considers politicians to be remote from its everyday concerns.

Talkback radio has achieved a level of notoriety because it has often promoted the expression of extreme conservative views, 'moral panics' and racism. Common topics discussed in talkback forums include immigration levels and policy, the prevalence of drugs in society, and the leniency of sentences handed down by judges and magistrates. Informed by a generally conservative political position, talkback often reproduces divisions in society. Targets of criticism in talkback radio cover a spectrum of the public—public servants, the unemployed, Aborigines, academics and homosexuals. The power of talkback radio to mobilise the public was graphically illustrated in Perth in 1991 when announcer Howard Sattler, then of station 6PR, organised the so-called 'Rally for Justice'. Around 30 000 people attended the rally at Parliament House to pressure the government for harsher juvenile sentences. Aboriginal youth were a particular target of the campaign. The campaign was successful and in February 1992 the state Labor government implemented the harshest juvenile crime laws in the country (Mickler 1998).

Talkback radio is also fascinating because of the kind of audience it attracts. Most scrutiny of talkback radio focuses on the celebrity power of the announcers or the more sensational topics raised by the programs. It is sometimes assumed that the audience is simply beholden to the views of the announcer, and there is little consideration of the reasons for the attraction of listeners to talkback radio. One of the reasons talkback radio is so popular is because it gives a voice to many people who feel they are marginalised and ignored by politicians and the political process. It is no coincidence that talkback is popular at a time when the political landscape is characterised by the perceived alienation of politicians from the public. Feelings of *political* alienation, however, only partly explain the popularity of talkback radio. More generally, people gain a sense of personal identity and a sense of belonging from regular listening to programs. Appleton notes that many callers to John Laws detail personal crises, which meet with a sympathetic response from the announcer. That is, the appeal of Laws emanates not only from his self-presentation as outspoken and knowledgeable on political matters but also as caring and responsive to tales of depression, family disputes and financial difficulties. The regular format and content of the program, together with the closing remark to 'Be kind to each other' while playing 'Try a Little Kindness', 'help engender a sense of belonging to the Laws "family"' (Appleton 1999, p. 93).

In understanding the political significance of talkback radio we need to note that it is primarily *entertainment*. As John Laws declared during the so-called 'Cash for Comment' scandal (see chapter 1): 'I am not a journalist. I am an entertainer'. The expression of political views and commentary on the news of the day circulate in a format together with music, gossip, competitions and mundane, everyday tales. Politics, then, is not presented as a separate subject, as it often is in other media formats, but is grounded more in the context of the ordinary person's concerns. This explains the common dismissal in talkback radio of the machinations that dominate much political news reportage. The emphasis on entertainment in talkback radio underlines how much the meaning of contemporary politics is determined by its articulation with broader cultural and everyday contexts.

The Triple J public

Talkback radio likes to present its listeners as representative of the general community and the views expressed by listeners as those of 'mainstream' Australians. While talkback radio does garner a large listenership, it appeals to sectional audiences, like much of the rest of radio. Generally, talkback attracts the largest share of the 35-plus age group but much fewer young people (Mickler 1998, pp. 82–3). Younger listeners are more likely to be tuning into either music-format-dominated commercial radio or the ABC's 'youth network', Triple J.

Triple J has evolved from a local, inner-city Sydney station when it started in 1975 into the 'national youth network'. The station, while not a ratings leader, does generate healthy enough ratings for commercial radio producers to complain about the draining away of young listeners to the national public broadcaster. Triple J has developed a distinctive profile through a range of on- and off-air features, which together facilitate the formation of a 'youth public'. On air, the station has a commitment to new Australian music, and the announcers possess an individualistic and eclectic mode of address, unlike the broadcast style replicated across most modern, music-format commercial radio. Off air, Triple J has created a popular website with music news and competitions, <www.abc.net.au/triplej.htm>. The station has developed a range of merchandise, which is available through the ABC shops. It also plays a prominent role in the organisation of public events, such as the Big Day Out concerts, the Unearthed competition and the promotion of the tours of particular performers.

Such on-and-off air features promote the station as a significant site for the expression of youth culture. Not only do young people listen to Triple J but the music, language and values expressed on the station inform the rhythms and patterns of their lifestyles. Listening to Triple J becomes a part of the identity of young people and provides them with a sense of belonging. This is particularly important, given that on much mainstream media 'youth' are disparaged and marked as a problem. On talkback radio and television, current affairs stories about drugs and unemployment often present 'youth' as a population that needs to be disciplined and controlled.

Contrary to much media interpellation the 'youth public' is not, however, a coherent grouping but a disparate, broad-ranging collection of different interests. There is no single 'youth culture' but rather numerous youth subcultures. There never has been a unified youth culture, although it could be argued that contemporary youth culture, has become more fragmented and that it has become more difficult to conceptualise different youth constituencies. This diversity, in turn, becomes an issue that must be negotiated by a station such as Triple J. While the station does employ various strategies to represent various youth subcultures, the diversity of groupings underlines the importance of the station image as a means of unifying youth culture. As Katherine Albury has written: 'Triple J, faced with the difficulty of serving a multitude of youth subcultures, has effectively constructed the network itself as a unifying source of capital, so that for the national youth audience, the act of listening to the radio becomes an embodiment of subcultural capital' (1999, p. 59).

The subcultural capital of Triple J arises from a certain vocabulary of musical and cultural style, which distinguishes what is currently in vogue. The subcultural capital of youth culture generally, and of Triple J specifically, works differently from most other forms of cultural capital where a 'classic status' is generated by its persistence over time. In contrast, the subcultural value of Triple J emanates from the newness of its music and the perpetual rotation of the music mix. Young people assume the subcultural value through their understanding of what is currently 'in'. The subcultural capital is generated not only by such knowledges but also through the particular public demonstration of that knowledge. Subcultural capital must be displayed for its social value to be realised, but it must also be displayed with restraint: ostentatious demonstrations of 'coolness' destroy the very basis of the claimed subcultural capital. This display of subcultural capital is manifested in the performance style of Triple J announcers, who are distinguished from other contemporary music station announcers by their casual and 'laidback' manner.

The subcultural capital of youth culture and Triple J, while giving the appearance of being effortlessly assumed, requires ongoing work and maintenance and is defined through its constant negotiation with other identities and expressions of cultural value. The subcultural capital of Triple J remains tenuous because of its *generalised* expression of a broad-based youth culture, unlike the more specific subcultural value of more clearly defined groups, such as 'goths' and 'mods'. The very popularity of Triple J represents a problem for the station. The subcultural capital of Triple J resides in its ongoing distinctiveness from other contemporary music stations, but its growing popularity makes its differentiation from the 'mainstream' more difficult. Triple J has been criticised for losing its 'radical' edge, but it is also the case that the 'mainstream' is fragmenting and becoming a much less coherent category.

The Triple J public is also an interesting phenomenon because it is constituted at a national level across several time zones. The establishment of Triple J as the national youth network involved a fundamental reorientation from the 'localness' of Sydney station 2JJ. Radio is effective at evoking 'the local', and so national broadcasting and networking poses problems. Announcers have had to develop strategies to bring together a national audience that is nonetheless not 'grounded' in geography. Albury argues that Triple J announcers have worked to construct a Triple J subculture which listeners are then invited into: 'Rather than having to transmit a generic onesided conversation into the imagined abstract "national audience", the presenting team invites "the nation" into their specific conversational space' (Albury 1999, p. 60).

As a national station, and as part of the national public broadcaster, Triple J has had a more practical obligation to represent marginalised and regional audiences. One successful strategy has been the localised band competition Unearthed, where bands from a particular region submit a demo tape to the station. Not only does the competition provide a national promotion of the region but it enables Triple J staff, who are largely based in Sydney, to establish some direct contact with local music, cultures and audiences. The ability of Triple J, and other national stations, to harness a national audience is also hampered by the different time zones across the country. Triple J is broadcast on a delay, interspersed with live news bulletins. The delayed broadcast gives a smoother feel to the programs but it hinders the general discussion of breaking news stories and talkback participation from listeners in South Australia, the Northern Territory and Western Australia.

Conclusion

The particular communicative forms of broadcast media have determined to a great degree how politicians and other public figures communicate to the rest of society. The content and form of television has thoroughly shaped our culture, over and above any specific effects. The visual requirements of television news and current affairs has elevated the importance of personal image in politics, which can be at the expense of matters of policy and 'substance' but which also underlines the centrality of bodily performance to all public communication. The ever-shrinking length of soundbites in television news works against detailed treatment of political issues, but great scrutiny of politicians continues in many current affairs interviews. The political importance of radio should not be underestimated, but its influence emanates increasingly out of talkback formats rather than news and current affairs, with the notable exception of ABC radio. Each of the various types of mass media brings about public formation in a mediated society but the particular form of radio, with its aural emphasis and the greater diversity of outlets, makes it very effective in organising constituencies of listeners.

6

Political image and performance

While watching and listening to our political leaders we witness dramatic performances. When we watch parliamentary debates or a television interview, or when we listen to the latest policy announcements, we also watch the style of dress, the deportment of our political leaders, and we listen to their manner of speech. We recognise the finger-wagging sternness of an Opposition leader, the nervous hesitations of a government minister, the confident smile of a Prime Minister. This is to be expected: human communication is embodied and performative. Whenever someone talks to us we not only decode the content of the speech—we attribute meaning to how they speak, their appearance, their gestures. The importance of political image in contemporary political communication is, nonetheless, an occasion for much consternation. Concern is expressed that political *style* is now almost as important as political *substance* and that political success is dependent more on media management than policy acumen.

Political leaders and public figures, always conscious of their performative powers, have always cultivated 'images' for political consumption. The importance of political image has, however, burgeoned in the age of television. The particular communicative contexts of television, with its audiovisual 'presence' of represented subjects, has leant personal features a significance they did not previously hold. (Abraham Lincoln, who had a speech impediment, might have found it difficult to assume public office today.) The greater importance of image and style in contemporary politics is partly due to changes in media, but it is also due to the changing political environment. As the major political parties in Australia, the UK and the USA have moved closer ideologically in recent decades, image and style have become increasingly important markers of difference.

The history of 20th-century politics is littered with famous stories about the successful employment of political image as well as salutary tales about political failures due to an inability to use the media to convey an appropriate image or persona in order to convince the public. Much has been written about Joseph Goebbels' use of the media in Nazi Germany to build an image of the party and to construct a stylised aesthetic for Hitler's political performances. In the United States, President Franklin Delano Roosevelt addressed the nation through a series of 'fireside chats', which connoted a domestic sense of security. Perhaps the most famous example of television's early influence on the political process occurred in the 1960 presidential debates, where the televisual John F. Kennedy assumed dominance over Richard Nixon, whose 'five-o'clock shadow' made him less telegenic and whose perspiration under the studio lights suggested he was under pressure. British Prime Minister Margaret Thatcher submitted to a famous image 'make-over' in the late 1970s. She was coached to speak in deeper tones, and her dress and hair style changed dramatically in order to convey a more authoritative image.

There was a time when politicians could have successful careers without close attention to matters of image and style, but now such image construction is an everyday part of political life and politicians cannot escape such a fate. The former British Prime Minister John Major was said to have been lacking in image when contrasted with his predecessor Margaret Thatcher and his Labour opponent in the 1992 election, Neil Kinnock. As a public figure, however, Major was not without an image: he simply projected an image of 'ordinariness' due to his modest social background, his more reserved and courteous manner, and his hobbies, such as his interest in cricket. Such an 'image' enabled him to be presented as more of a 'real person'. The subsequent election victory of Tony Blair's New Labour in 1996 dispelled any suggestion that such a strategy would always be successful, and indeed Blair's victory underlined how central the politics of image and style were to the political process (see later in this chapter for an analysis of Tony Blair).

Constructed selves

Any consideration of the importance of political image and style in media representations of politics must be based on fundamental conceptualisations about the nature of 'the self'. The idea of the self as a free and autonomous individual is a legacy of Enlightenment thought and still carries considerable weight in contemporary Western cultures and political systems. This idea of an 'unconstructed' self emphasises that the individual is the product of their own initiative and intelligence. The idea of the self as a free and autonomous individual has been critiqued by various theorisations of subjectivity throughout the 20th century (see Mansfield 2000). Indeed, the use of the term 'subjectivity' instead of 'self' emphasises how the individual is not a discrete entity but is the product of, or *subject to*, political, social and cultural forces.

Theorisations of subjectivity are wide-ranging and complex and cannot be considered in detail here. As Nick Mansfield notes, one way of classifying the dominant theorisations of subjectivity is to distinguish those positions which attempt to articulate and reveal the 'true' nature of the subject (associated most famously with Freud and psychoanalysis) from theories which see subjectivity as the product of culture and power (2000, p. 51). Both dominant positions see subjectivity as a *construct* and are critical of the idea of the self as a free and autonomous individual. The latter dominant position, associated with the work of a theorist such as Michel Foucault, argues that we are constituted as subjects through the discourses, rules and norms of social and institutional life. The exercise of such power is effective not because it is 'forced' on people but because it is 'freely' enacted through the lives of subjects.

Another account of the self also understands the self as constructed, and it gives emphasis to the agency or making of the self within the contexts of available resources. John Thompson (1995, p. 210) writes that the self is viewed:

> . . . neither as the product of an external symbolic system, nor as a fixed entity which the individual can immediately and directly grasp; rather, the self is a symbolic project that the individual actively constructs. It is a project that the individual constructs out of the

symbolic materials which are available to him or her, materials which the individual weaves into a coherent account of who he or she is, a narrative of self-identity.

Such an understanding of the self does not posit a constant, unified entity, but it acknowledges that the self is differentiated and that the presentation of the self changes in different social and cultural contexts. Erving Goffman's well-known work (1969) notes how the actions and performances of an individual are informed by particular interactive frameworks. He observed how people often orient their appearance and behaviour to project a self-image that is compatible with the particular communicative encounter. This applics most obviously in communicative encounters such as job interviews and formal, ritualised events such as weddings, but it is more generally an integral part of everyday life. Goffman describes the interactive framework and the features of the individual self that are promoted as the 'front region', and those actions and views that are suppressed and reserved for other communicative encounters as the 'back region' (Goffman 1969).

The self, then, is a constructed entity that is variously produced in different communicative encounters, but this process of self formation and presentation is further complicated by the insertion of the self into a media environment. As we note in chapter 3, the process of becoming a 'public figure' involves the creation of a 'new' subjectivity, which involves the negotiation between the existing self, their media representations and, in turn, the public interpretations of those representations. An integral component of any successful public figure is a skilful use of the media together with an ability to communicate a self-image to the public. The successful production of a 'media image' by a public figure is based on the public acceptance of the alignment between media representation and the underlying reality of that self.

The media, then, do not 'mask' some 'essential' self but rather, in a mediated society, are necessarily involved in the production of the subjectivity of public figures. We cannot ascribe to the media a function of transparency in the presentation of subjectivities but, as with other cultural and communicative contexts, the production and presentation of the self is informed through its negotiation with media contexts. We do have to consider, however, whether the increasing volume of media images and the increasing sophistication of image making is altering the terrain of politics so that substantive matters are insufficiently considered and whether the public have sufficient skills and knowledge with which to judge sophisticated media images. Nonetheless, contemporary politics is substantially centred around the production of media images and public judgements about those images.

Public judgements about constructed selves is itself an important domain of contemporary politics and public life. As I have noted elsewhere, newspaper assessments of Princess Diana's performance in the famous television interview on the *Panorama* program, where she confessed she had been unfaithful to Prince Charles, were split by very different conceptualisations of subjectivity (Craig 1997). The left-of-centre newspapers, such as *The Independent* and *The Guardian*, offered a generally positive appraisal of Diana's performance based on a perspective on subjectivity which emphasises a notion of identity that is more multiple, fluid and self-reflexive. In contrast, the more conservative broadsheets, such as *The Times* and *The Daily Telegraph*, criticised Diana based on a more traditional view of subjectivity which emphasises a unified, stable and unchanging identity. For the conservative newspapers, the juxtaposition of Diana's 'performance' with an assumed existence of an authentic or essential self was the basis on which Diana could be criticised as not presenting her 'true self'.

Performance in political communication

Subjectivity is not an identity that is independent of actions but is produced through our embodied *performances*. A 'rational' and 'normal' self is produced and exhibited through appropriate actions in particular cultural contexts, which involves a disciplining of the body. So much popular discourse in our society equates a 'normal' subjectivity with the production of a 'healthy' body. Political subjectivity is also manifested in performance, including factors such as dress, physical appearance and manner of speech.

Performance is central to contemporary public life. Baz Kershaw argues that 'widespread changes in the processes of the social . . . are producing what [he] call[s] the *performative society*' (1999, p. 13, author's emphasis). Kershaw says that performative societies are found particularly where democracy and capitalism meet: performance becomes a major element in the negotiations of power and authority, and the performative dimension is also foregrounded where the market is central to social organisation (1999, p. 13). The designation of the performative society suggests how much politics occurs in 'dramatic' and 'theatrical' contexts. From the ritual of parliament to election campaigning, to a doorstop interview, political communication necessarily involves 'performances'.

Political communication, more so than other forms of media communication, emphasises its rational character, but the body remains central to the meanings of any political communication. As stated in the opening of this chapter, human communication is embodied, and this refers not only to high-profile celebrities whose bodily presence is foregrounded in their public image but also to the most ordinary politician in a suit and tie. The site of the body as the bearer and initiator of discursive values has been explored in great detail in a number of areas of study, including sociology (Falk 1994; Crossley 1995) and feminism (Grosz 1994; Gatens 1996). At one level, it is readily apparent how the bodies of politicians, such as former Australian Democrats leader Natasha Stott Despoja and British Deputy Prime Minister John Prescott, convey certain values and inform the public perceptions of them. While we can debate about the degree of media emphasis given to particular political bodies, we cannot avoid analysis of political communication as instances of embodied communication.

Of course, we do not encounter the bodies of politicians and other public figures but *representations* of those bodies. 'Bodies', for all their materiality, do not themselves contain essential or fixed meanings but are attributed with value through their presentations and subsequent readings. As Moira Gatens notes: 'the human body is always a signified body and as such cannot be understood as a "neutral object"' (1996, p. 70). Our readings of the media images of the bodies of politicians and public figures, then, are highly mediated and are but part of a complex process of meaning production: our readings of a body follow both the presentation of that body by the person concerned and the subsequent readings of the body in its media representations. Public judgements about bodies, in turn, inform the subsequent presentation of that body and its media readings. To highlight the discursive basis of the bodies of politicians and public figures is not to argue that material bodies and their actions are of no consequence. The material body is the basis of human action, and, as we have noted, subjectivity is grounded in its materiality and its outward orientation to others.

The management of visibility

The management of visibility must be, logically, a central feature of politics in mediated public life. When the public domain is encountered on our television screens and in our newspapers, when we experience politicians and public figures as media representations, then politics must be concerned with image. The political management of visibility occurs throughout the spectrum of political practice, from the organisation of large-scale 'media events', such as elections, state visits, mass protests and forms of national celebration, through to everyday political practice. One consequence of the importance of the media in politics has been a growing focus on individual political leaders: governments and political parties are increasingly identified with individual leaders (Fairclough 2000, p. 95). The management of visibility often involves the policing of the division between the private and the public spheres. As we see later in this chapter, for example, negotiation of the publicness of the birth of Tony Blair's son, Leo, was subject to careful political management. The management of visibility incorporates a range of political practices (which we consider in chapter 7), such as leaks and 'spin doctoring'. We will focus here on the management of the image of the individual politician.

The management of the public images of politicians occurs prominently through the staging of events for media consumption. Media coverage of prominent political and public events is not an incidental feature of the event but is rather a constitutive feature, informing the planning and structure of the event. Politicians at such events are well aware they are performing for a media audience as well as the audience physically present at the event. The status of the media event has attracted interest since Daniel Boorstin in the early 1960s wrote about the rise of 'pseudo-events'—stage-managed events that informed the manufacture of the news (Boorstin 1963). More recently, Daniel Dayan and Elihu Katz have defined media events as live events with an existence independent of the media: the events are organised by public bodies with which the media cooperate. Dayan and Katz's media events are celebrations of unity rather than conflict; they integrate societies and often the public is given an active role in the event (1994, pp. 5–14). An example of a media event, according to Dayan and Katz's definition, would be the 2000 Sydney Olympic Games. The meanings of modern media events are not limited to their fixed geographical occurrence but are the product of the event itself together with its media representations and interpretations, which sometimes feed back into the event itself. One famous example of this occurred when Western media coverage of the 1989 Tiananmen Square protest influenced the subsequent actions of the protesters and political authorities in Beijing. The Chinese state authorities used Western news media coverage of the protest against their one-party rule and restrictions on individual and group freedoms to respond to protest actions and to identify student protesters (Wark 1994).

Media events are not only singular, large-scale occurrences: they are also more mundane and regular features of political practice. Most attention might be directed to special spectacular events, but in mediated public life the management of visibility is a part of everyday political practice. The everyday management of the public images of politicians occurs through activities such as press conferences, community functions and photo opportunities. Public figures who squeeze into every photograph in the local newspaper are often the object of derision, but they realise that public visibility and access are a political necessity. Successful practice as a public figure depends on the regular negotiation of the public/private divide when handling issues and crises. Do you produce a press release and conduct media interviews on an issue or do you manage the issue privately, making telephone calls to the respective people? Part of the successful management of visibility also derives from the correct timing of the public release of information.

The management of visibility of a public figure centres around individual appearance and personality. Enhancing the positive physical features of an individual and suppressing less desirable physical features are an essential part of contemporary political practice. How someone looks and sounds—their weight, their hairstyle, their dress sense and their voice presentation—all conveys meaning and value and is always integral to the political communication of that individual. The stylish dress sense of former Prime Minister Paul Keating, for example, was cited by his critics as a manifestation of his remoteness from the life of the average person. Criticism that contemporary politics focuses too much on individual appearance and personality may carry merit, but it is often overlooked how closely individual appearance and personality are linked to political values. Some politicians, who have been adept at manufacturing a personal image, have foundered because of the public perception that there is no substance behind the image.

While physical features are important in the image of a public figure, the personality of the public figure and their ability to capture or represent the mood of their constituents is integral to success. The public figure must display a personality that encompasses an emotional range which can be used to respond appropriately to every situation, from sporting success to mourning after a natural disaster. More so than ever before, the authority of public figures resides in their ability to make manifest, to literally embody, human qualities and characteristics. Politicians, of course, must negotiate particular binaries, such as showing strong leadership while also demonstrating a common touch. But public figures must have the personality depth and range in order to forge an emotional connection with the public. This connection could be manifested in a range of public feelings, from genuine affection to a reserved respect. The *emotional* basis of the connection between public figures and their constituency should not be dismissed as trivial and peripheral to more substantive matters. We necessarily always adopt an affective position to others, and emotion—as with language and forms of practical action—is an integral feature of public formation (Crossley 1995; G. Little 1999).

The modern emphasis on the personal images of politicians is partly a consequence of changes to the political culture in recent decades. Traditionally, political parties were more clearly differentiated along ideological lines, and could rely on electoral support from particular social classes. Social and economic changes, including the decline of the manufacturing sector and the dominance of ideas popularly known as 'economic rationalism', have meant that such class divisions no longer carry the same currency, and political parties have had to contend with voters whose political allegiances could not be so easily categorised and retained. The erosion of ideological differences between political parties has lent the individual character of politicians a greater significance. Voters focus more on the ability of individual politicians to govern the society and manage the economy. In this political culture, described as the 'politics of trust' (Thompson 2000, p. 111), the credibility and character of politicians becomes a crucial site of political attention and struggle.

The careful construction and meticulous management of the personal image of politicians often enables considerable control of the political process and a limitation of public scrutiny. A politician well trained in dress sense, personal appearance, voice presentation and general media management skills (e.g. the provision of effective 'sound bites') can project a polished persona that thwarts to some degree the critical, probing gaze of the media. The organisation of media events that provide good visual images and promote the personal image of the politician can deflect attention away from more thorough investigation of issues. The amount of media scrutiny of the character of individual politicians and public figures does mean that analysis of public policy can be diminished.

The media are not, however, rendered impotent by such media management, and the disciplined personal presentations of politicians and other public figures are never immune to failure and interrogation. As we note in chapter 1, no matter how polished the personal image of politicians may be, political behaviour in mediated public life is always subject to media examination, and there is never a guarantee about the control of disseminated images and information. That is, while modern political and media culture is highly structured, contemporary mediated public life is characterised by a fundamental democratic indeterminacy.

The carefully presented images of public figures can be undermined by gaffes and outbursts. Gaffes can be quite trivial misstatements or silly mistakes (most famously, former US vice-president Dan Quayle's misspelling of 'potato') or they can be more serious lapses in judgement, displaying a lack of knowledge on an issue. Gaffes reveal a level of incompetence by the politician, and their significance resides in the widespread public display of the mistake. Outbursts are similar to gaffes but these more explicitly reveal a lack of control by the public figure: the outburst may be limited to verbal exclamations but can also extend to physical actions, such as John Prescott's punching of a protester in the 2001 British election. Gaffes and outbursts are mistakes on the part of the public figure, but sometimes a media event or personal presentation will backfire. Here, the intended interpretation of the event is not taken up by the media and an unintended interpretation is produced, with serious consequences for the public figure. Scandals are the most serious type of damage to the personal image of public figures. In chapter 1 we outlined some of the negative effects of scandals in assessments of media performance, but scandals can also be judged more positively: they reveal individual hypocrisy, they often stimulate important debates on the conduct and accountability of public figures, and they trigger analysis of issues and values in public life (Thompson 1995, pp. 140–8; 2000).

Working on the image: media coaching

The centrality of the management of visibility to contemporary political practice has resulted in politicians obtaining coaching on media relations. The rise of media coaching has received little academic or even general media attention, but it is an important part of a public figure's armoury. Some politicians, notably former US President Ronald Reagan, have backgrounds in the media or acting and already have the skills to present a polished public image, but most struggle initially in their encounters with journalists and are unaware of how to package information for media consumption.

Media coaching covers a broad range of skills required to handle successfully a variety of media encounters, such as one-on-one interviews and large-scale press conferences. Media coaches are usually former public relations practitioners or journalists, and their clients include politicians, corporate executives, industry or trade organisation leaders and other public figures. Media coaching is much more than simple public speaking training and extends to instructions on journalistic practice, including deadline pressure and identification of news values; it covers body language, dress sense, voice training, and detailed instruction in the language and rhetorical skills necessary for a successful interview. The language skills include 'bridging', where a question is rephrased by the interviewee in order to focus on particular aspects of a question, and 'flagging', where key messages and phrases are repeated throughout the interview using slightly different language each time. A key skill covered in media coaching is the difficult task of translating technical terms and ideas into everyday language for general media consumption.

Media coaching is not just about the presentation of a slick, media-savvy politician: it also provides politicians and other clients with knowledge about their intended audiences and tools for more effective political communication. As one media coach (Cowlett 2001) said:

> What media coaching gives you is the ability to analyse audiences, anticipate questions and package your information . . . It helps you practise themes and soundbites, weave them into the conversation to influence how the audience thinks and feels about you.

Tony Blair and New Labour

British Prime Minister Tony Blair has been one of the most successful politicians on the global stage, and his success has been facilitated partly by the creation and management of a particular personal image and a sense of style. Blair himself and his government have attracted criticism because of their zealous control of their media images. During the term of the Blair government the activities and powers of political and media managers, commonly referred to as 'spin doctors', have assumed tremendous influence and public attention (see chapter 7). The personal image of Blair has been produced through such factors as his relative youthfulness (although commentators noted after the war in Iraq how much he had 'aged'), his physical appearance, his charisma and demeanour. This image has been successful because it has negotiated a number of binary oppositions: Blair's youthfulness has been tempered by a valuing of 'tradition', the appeal of his looks and physical appearance have been balanced by his family life and spiritual beliefs. Blair has produced a personal image which, while emphasising a generational change, also projects moderation and continuity.

Blair has distinguished not only himself but his political party from older, more conventional representations of the Labour side of politics in Britain. Under Blair, Labour has effectively created a 'new' political party by 'rebranding' Labour as 'New' Labour'. The updating of the party's image has worked because it has been manifested in the person of Blair.

The magnitude of Blair's success has prompted close analysis of his individual character and rhetorical style (Fairclough 2000). An important feature of Blair's rhetorical style is its flexibility: he is able to successfully employ different ways of speaking in a range of contexts, from formal party conference speeches to the informal and intimate responses to individual talkback callers. His rhetorical style is also captured in his middle-class accent, his facial expressions (e.g. his grin), and his body language (e.g. his emphatic hand movements when emphasising a point). Blair's character is manifested in his interview manner: unlike Margaret Thatcher and her combative style, Blair conducts himself politely, not interrupting the interviewer and complying with shifts in the interview subject matter (Fairclough 2000, p. 109).

An important feature of Blair's personal image is his ability to project a sense of being an 'ordinary' or 'normal' person. Blair is not alone in his ability to convey this sense of 'normality': other politicians, such as former US President Bill Clinton, and celebrities, such as Princess Diana, have exhibited this character trait. A paradox of contemporary politics resides in this privileging of 'ordinariness' together with an increasing emphasis on political style and presentation. Many successful modern politicians seem relaxed and comfortable in the public spotlight and are able to convey a sense of honesty and 'genuineness'. This type of political style differs from previous generations, where political rhetoric and charisma were expressed through more formal behaviour. This political and cultural production of 'normality' obviously facilitates connections with the public, and it assumes great significance in a public life that is increasingly mediated. As noted in chapter 3, it is surprising how often the 'ordinary' features of 'extraordinary' public figures are publicised and the ongoing success of public figures depends on their negotiations of the extraordinary/ordinary binary.

The public promotion and management of the 'ordinary' features of Tony Blair and his family life is a vital part of the politics of style exercised by New Labour, and it is an integral means through which public support is maintained. Blair has sought to protect his family from the media, but such events as the birth of his son have prompted much public discussion and debate, which has reflected on the individual character and performance of the Prime Minister. Leo Blair's birth generated much public goodwill (one journalist declaring that Blair would be the first Prime Minister of the television age with his own baby to kiss!), but it became a problem with the acknowledgement of a fine line between good publicity and exploitation of the baby for political purposes (Ahmed 2000). The birth mobilised a range of political, social and gender issues that had to be politically negotiated and exploited. The simple joy of Blair as a new father talking about changing his first nappy worked to promote the Prime Minister as an 'ordinary' man experiencing one of life's extraordinary moments (Smith 2000). Tony Blair's role as a new father was located in broader contexts of changing notions of masculinity when the Prime Minister was grouped with celebrities, such as soccer star David Beckham and the Gallagher brothers from the band Oasis, likewise discovering the joys of fatherhood (James 2000). The birth also raised important policy concerns, such as governmental provisions for maternity and paternity leave, which the Prime Minister's public ponderings about his own leave only highlighted. Finally, the arrival of a baby at 10 Downing Street generated discussion on the broader social dilemma of juggling family and career in modern times. This one event illustrates that political image management is much more than the organisation of some favourable media coverage through the provision of an official portrait and a couple of photo opportunities. Political images also resonate with political and cultural values, and successful public figures must manage the public circulation of those values both to further their own popularity and to convey their own value positions to the public.

Anti-global capitalism protests

Political image and style is also central to another contemporary political phenonomen—the so-called 'anti-globalisation' protests (Craig 2002).

The protests at international economic, business and political meetings have become a new 'genre' in global politics. This genre has captured the world's attention ever since the protests on the streets of Seattle disrupted the World Trade Organisation (WTO) meeting in 1999 in such spectacular fashion. While the terrorism against the World Trade Center buildings has tempered the public visibility and media coverage of the protest movement, we can also argue that such an act of terrorism and the ensuing events make analysis of such global events more pressing (Klein 2001). The manner of the 'anti-globalisation' protests (although it is more accurate to call them the 'anti-global capitalism' protests) and the protesters themselves are a fascinating phenomenon for many different reasons: the use of the Internet, imaginative protest strategies, and the huge variety of groups that have been brought together in a loose coalition in their opposition to various manifestations of globalisation.

In addition to the expected presence of political groups, such as socialist and other anti-capitalist organisations, and environmental organisations such as Friends of the Earth, there has arisen a plethora of unusual activist groups, including the WOMBLES (White Overall Movement Building Liberation through Effective Struggle), a highly disciplined, non-violent group in white overalls and crash helmets who brandish water pistols and fake weapons. The WOMBLES (named after the fictional TV creatures who pick up litter on Wimbledon Common) are based on Ya Basta! (Enough is Enough), an Italian support group for the Zapatista rebels in Mexico. Other groups are Reclaim the Streets, which holds impromptu street parties by blocking off roads, and the Guerilla Gardeners, who dig up streets and other public spaces to plant flowers and turf.

The 'anti-global capitalism' protests are an excellent example of how central the management of visibility is to the contemporary political process. The protests render visible and public the issues relevant to the expansion of global capitalism, such as the lack of democratic accountability, the degradation of the environment, cruel and exploitative labour practices, and international debt structures. The protests give the international economic, business and political meetings a public profile and a degree of scrutiny they would not otherwise have encountered. The management of visibility, however, is not practised only by the protesters. The authority of meetings of such organisations such as the World Economic Forum (WEF), the World Bank, the International Monetary Fund (IMF) and the WTO may have been produced previously through their status as closed to the public and undermined by their increased public scrutiny as a result of 'anti-global capitalism' protests, but such groups are increasingly exercising their authority through the deployment of strategies of visualisation. A particular feature of such 'global capital' meetings is the presence of international business celebrities, most notably Microsoft chief Bill Gates. Indeed, it could be argued that such global capital meetings have been promoted increasingly as media spectacles of the making of the new global order.

Visibility, through extensive media coverage, is not in itself a guarantee of the protests' success. Much media coverage of the protests is negative, condemning the protesters for the violence that often occurs and dubbing the protesters variously misinformed, irrational, not interested in dialogue, and anti-democratic. The success of the protesters in raising the issues for public attention is followed by a struggle in the media and in public debate over the meanings and future directions of 'globalisation'. The interpretation of the actions of the protesters is highly dependent on news values, and this works for and against the anti-global capitalism movement. The conflict with police generates much media coverage, but the emphasis on the physical clashes can misrepresent the overall tone of the protests and result in the issues not being thoroughly investigated. An important feature of the anti-global capitalism protests, then, is the management of the journalistic coverage of the event: the protesters have to varying degrees captured media attention with imaginative protest strategies, and they have worked closely with journalists foregrounding the perspective of the protesters at the rallies. At the Melbourne meeting of the WEF in 2000, S-11 (umbrella name for activist groups after the opening day, September 11) protest spokesperson David Glanz played a prominent and effective role in media coverage prior to and during the Forum. Glanz's success was particularly evident on the opening day, when his claim of victory for the protesters was often the news angle adopted by the newspapers. Glanz thanked the police for erecting the steel fence and barricades, thereby concentrating protester action on a few key sites. In *The Australian* this earned a headline: 'S11 thanks officers for "victory"' (Mitchell 2000, p. 3).

The anti-global capitalism protests have attracted worldwide attention, not just because of their size and sometimes violent nature but because they represent a new style of protest. They are becoming increasingly theatrical and are marked by a playful and ironic tone that distinguishes them from earlier protest movements. Even with the media focus on the front-line clashes, it is apparent that the protests employ street theatre, banners, games and music to produce a movement with a strong carnival atmosphere. The 2001 May Day protests in London, for example, used the Internet and pamphlets to promote 'MayDay Monopoly', using the famous game to inform people of targeted city sites for the protests. This historical shift between the 'old' Left and the 'new' Left was also manifested in the differences between the trade union protest and the S-11 protests at the Melbourne WEF. As one journalist noted: 'One side had a conga line and ferals in reindeer horns and the other side had Moss Cass ... a relic of the Whitlam government. Said [a] dispirited union official, "It was like a funeral"' (Wynhausen 2000, p. 31).

Conclusion

In contemporary public life there is often concern expressed about the importance given to the personal images of politicians. Similarly, there is often consternation about the tendency to present modern politics as a performance acted through 'media events'. There are legitimate concerns about such developments: too much attention is devoted to political leaders while ignoring a broad range of other political participants; and scrutiny of policy is sometimes squeezed out of media coverage. But we need to be critical about some of the assumptions that underlie such familiar laments about modern politics. The subjectivity of politicians and other public figures is always a construction informed by different communicative encounters. A politician may receive media coaching and construct a 'media image' at odds with their 'everyday' self, but more fundamentally the 'media image' of a public figure is a necessary feature of their communicative powers. The creation of a media image is not limited to the superficialities of a haircut and a good set of teeth but extends to the personality and character of an individual and their ability to forge an emotional connection with the public. Similarly, observations about the 'performances' of public figures need to move beyond concern about 'artificiality' and to recognise how fundamental performance is to subjectivity, also to understand the dramatic and theatrical basis of modern public life. This is relevant across the entire political spectrum, from the parliamentary speech of a Prime Minister to the street demonstrations of a political activist.

7

Political information management

The personal image of political leaders is a focus of contemporary political communication, but the looks, style and character of politicians is only the most prominent product of a process in which a broad range of personnel deploy their sophisticated skills to produce political texts and images, control the flow of information within and across organisations, and manage relations with the mass media and the public. The professional communicators employed by politicians and political parties include media advisers, public relations consultants, speech writers, advertising executives, political strategy consultants and pollsters. In addition to these professional communicators, political personnel such as party leaders and government ministers or other members of parliament perform important strategy or planning roles. Graham Richardson, for example, was an important strategist in the Australian Labor governments of Bob Hawke and Paul Keating. In Britain, Peter Mandelson managed the public image of Labour, initially as the party's communications director and subsequently as an MP.

Politicians or political parties may themselves employ a range of personnel to manage their public communications, but there are a great number of professional communicators who are employed by other individuals, corporations and organisations seeking to influence the political process. The public relations industry has experienced phenomenal growth in recent decades, outstripping the employment growth of journalists, and it continues to shape the news agenda. Corporations and other organisations have well-staffed media relations or communications offices to ensure that their messages and images receive a favourable public response. Political lobbyists offer skills in direct, targeted negotiations with politicians and political parties over issues important to their clients. Media monitors and polling agencies are used to gauge media coverage and public opinion in order to tailor and strengthen public communication strategies.

The contemporary political media landscape, then, is an extraordinarily complex terrain on which a tremendous variety of information, stories, images, statistics and rumours circulate at great velocity on a daily basis, all subject to a multitude of interpretations. It is a considerable feat that in such a landscape professional communicators often have their messages received with the intended effect. On the one hand, the proliferation of these professional communicators and the deployment of their sophisticated media skills does result in the slicker presentation and more tightly controlled flow of information to the public arena. On the other, political messages are subject to increased competition and closer media and public scrutiny. Either way, media and information management is central to the political process.

Political advertising

Political advertising is one of the most powerful forms of political communication. It is powerful because it is a format that allows political actors to impart their messages direct to the public, without mediation by journalists. Political advertising is used across a range of media, including television, radio, press, billboards and the cinema. It has been credited with roles in famous election victories and defeats. In the 1972 Australian federal election the 'It's Time' theme captured a mood for change and helped Labor to victory. In the 1988 US Presidential elections, the Republicans devastated the Democrats' campaign by using a political advertisement featuring convicted murderer Willie Horton to claim that the Democrat candidate, Massachusetts Governor Michael Dukakis, was soft on crime. Political advertising does inform the electorate about candidates, policies and issues but it also aims to be highly persuasive and to associate particular feelings and values with candidates and opponents, often invoking treasured national myths and deep-seated fears. The rhetorical power of political advertising has often raised concern that electoral judgements are not grounded in rational choices, that voters are addressed more as consumers than citizens, and that political parties and candidates have been reduced to mere products. We should be cautious, however, about damning contemporary political advertising with evocations of a golden past in which voters soberly contemplated political advertisements composed of detailed and rational arguments. As Kathleen Jamieson (1986, p. 12) notes of US political advertising:

> those . . . who see our nation's political decline and fall mirrored in the rise of political spot advertising remember a halcyon past that never was. The transparencies, bandanas, banners, songs and cartoons that pervaded nineteenth century campaigning telegraphed conclusions, not evidence . . . Their messages were briefer . . . than those of any sixty second spot ad. The air then was filled not with substantive disputes but with simplification, sloganeering and slander.

The effects and costs of political advertising have raised questions in a number of countries about its regulation and control. In Britain, for example, political parties can place advertising in newspapers, cinemas and billboards but are prohibited from buying advertising time on television and radio. Instead, political parties are allowed to screen party political broadcasts (PPBs) and party election broadcasts (PEBs), with the amount of airtime allocated on the basis of the number of candidates a party stands at a general election. While the amount of broadcast advertising is regulated, the campaigns are still produced by advertising agencies and so employ sophisticated techniques of persuasion, which is expensive for the political parties (McNair 1999, p. 95). In Australia and the United States there are no such controls on political advertising, although in Australia there is a black-out on political broadcast advertising in the last days of an election campaign.

The costs of political advertising have skyrocketed over the past couple of decades. In the United States total television advertising costs were estimated as high as US$1 billion in the 2000 Presidential election race, up from $600 million during the 1996 Presidential campaign

(Kettle 2000). Attempts to control political advertising are countered with arguments about limits on freedom of speech, as we saw when the Hawke Labor government attempted to proscribe the broadcasting of political advertising in 1991 (Ward & Cook 1992). Alternatively, we can argue that contemporary political advertising is far from 'free' speech, and that the exorbitant costs of advertising hinder democratic development because it restricts the ability of minor parties and other groups to publicly distribute their ideas and policies. In addition, the growing cost of political advertising has meant that the major political parties, suffering falls in membership numbers, have been increasingly reliant on donations from corporations. There are fears that such financial assistance gives the business sector more leverage over major political parties. Regulation of the amount and type of political advertising may be a relatively achievable task, but political advertising will always be controversial because of its content. Attempts to render political advertising more rational and informative face much greater difficulties. As Henry Mayer once stated, to regulate slogans, jingles and references to trust and fear in political advertising would '*eliminate politics as we know it*' (1994, p. 116, author's emphasis); and (1994, p. 119):

> Truth is hardly ever simple or short in politics. Truthful political promotion would have to stress context and complexity and imperfection to such a degree as to bore the pants off most men and women and send them to sleep.

Truth may be neither simple nor short in politics, but political advertising is often so characterised. Just as the average soundbite length on the television news has diminished over the years, so has the average duration of television political advertisements fallen. Most political advertisements now run the length of other television advertisements (30–60 seconds). This means that complex explanations of policy are replaced by simple statements and the repetition of party slogans. The shortness of political advertisements also partly determines an image-dominated content that communicates pre-existing beliefs and values. One of the most famous political advertisements was the 'Morning in America' spot for the Ronald Reagan campaign in the 1984 US

Presidential election. The advertisement evoked the 'American dream' and traditional values as it depicted decent, hard-working people, often in beautiful rural locations. Such texts highlight political advertising as a dramatic, emotional and rhetorical genre.

Political advertisements are used in a variety of contexts, and sometimes their status is difficult to determine. Usually, political advertisements feature most prominently during election campaigns, but governments are increasingly promoting their policies in the guise of public service announcements. During an election campaign a narrative of political advertising is organised by the advertising agency. Diamond and Bates identified these four phases of a typical US political advertising campaign: the identity of the candidate is established; the candidate's policy positions are broadly established; the opposition candidate is attacked through negative advertisements; finally, the candidate's image is enhanced through an association with positive values (Diamond & Bates 1992).

Political advertising allows the candidate or party to retain complete control of the production and distribution of the message, but it is also undermined by its status as advertising. Members of the public, regardless of whether they agree or disagree with the advertisements, are aware that the texts reflect unproblematically the point of view of the candidate or party. Political actors are aware that more effective political communication can occur through the use of news media or 'free media'. Political messages carry greater weight through free media because they have been subject to scrutiny, but the use of news media also carries risk because the meanings of a political interview or a promotional appearance are outside the control of the political actor and sometimes the desired message is undermined. The challenge for political actors is to minimise that risk through careful control of the delivery of the information and of the media interpretation of the political messages.

Public relations and crisis management

Politicians, the media and the public are the recipients of a barrage of information from a range of personnel who seek to influence the political process. These groups of individuals and organisations are wide-ranging: we will focus here on the activities of public relations practitioners, pressure groups, thinktanks and political lobbyists. Public relations is a massive industry: it has been estimated that the Australian public relations industry is growing by 20 per cent annually and that it has a turnover of $1 billion per year, with about 7000 practitioners (Cadzow 2001, p. 1). Public relations is a disparate field and difficult to define singularly: research has revealed 74 different job titles that conduct public relations work, such as 'corporate affairs manager', 'media liaison director' and 'communications manager' (Johnston & Zawawi 2000, p. 3).

Public relations exercises tremendous influence over the news agenda and the content of news stories. Research suggests that public relations was the source for 60 per cent of news stories and 80 per cent of business news stories in some Australian metropolitan newspapers (Cadzow 2001, p. 1). Such influence is partly attributable to dwindling numbers of journalists in newsrooms and growing deadline pressures, but it is also a measure of the greater resources of public relations practitioners and their growing communication skills. The integral role of public relations to news content is a cause for concern when it corresponds with less independent journalistic scrutiny. The influence of public relations underlines that news is the end product of a series of negotiations between institutional participants. News content often arises from persuasive strategies of public relations staff and other news sources with an interest to promote issues, events and ideas and the interactions of such sources with journalists.

Ironically, the public relations industry struggles with its own public image, despite the industry's claims that public relations practice is informed by principles of accuracy and truthfulness. The contribution of public relations to public life can generate concern because, unlike a journalist, the public relations practitioner promotes the particular point of view of a client. The rapid expansion of public relations is, however, to be expected given the increasing complexity and character of modern public life. Public relations deals with a variety of communicative contexts, both 'internal' (company employees, organisation members etc.) and 'external' (mass media, general public etc.) 'publics'. And public relations is much more than just the provision of information for news outlets: it also involves a broad range of advocacy activities for clients.

Crisis management is a growing feature of public relations practice. With the onset of a crisis a company, organisation or public figure comes under intense scrutiny, which can destroy the company or damage reputations. Successful crisis management involves identification of possible crises and response planning, a quick response to the crisis when it occurs, clear and definite articulations of the problem and claims of responsibility, the balancing of legal, political and public opinion demands, as well as a dose of good luck. Crisis managers formulate a comprehensive communications strategy oriented towards the media, the general public and the stakeholders implicated in the crisis. An important component of crisis management is the media coaching of the client, and its first rule not to conceal information (which will only subsequently prolong and magnify the crisis) but to manage the crisis through the truthful disclosure of relevant information. In the words of one crisis manager: 'What you say is "This is the information that we have so far, we don't know whether it's 100 per cent correct; if it changes we'll come back to you", as distinct from "I couldn't possibly comment, the matter's in the hands of our lawyers"' (J. Little 1999, p. 7). Legal issues are, nonetheless, prominent in a crisis management strategy, and clients are coached in ways to express concern without admitting liability. Clients are coached not only in the content of their message but in the production of their image and the cultivation of public perceptions. The same crisis manager (J. Little 1999, p. 7) declares:

> The formula now is confess fast. Communicate. If it's an oil spill, don't appear in a suit; appear on the dock with tousled hair as though you were putting your kid to bed and the phone rang and you put down the nursery rhymes and came running.

The influence of public relations does have significant ramifications for the structure and operations of contemporary public life. The proliferation of public relations is a consequence of a public life characterised by promotion, performance and the management of visibility. Public relations practitioners argue that they simply present their clients' points of view before 'the court of public opinion'. In this sense, the power of public relations is diminished to its informational functions and the industry is posited as a necessary tool in a democratic society. Such arguments, however, are blind to issues of structural access to the public domain and the persuasive powers of public relations. Public relations activity is not just 'another voice' contributing to public debate but, as a result of capital and organisational resources, it is also 'a tool for the already powerful, promoting and defending them by mobilising consent' (Wilson 1989, p. 178). Increasingly, the public sphere is not a neutral domain where opinions are considered irrespective of financial resources or someone's status. Indeed, it can be argued that the pervasiveness of public relations has closed off public life by increasing competition for news space and making it more difficult for organisations without public relations and financial resources.

But the power of public relations can be overstated. As several studies have noted, many public relations campaigns fail (Wilson 1989, p. 178; Tiffen 1989, p. 85). As already noted, the fragility and indeterminacy of public life means that even the best-planned campaign can founder. As with political advertising, overt public relations campaigns can fail because of public scepticism, informed by the knowledge that the campaign uncritically presents one side of an argument. Public relations is thus most successful when it is 'invisible', as in the reproduction of a press release in a news story. Public relations campaigns can also be undermined by other public relations campaigns. Any political public relations work that deals with controversial topics encounters vigorous counter-arguments by other interested parties and careful media scrutiny.

Pressure groups, thinktanks and political lobbyists

Public relations is often allied with the corporate world, but public relations strategies are also employed by a variety of organisations seeking to influence government policy and public opinion. Pressure groups are a prominent part of the political landscape, and many of these have become very proficient in the use of public relations to draw attention to their cause. Pressure or interest groups are organisations that represent certain sections of society and promote particular issues, and they seek to influence the political processes of government. Pressure groups must be distinguished from social movements, which are less systemic, more interested in changing cultural values than lobbying parliaments, and often do not have formal administrative structures (Stewart & Ward 1996). Pressure groups may be closely allied to political parties but do not usually seek election to office. Some pressure groups, such as the Australian Council of Trade Unions (ACTU) and the National Farmers' Federation (NFF), have institutionalised and direct links to governments, and are called on by government to contribute to the formulation of policy. Pressure groups without such institutional links to government are more likely to implement media strategies to publicise their cause and influence policy. Pressure groups represent a range of sectors of society and issues, including business (e.g. Business Council of Australia), labour (e.g. ACTU), professions (e.g. Australian Medical Association), consumers (e.g. Australian Consumers Association), gays and lesbians (e.g. Gay and Lesbian Rights Lobby) and the environment (e.g. Greenpeace). Pressure groups engage in such tactics as the staging of public rallies and demonstrations, organising petitions, publishing newsletters and leaflets, lobbying politicians, and providing information and expertise to government.

Pressure groups have become more important over the past few decades due to broad social and political changes. The general weakening of the institutions that once provided a greater degree of social consensus has meant that sectional interests have become more autonomous and involved in political struggle. The political domain has been characterised by greater executive power and declining parliamentary influence, together with growing public distrust in the ability of political parties to bring about change. These political developments, combined with the increasing complexity of modern life, have resulted in people seeking more direct forms of political expression and representation through pressure groups. Social and political changes have also resulted in the growing importance of the mass media to the various forms of political struggle. As we have noted, pressure groups will rely on the media to differing degrees, depending on their institutional links, but the declining authority of institutions and the parliamentary domain has meant that the media have become increasingly the site of political struggle. While some groups benefit greatly from media publicity, often the most successful pressure groups are able to influence policy makers more directly, out of the public gaze (Stewart & Ward 1996, pp. 191–2).

'Thinktanks' can also influence the political landscape. A thinktank can be defined as 'an independent organisation engaged in multi-disciplinary research intended to influence public policy' (James, in Bakvis 1997, p. 97). Thinktanks are distinguished from most pressure groups because they offer advice on broad programs of social action and direction as well as on individual policy areas (Bakvis 1997, p. 94). They gain prestige to some degree through their independence from funding by either government or other specific political interests, but they are often identified with particular ideological positions: in Australia, for example, the right side of the political spectrum has the Institute of Public Affairs while the left side has the Evatt Foundation. The Liberal and Labor parties have links with the Menzies Research Centre and the Whitlam Institute respectively.

Pressure groups and other organisations that seek to influence government often rely on the specialist skills of political lobbyists. As Peter Sekuless has noted, political lobbying has swelled from a handful of consultants in the late 1970s to the so-called 'government relations industry' in more recent times, with the introduction of multinational public relations companies such as Burson-Marsteller and Hill & Knowlton (1991, p. 2). While political lobbying has grown in Australia it does not match the size and influence of the government relations industry in the United States, where some lobbyists specialise in one congressional committee. Political lobbyists supply their clients with relevant governmental information, such as departmental annual reports, speeches, statistics and media releases. As their name suggests, they also lobby politicians and bureaucrats through a range of activities. Lobbyists will cultivate ongoing political and public service contacts and seek to persuade political decision makers to particular actions, such as the modification of a regulation or the content of a proposed bill. Lobbyists advise clients on how to define a problem and how to prepare a case; they mould information supplied by their clients into acceptable formats and advise their clients on when and to whom the information should be distributed. Political lobbyists are political insiders with detailed knowledge of the political process, but they are also skilled users of the media given that it is often quicker and more effective to influence the government through more public means.

Spin doctors

Corporations and other organisations benefit from their deployment of public relations strategies in the management of information and the media, but such skills are crucial to the success of political parties. Political parties are absolutely dependent on public support for their ongoing survival, so it is not surprising that they have become adept at the deployment of sophisticated media strategies. Indeed, the degree of their success in managing the media has provoked concern that the balance between political power and media scrutiny has tipped too far in the politicians' favour. Such concern has focused predominantly on the figure of the 'spin doctor'. The term has been widely and loosely used, but 'spin' generally refers to the 'highly professional selling of the political message that involves maximum management and manipulation of the media' (Grattan 1998, p. 34). 'Spin doctors' are usually political staffers and operators, such as press secretaries or media advisers, but the term has been also applied to non-political public relations practitioners and to politicians themselves, sometimes the most skilled of all in the practice of spin. Spin doctors have been attributed with extraordinary powers and a mysterious repertoire of persuasive strategies, but their functions generally include the control of media access to politicians, the packaging of information for media and public consumption and, most notably, various forms of direct communication with journalists about the interpretations and meanings of political events and comments. It is difficult sometimes to distinguish between the actions of spin doctors and the general persuasive strategies that have always been an integral part of political communication. The rise to prominence of the term, with its nefarious connotations, is perhaps a marker of how much more sophisticated media management has become and how much more important media relations have become to the successful functioning of political parties.

Spin doctors are known chiefly for their attempts to persuade journalists to construct positive interpretations of a politician's comments.

They provide a 'spin' or 'angle' on a speech or a news conference, helping to make sense of the issues, or they highlight and clarify points. They may issue press releases following up on a speech or interview, they may speak personally to journalists, and in some instances (mainly in the UK and the USA) they themselves give news conferences. Sometimes the spin doctor's attempt at persuasion will be a few quiet words in a journalist's car after a news conference; sometimes the tactic will be a bullying and intimidating telephone call after a critical news story has been released. Outbursts are not uncommon, and, while they may not influence the way a journalist covers a story, they do put pressure on journalists aware of the ramifications of getting 'offside' with a politician. Journalists can have information withheld from them, or they can be, as former Australian Prime Minister Paul Keating once declared famously, 'put on the drip', and given regular and quality access and information.

Spin doctors, and the media management that goes along with such an 'occupation', are now an integral part of the political process throughout much of the world—although, as Michelle Grattan notes, spin doctors are more prominent, and arguably more influential, in the UK and the USA than they are in Australia (Grattan 1998, pp. 33–4). In Britain, 'spin doctoring', as employed by Tony Blair and New Labour, has been a very public and powerful tool. Blair's colleague Peter Mandelson was for a long time the chief architect in news management, both within and outside the party. Blair's press secretary, Alastair Campbell, has been also influential in his daily briefings with journalists. Indeed, Campbell had been reported as assuming a less prominent role following Labour's 2001 election victory because he had become the focal point of public concern that Labour was driven too much by spin. As one government minister stated: '[Campbell] is too high profile. He has become the story. The government looks as if it is run by spin instead of just using spin' (Watt 2001). In the United States, the position of presidential spokesperson has a much more formalised public profile. The spokesperson gives regular news conferences at which it is a conventional understanding that their comments represent the views of the President and his administration. Putting a spin on Presidential comments and actions can be an arduous task, as Mike McCurry found when he was the spokesperson for the troubled Clinton administration (Kurtz 1998, p. 15):

Each day, it seemed, McCurry faced a moral dilemma. He stood squarely at the intersection of news and propaganda, in the white-hot glare of the media spotlight, the buffer between self-serving administration officials and a cynical pack of reporters. The three principles of his job, he believed, were telling the truth, giving people a window on the White House, and protecting the president, but the last imperative often made the first two difficult.

In Australia, spin doctors (such as Prime Minister John Howard's media adviser Tony O'Leary) can at most be glimpsed in the background of television news footage. While they may not be public figures themselves, Australian spin doctors are engaged in the same kind of strategies and activities as their overseas counterparts.

Spin doctors ensure that their bosses benefit from publicity but they also control the public presence of their political masters to gain publicity with minimum scrutiny. Paradoxically, then, a politician may have a high public profile while remaining protected from the public. John Howard, for example, is said to be 'simultaneously over-exposed and under-available. He is all over the media, but that doesn't mean he is accessible to answer media questions from other than those on whose programs he has decided to appear' (Grattan 1998, p. 38). This is particularly true for US Presidents, who do not have to face political opponents in regular forums (unlike a Prime Minister, who at least appears in parliament). Spin doctors will protect politicians from media scrutiny through a variety of strategies: they will hold fewer news conferences, hold more 'doorstop' interviews where they can exert greater control over the discussion, and select more favourable television and radio interviewers. As discussed in chapter 5, one strategy is appearing on talkback radio so politicians can talk more directly with members of the public without the intervening journalistic scrutiny and interpretation. Spin doctors not only limit which journalists get direct access to the politician and the kind of interactions with the media—they also control the range of sources on which journalists can draw. Spin doctors designate the limited few individuals who can speak to the media on a given topic, thus ensuring that a consistent message is communicated.

Party political communication

Spin doctors are only part of the broad communications structure that is a necessary feature of mainstream political parties. While an individual spin doctor may control the breadth of sources on a particular topic, political parties must more broadly implement and coordinate internal communication channels and strategies. Party officials and members need to be informed of policy developments and other information to ensure that the party functions effectively and that a united party image can be projected. Political parties need to coordinate policy developments and the promotion of issues with a variety of media campaigns and communication strategies. The successful media management of the modern British Labour Party can be traced back to the 1980s, when the party formed a communications and campaigns directorate that brought all of the party's media, marketing, advertising and public relations activities under one management unit (McNair 1999, p.146). The unit, headed by Peter Mandelson and involving a range of media personnel such as advertising professional Philip Gould, developed a total management plan for the party. As Hughes and Wintour (1993, p. 183) state:

> Mandelson and Gould succeeded, not because they exploited slick advertising and media management more effectively than the Conservatives, but because they forged between themselves an approach to political strategy which has never before been seen . . . They welded policy, politics and image-creation into one weapon.

The importance of such party communication units is most evident during election campaigns, when political strategy and media management becomes fraught and frenzied. The party communications unit will draw on a range of skills from outsiders such as advertising experts, pollsters, and political strategists. The party communications unit and political strategists will engage in a wide variety of tactics during an election campaign. One tactic, successfully used by the New South Wales Labor Party in the 1999 election, is to target the advertising of the political Opposition, checking for errors or misleading claims in the hope of having the advertisement withdrawn. As one political strategist (Bailey 1999, p. 14) noted:

It's enormously destabilising for a political campaign to have your ad knocked out . . . It goes right to the heart of the campaign office. The director has to spend time rectifying a problem he's already dealt with and so he can't deal with other problems. It distracts the leader because they're forced to handle it, they're held responsible. And it can set up a panic among staff.

Management of the election campaign extends through to cultivating perceptions about the election result. A narrow loss for an Opposition that was not expected to win, as occurred for Labor in the Australian 1998 federal election, needs to be portrayed positively to ensure continued momentum for the party (Bailey 1999, p. 15).

The rise of spin doctors and sophisticated party communication units has had profound effects on the journalistic reportage of politics. It has long been a complaint that the news media focus too much on political image and strategy and not enough on issues and policy. The political emphasis given to leadership style has resulted in news coverage reporting elections as a 'horse race' rather than providing comprehensive reportage and critical evaluation of issues. Journalistic scrutiny of the careful packaging of information and the management of the media reduces politics to a 'game'. While such behaviour diminishes the political culture, news media coverage of media management at least draws attention to the techniques and actions of the spin doctors and media strategists.

Leaks and background briefings

Leaks are part of the weaponry of a spin doctor but they are also a more generalised part of political communication, practised by others such as politicians and public servants. As Tiffen notes, 'leak' is a loosely used term but it can be defined as 'the unauthorised release of confidential information' (Tiffen 1989, p. 96). The nature of the leak will vary from innocuous to highly sensitive information, and it may be the premature release of information or it may be information that was intended to remain private. Sometimes briefings are distinguished from leaks only through the negative connotations associated with the latter (hence former British Prime Minister James Callaghan's famous remark: 'Leaking is what you do; briefing is what I do'), but generally background briefings are distinguished from leaks in that 'they are semi-institutionalised; and are usually given to a group rather than to an individual. The convention is that the information may be used but not attributed to the source' (Tiffen 1989, p. 97). Leaks are also distinguished from 'whistle blowing' by being conducted usually by politicians or political figures rather than public servants or other career personnel. Whistle blowing, like leaking, involves the unauthorised release of information, but it usually occurs to right a wrong, while a leak may occur for personal or political advantage; whistle blowers are, moreover, sometimes willing to disclose their information publicly (Negrine 1996, pp. 36–7).

Leaks and background briefings transgress the divisions between the public and private domain, between official and unofficial information, between the 'front' and 'back' regions of organisations and institutions. As we have seen, the meanings of politics are often generated through the careful management of a public image, and leaks are an indispensable type of political communication precisely because they are not contained by formal channels and conventions. Leaks are often motivated by conflict: they are usually signals of a disagreement between two parties, and the leak's covert nature suggests a betrayal or a breakdown in a relationship. Leaks are often a power strategy of weaker participants in a conflict: the unauthorised release of information often undermines the power of those with authority and challenges the official public position on an issue. Sometimes the conflict behind a leak will reside in a single person: a political figure, pressured by requirements of diplomacy or the need for party unity, may leak information to signal personal views at odds with public pronouncements. Sometimes leaks occur as a strategy to avoid conflict. It is a common strategy of political parties to engage in 'kite flying': this is where a proposal is leaked to gauge public opinion, enabling the party to publicly retreat from the proposal if sentiment is adverse. The significance of leaks is often determined by their timing: a leak may, for example, undermine the political impact of an opponent's announcement.

Leaks and background briefings facilitate the public disclosure of information and in many instances do allow for a more accurate and comprehensive understanding of issues, policies and personal strategies. Increased political control over information has meant that leaks are less frequent than they once were: cabinet leaks, for example, are rare while they were once almost routine (Steketee 2001, p. 7). Leaks and background briefings remain, however, an integral part of political communication precisely because of more sophisticated media management. Leaks can have a deleterious effect on the quality of the news and public information. They can distort news judgements: otherwise routine information can become front-page news simply because the information was leaked and was obtained exclusively by a journalist. The covert nature of leaks also permits source irresponsibility and makes evaluation of the information difficult. Their secretive character can allow the concealment of journalistic incompetence and even invention (Tiffen 1989, pp. 121–4).

The British Labour government suffered a number of serious leaks in 2000, most notably of the full text of a private memo by Tony Blair which acknowledged that his government was publicly perceived to be 'somehow out of touch with gut British instincts' on a range of issues such as crime and asylum seekers. The leaks occurred at a time when Labour was declining in the opinion polls, intensifying public debate over the performance of the government. They highlighted conflict and division within the party, allowing certain ministers to question publicly the influence of the Prime Minister's advisers. The leaks also overshadowed policy implementation, such as Chancellor Gordon Brown's announcement of a £43 million spending plan. Despite the controversy of these leaks and New Labour's diligence in seeking to control information, figures suggest that the Blair government's formal leak inquiries average of about 25 per year is not unusual in the context of the past two decades of British politics (Walker 2000).

Governmental communication

Aside from the high-profile and often controversial activities of spin doctors and party political communication offices, governments are routinely involved in significant forms of information management. These processes of information management constitute a significant feature of the machinery of government, covering a diverse range of legislation, government offices and types of communication, such as freedom of information legislation, the publicity offices of individual government departments, the government media unit, government advertising and public information campaigns. Such structures and types of government communication disseminate information to the public about the activities of government—a necessary and vital function of government in a democratic society. But governments do not only disseminate information to inform the public and involve them in the political process: information is also suppressed and manufactured, and the timing of its release is controlled, in order to manage public opinion and to further the interests of the government.

Governments have official secrecy provisions that restrict the flow of information to the public. It is argued that some information needs to be classified because it represents a threat to national security. The British government has four categories for classified information, from 'restricted', which is information deemed to be 'undesirable in the interests of the nation', through to 'top secret', which is information that could pose 'exceptionally grave damage to the nation' (Ponting, in Negrine 1996, p. 37). Governments impose restrictions on information through Official Secrets Acts, and they have disclosure rules which allow only some information to be released publicly decades after the event. Cabinet documents, for example, are released in Australia 30 years after the meetings. In Australia, the government can issue a 'D-notice', whereby the federal Defence, Press and Broadcasting Committee asks the media not to release information on a specific issue. The issuing of D-notices relies on the cooperation of media companies: there are no penalties for breaches (Conley 1997, pp. 118–19). More recently, governments have been restricting the release of information for reasons of 'commercial confidentiality'. Such decisions relate to information on tenders for government business and projects.

At the other end of the spectrum governments now have Freedom of Information (FOI) Acts, which enshrine in legislation the rights of individuals and organisations to access information about themselves and their government. The Australian federal government introduced FOI legislation in 1982, and the Northern Territory was the last

Australian government to introduce FOI legislation almost 20 years later, in 2001. The objectives of FOI laws have been to improve the quality of government decision making by reducing secrecy, increase the opportunities for the public to participate in decision making, and allow people to see information about themselves that is held on government files. When FOI was introduced it was lauded as a valuable tool for journalists, but the costs involved, the difficulties of correctly framing applications in order to obtain the requested information, and the considerable time frames needed for processing applications, has meant that it is not commonly used by journalists. There is a variety of information that is exempt from FOI, such as cabinet and executive documents, information relating to national security, law enforcement matters and information given under legal professional privilege.

On a more everyday basis, governments communicate with the public through government media offices. Governments also communicate with the public through advertising, which includes public information campaigns, also information about tenders, electoral matters etc. Public information campaigns (discussed in more detail in chapter 10) cover a broad range of behaviour and actions, from anti-smoking drives to neighbourhood watch organisation. As noted in chapter 2, government media offices are supposed to distribute governmental information in a neutral manner, but this is increasingly an ideal that is not realised in everyday political practice. Under the Howard government, the Office of Government Information and Advertising has been renamed the Government Communications Unit and moved into the Prime Minister's own department. One way to try to justify such a move is to declare that at least this makes the political control of the office more transparent. The political effect of this move, however, is to allow policy makers to retain control over the subsequent public promotion of policies (Brenchley 1999, pp. 30–1).

The higher levels of governmental advertising and the blurring of the line between governmental and party political advertising is a cause for concern. In 2000, the federal government was the biggest spender on advertising in the country, laying out $145 million and outstripping such companies as Telstra, Coles Myer, Toyota and McDonald's (Lloyd 2001). While governments do need to incur expenditure on advertising in a mediated society, it is the growing tendency to politicise such information distribution that has caused most alarm. The Howard government's GST advertising campaign, for example, was much criticised because it was judged to have been motivated more by the desire to improve the government's electoral stakes than the task of providing substantive information for citizens about the tax changes. Such trends are not limited to Australia: in the year 2001/02 the British Labour government spent £272 million on government advertising, more than double that for the year in which it first assumed office (Day 2002).

Conclusion

Political information management involves an extraordinarily broad range of communicative strategies, from the very public jingles of political advertising through to the most covert of leaks. Political information management involves a great diversity of political personnel—the political leaders themselves, media advisers and public servants. There are also a variety of media- and information-based professions that feed into political information management, such as advertising executives, lobbyists and public relations personnel. The sheer amount of political information production and management should be expected in the mediated and promotional culture in which we live. In a vibrant and active democracy we should not bemoan 'special-interest groups' and 'lobbyists' but rather expect and welcome such expressions of interest and contributions to political debate. We need to remember that while extraordinary amounts might be spent on political advertising, while spin doctors may deploy their skills with great sophistication, it remains the case that political advertising often meets with a sceptical public response and that the strategies of media advisers sometimes fail dismally. Still, there is very real concern for the democratic health of a society when the processes of information management become big business and subject to massive expenditure. We, the public, need a critical news media that is not beholden to the public relations industry. We also need governments that put the public interest ahead of corporate and other special interests and are able to distribute information to the public in a responsible and non-partisan manner. Finally, we need to enhance our own media literacy to better understand the complexity of modern political information management.

Part 3
Mediated Public Life

Opinion polls and public opinion

8

Contemporary public opinion is synonymous with methods of opinion polling, yet public opinion is also a broader phenomenon that is manifested in forms other than polling. The various forms through which public opinion is expressed provide for a variety of political effects. Modern forms of opinion polling, which provide for individualised responses to set issues and options, have been characterised as a means of social control. Alternatively, public opinion can erupt in unpredictable and violent ways, as we have seen in the anti-global capitalism protests (detailed in chapter 6). Also, some theorists have questioned the validity of linking the findings of opinion polls to expressions of public opinion. In complex and large-scale modern democracies, however, there is a need for means of measuring and allowing expressions of public opinion. The media, in particular, given their functions in a democratic society, have the difficult task of ascertaining public opinion so they can address relevant issues. The relationship between public opinion and opinion polling, then, is complex and problematic, yet it is also a vital topic to investigate given its everyday importance to the media and politics.

The production and expression of public opinion is not limited to politics. A broad range of surveys and forms of market research inquire routinely into a multitude of matters, including our lifestyle choices, our values, and our consumption of goods and services. Extensive databases are compiled from such information and become valuable commodities for businesses, organisations and governments.

Such forms of market research are a more pervasive phenomenon in modern life but they address us primarily as consumers, and our emphasis here will be on public opinion as it pertains to the news media and politics.

History of public opinion

Public opinion has a strong and positive political resonance: politicians can dismiss opposition to policies on the grounds of public opinion, and journalists can justify interrogations on the basis that they inquire on behalf of public concern. The political power of public opinion, of course, stems from the principles of a democratic political system. Public opinion mobilises principles of 'classical democracy': it is assumed that the opinion has been freely formed through the rational evaluation of arguments; it is the expression of a majority view, or the most popular opinion of the voting population; and it represents a means by which people can participate in the life of the society. The positive political resonance of such principles invokes ancient Athenian democracy, even though the modern reality of public opinion production may be far removed from such classical ideals.

The ideals of contemporary public opinion may be informed by the principles of classical democracy but public opinion is nonetheless a historical concept, and its forms and social values have changed dramatically over time. As noted in our discussions of democracy and citizenship in chapter 2, public opinion is also not a static 'category' but a concept that is the product of economic, social and technological contexts. Equally, just as the concept of 'the public' has undergone historical development, so has the manifestation of the 'opinions' of those publics changed. Indeed, the concept of public opinion is closely aligned with the understanding of the 'public sphere', as articulated in the work of Jürgen Habermas (see chapter 3). The free and wide-ranging expression of opinion is integral to the functioning of the public sphere (Habermas 1989, p. 49):

> Citizens behave as a public body when they confer in an unrestricted fashion—that is, with the guarantee of freedom of assembly and

association and the freedom to express and publish their opinions—about matters of general interest.

Public opinion has always been articulated in a variety of forums with diverse mixes of rationality and passion. Eighteenth-century England, the focus of much of Habermas' historical interest, saw the rise to prominence of the bourgeois class and their generation of public opinion through discussions in the coffee houses, reading rooms and libraries of the day, supplemented by a more active, critical and regular press. The public opinion produced in the coffee houses was dynamic and open-ended, the result of dialogue among many participants. Petitions were another popular form of public opinion expression, and were drawn up at mass meetings after discussion and debate. Alternatively, public opinion was expressed on the streets through rioting and demonstrations. Dramatic displays of public opinion through the formation and actions of crowds provoked concern about the potential power of the general populace, manifested in expressions about 'mob rule'. Of course, such displays reached their apex in the rise of revolutionary movements—most notably in the French Revolution, where the power of the masses overturned the divine right of monarchy. Political struggles to enlarge the franchise in Britain were played out through the 19th and 20th centuries, as working-class men and women respectively engaged in strikes and demonstrated in the streets to claim their democratic rights. These types of public opinion expression, from street demonstrations to the bourgeois dialogue of the coffee houses, were divergent ways of expressing public opinion, but they all took place in public and were all relatively unstructured.

The history of techniques for public opinion expression generally shows the rise to prominence of more structured and privatised forms of public opinion expression. Straw polls, which are unofficial or rough votes to assess the relative strengths of candidates or issues, made their debut in the 1820s. Straw polls most often consisted of coupons in newspapers which readers were encouraged to complete and send in, although they also consisted of polls of groups of people, such as theatre audiences and patrons in bars. The introduction of more regular general elections from the 18th century also marks the beginning of the increasing rationalisation of public opinion (Herbst 1991).

As Susan Herbst and James Beniger note, the latter half of the 19th century in the United States saw public opinion structured around a diverse range of groups, most notably political parties. Political activity was still grounded in local communities, and political parties relied more on local knowledge than polls to assess the mood of the public (Herbst & Beniger 1994, p. 104).

The era of modern polling started in the USA in 1935, when *Fortune* magazine published its first poll and George Gallup began a syndicated polling service to newspapers. The defining moment in modern polling occurred in the following year, when the old form of straw polls—most famously conducted by the *Literary Digest*—and the new scientific form of polling confronted each other in the Presidential election. The *Literary Digest* predicted a victory for the Republican candidate because it sent its ballots to more affluent households with telephones and cars, while the new scientific survey method correctly predicted a Roosevelt victory (Gawiser & Evans Witt 1994, pp. 18–19).

The historical rise of methods of opinion polling created a fundamental change in perceptions of public opinion. As Herbst (1991, p. 226) has noted:

> Since the beginning of the straw poll in the 19th century, politicians and scholars began to think about public opinion as the sum total of all individual opinions. This aggregation-oriented approach to understanding the public sentiment was intertwined with survey research techniques: as sampling techniques were refined, many public opinion scholars began to lose interest in the meaning of public opinion and instead concentrated on measuring it.

The dominant forms of modern public opinion expression, then, represent a significant transformation from earlier expressions of public opinion. In contemporary times public opinion is expressed through 'top-down' strategies, where public opinion is sought from the state or the media or other commercial organisations, unlike earlier expressions of public opinion, which tended to be 'bottom-up' strategies. Modern forms of polling produce public opinion through privatised forms of expression and, rather than encouraging debate and discussion, public opinion polls present to citizens already complete public opinions. That is, in public opinion polling, organisers select questions and dictate respondents' choices. Of course, other forms of public opinion expression continue to exist, but public opinion has increasingly become synonymous with the findings of opinion polls.

Criticisms of opinion polls

This historical development that has seen public opinion polls assume the place of the dominant technique of public opinion expression has attracted considerable criticism from scholars. An early critique came from Blumer (1948), who maintained the importance of the dynamic cultural and social contexts in which public opinion was produced. Public opinion, he argued, is not just the aggregation of individual viewpoints but is generated through discussion among social groups. Most provocatively, Pierre Bourdieu declared his intentions on the issue in the title of his article 'Public Opinion Does Not Exist' (1979). Bourdieu does not denounce opinion polls per se, and he acknowledges that they can make a contribution to social science, but he challenges three assumptions that inform opinion polls: that all individuals have opinions, that their opinions have the same value, and that social consensus exists regarding which issues should be addressed in the opinion polls (Bourdieu 1979, p. 124). Bourdieu offers a critique of several technical features of opinion polls, including the treatment of the 'no replies' or 'no opinion', and argues that opinion polls are ultimately the instruments of political agents (1979, p. 125):

> This is the fundamental effect of the opinion poll: it creates the idea that a unanimous public opinion exists in order to legitimate [sic] a policy, and strengthen the relations of force upon which it is based . . .

This point is elaborated in Benjamin Ginsberg's work, the title of which, *The Captive Public: How Mass Opinion Promotes State Power*, also clearly suggests the author's perspective on the effects of modern opinion polls. Ginsberg notes four fundamental changes that have occurred to public opinion, which stem from the growing influence of opinion polls. First, he notes that opinion polling has transformed public opinion 'from a voluntary to an externally subsidized matter' (1986, p. 63).In the absence of polling, an individual must involve themselves in expenditures of money, effort and time in order to communicate their views publicly, whereas opinion polls subsidise or underwrite the costs of that public expression. This weakens the relationship between public opinion and the intensity or extremity of opinion because those who do not hold strong opinions on an issue are included in formulations of public opinion. This, in turn, has political effects: politicians are more likely to prefer scientific, statistical expressions of public opinion over demonstrations, letter-writing campaigns, and other forms of public opinion expression that are deemed to be more personal, more informed by 'special interests', and less 'rational'.

Second, opinion polling has transformed public opinion from a behavioural to an attitudinal phenomenon. Before the advent of polling, public opinion was mainly manifested in forms of behaviour, such as riots, strikes and demonstrations. Opinion polls, however, elicit public opinion without any action required by the opinion-holder. As Ginsberg notes, such a form of public opinion expression makes it possible for authorities to recognise and deal with public opinions before they are manifested in disruptive behaviour (1986, p. 69). Third, as has already been noted, the dominance of opinion polls has transformed public opinion from the property of groups in society to an attribute of individuals. While it is true that the opinions of groups in society have always been articulated by group leaders, such as the church hierarchy and trade union officials, opinion polls have facilitated the production of a more generalised and individualised form of public opinion. Again, this has important political ramifications: '. . . by undermining the capacity of groups, interests, parties, and the like to speak for public opinion, polling can also diminish the effectiveness of public opinion as a force in political affairs. In essence, polling intervenes between opinion and its organized or collective expression' (Ginsberg 1986, p. 74). Finally, Ginsberg notes how polling to some degree removes individuals' control over their own expressions of opinion by transforming them from spontaneous assertions to a constrained response. 'Public opinion', then, is produced only in response to the issues of concern raised by the governmental agencies, businesses and media outlets that conduct the opinion polls.

Noelle-Neumann (1984) has also speculated on the power relations produced through the modern production of public opinion, but focuses more on how individual viewpoints are affected by perceptions of others in society. Her 'spiral of silence' concept argues that fear of isolation causes people to assess the climate of opinion and that perception prompts people to act in accord with the perceived majority opinion, or makes them less willing to express their own opinion. Such a concept adopts a broad perspective on the production of public opinion, including the prominence of interpersonal communication and social relations as well as the effects of media reportage of public opinion. While this concept locates media influence in social contexts, it nonetheless posits a 'powerful media' viewpoint, arguing that a dominant perspective offered in media reportage will strongly determine public opinion. Noelle-Neumann's theory has been subject to much testing over the years, with mixed support from researchers (McQuail 1994, pp. 361–3; Sligo & Williams 1999, pp. 40–1).

Public opinion in mediated society

As noted throughout this book, modern public life is a mediated phenomenon. We tend not to encounter public opinion directly but rather read about representations of public opinion as expressed in the findings of opinion polls. Opinion polls have been subject to much critique, but their presence and influence in modern society underlines how the techniques, or technologies, of public opinion expression are integral to the formation of public opinion. In a mass society, opinion polls are a necessary and efficient technology through which public opinion can be measured. Publics have always been formed through their interactions with communication technologies: the emergence of early reading publics became possible with the invention of printing technology. As Gabriel Tarde noted a century ago, 'the transportation of thought across distance' distinguishes a public from a crowd (in Herbst & Beniger 1994, p. 97). Publics are bound together by common concerns and ideas which are shared by means of communication technologies.

The significance of opinion polls in mediated public life does prompt concern about our ability to distinguish public opinion, from mass media representations of public opinion. When the media make pronouncements on public opinion, are they articulating the views of the society that exist independently of the media or are the media merely speculating on a product of their own creation, which may or even may not have some grounding in reality? The media are central to the production of public opinion in a mediated society, which is not to conclude that modern public opinion is a charade. The media do, nonetheless, perform an integral role in the framing and shaping of public opinion, and the nature of that role has always interested media and cultural studies scholars. In *Policing the Crisis*, public opinion is conceptualised as the crystallisation of the pre-existing public opinion of citizens together with its uptake by the media; the media do not simply transmit those opinions of the public but work them into public opinions that 'underpin and support the viewpoints already in circulation' (Hall et al. 1978, p. 137). The media can give voice to public opinion by articulating what they consider the majority of people to believe, or the media can take an even more active role in public opinion formation where they take it on themselves to speak directly for the public, most notably in editorials. As Negrine (1996, pp. 102–4) notes, while such a conceptualisation of public opinion formation does allow for the expressions of public opinion separate from the mass media, it runs the risk of devaluing the separate opinions of the public or, at worst, emptying the opinions of the public of any political force and rendering them a mere instrument of social control.

The media are integral to the production of modern public opinion in mediated public life, and public opinion production is used as a means of social control; but public opinion is also a more productive phenomenon, the result of a more complex dialogue between the media and the public. To see public opinion formation as merely the way the opinions of people are taken up and transformed by the media to further established positions in society is to ignore the dynamic, dialogical and indeterminate nature of modern public opinion. While public opinion can be defined, measured and used for particular political purposes, it is also the ongoing discussion a society has with itself, which is based on the interpretations and uses of public opinion that circulate in the media and throughout public life. As McKenzie Wark notes: 'The media proposes, publics form themselves by reading what is proposed, and images of what those readings decide are proposed back to the public via opinion polls and surveys' (1999, p. 136).

Such an argument about public opinion in mediated public life emphasises its *imaginary* status: public opinion in this sense is not a fiction but has a fundamentally *indeterminate* character. Wark (1999, p. 32) expresses this view in his idea of Australia as a 'virtual republic':

> What makes it a virtual public thing is the paradox that while it is shared by all who make it real by imagining it and articulating it, everyone imagines and articulates it as something different. Its existence is not predicated on any agreement as to its essential features . . . Rather, its existence, like the existence of the 'fair go', is predicated only on the possibility of disagreement about its qualities. Australia is that which Australians disagree about . . .

Public opinion in mediated public life is dominated by opinion polls but is also expressed through many other techniques. Of course, public opinion is expressed in what the politicians are fond to call 'the only poll that matters'—elections. Election campaigns are times when public opinion assumes a heightened importance and is expressed in a variety of forms, through mass media and other public forums and interpersonal channels. Public opinion is expressed more directly in the mass media: we tune into expressions of public opinion daily as we listen to talkback radio programs; similarly, we encounter the opinions of the public as we read the letters to the editor in the morning newspapers. There are many other media audience feedback mechanisms that facilitate the expression of public opinion.

Public opinion is also communicated through the memberships and public pronouncements of social groups and associations. As noted in chapter 7, such groups will try to promote their issues through the media, mobilise the general public, and lobby politicians. Such groups as Friends of the ABC have been successful in highlighting the dilemmas of the national broadcaster in the media, harnessing the general public to their cause and pressuring politicians to change policies or soften funding cutbacks. Such groups will often use email or letter-writing campaigns to impress on public figures the weight of public opinion. And public opinion is expressed through those forms highlighted in our discussion of the history of public opinion. Demonstrations and public rallies continue to be powerful technologies of public opinion expression. It is a strangely exhilarating experience for modern subjects to be in the middle of demonstrations and marches because they are profoundly embodied experiences of public opinion. These more physical forms of public opinion expression can influence judgements about the perceived public opinion on issues. When striking waterfront workers around the country in 1998 were joined by general members of the Australian public on the picket lines, public perceptions of the issue changed. Public opinion is clearly not singularly captured in the findings of opinion polls but is the complex product of negotiations between various forms of public opinion expression.

Major pollsters and types of polling

The political influence of public opinion polls and their increasing importance as promotional tools for news media means that the major polling companies have themselves assumed a significant public profile. Newspoll, which is 50 per cent owned by News Corp, publishes its polls in News Corp newspapers throughout the country. Newspoll, headed by managing director Sol Lebovic, has been judged to be the most accurate opinion poll. Murray Goot concluded that Newspoll had the best record, after an analysis of 13 federal, state and Northern Territory elections conducted between 1990 and 1996 (Steketee 1999a, p. 7). Other polling companies include AC Nielsen, which conducts polls for the Fairfax organisation and Roy Morgan, headed by Gary Morgan, another high-profile company—although it suffered a blow to its reputation when it predicted Labor would win the 2001 federal election. Sometimes pollsters move beyond the provision of opinion poll results and act as advisers to political parties. Most famously in Australia, Rod Cameron's company ANOP was instrumental in Labor party victories during the 1980s.

The major polling companies and their political polling attract the most attention because their results are published on the front pages of newspapers, but polling companies conduct public opinion polls for a wide variety of commercial clients and political polling may represent only a small percentage of company business. Public opinion polling is also conducted by a wide range of groups and organisations: companies may do their own polling in their market research, and pressure or interest groups often conduct their own polling to determine the best strategy to mobilise public opinion behind their cause. Political parties rely heavily on their own opinion polling, conducting long-term polling to track changes over an election cycle, or conducting opinion polls that influence daily strategies during an election campaign. Political parties conduct their own private polling to assist in the formulation of policy, to ascertain public opinion on the image of the party and the party leadership, and to gauge the most appropriate timing of elections.

Polling is now a ubiquitous feature of public life. As noted at the start of this chapter, political polling is only a small component of the overall questioning of the public: as consumers we are often interrogated by market researchers about our preferences and practices. We are confronted on the telephone, at our front door and in the shopping mall, and asked to answer everything from a 'quick question' to a comprehensive survey. Marketing is driven by the tension between the fundamental difficulty of 'knowing' the public in a mass, mediated society and a need to understand with increasing accuracy and specificity the opinions, needs and desires of that public. Our interest here is in political opinion polling but within that focus there are various types of polling. Most public opinion polling uses quantitative research methods, but pollsters can also employ qualitative research methods. Quantitative research, which produces numerical results and can express public opinion in percentages, is helpful in telling us how many people hold particular beliefs or preferences, but sometimes further information is required about the nature of those polled beliefs or preferences. In-depth interviews may be conducted in various formats, but the most common form of qualitative research for pollsters is the focus group. There are normally 6–12 people in a focus group who discuss issues raised by the pollster or researcher. Pollsters facilitate the discussion and keep the group on the topic but do not usually actively express their own views. The focus group combines the advantages of observation and in-depth interviews in a group context (Bouma 2000, p. 181).

The increasing prevalence of public opinion polling has given rise to new types of opinion polling which have no scientific basis and which are sometimes used to manipulate rather than to measure public opinion. 'Call-in' polls are a common form of polling used by television current affairs programs. These polls usually take the form of a posed question, with separate telephone numbers to call if you agree or disagree with the question. These types of opinion poll are sometimes called SLOPS (*Self-selected Listener-Oriented Public opinion Surveys*), an acronym which suggests their scientific merit (Gawiser & Evans Witt 1994, p. 99). Call-in opinion polls may seem powerful expressions of public opinion with tens of thousands of responses, particularly when contrasted with a sample size of only 1000 people from a reputable opinion poll. The major flaw to call-in polls is that there is no way of knowing whether the results can be projected to the general population. There is nothing to stop people from ringing the same number multiple times to inflate the numbers of their chosen response. After a US Presidential debate in 1980, a call-in poll recorded 727 000 responses with a 2-to-1 margin for Ronald Reagan over Jimmy Carter, a result contrary to a reputable opinion poll which found that viewers were evenly split. Both the Reagan and Carter campaigns subsequently admitted they had volunteers calling in regularly from banks of telephones (Gawiser & Evans Witt 1994, p. 101). Another form of 'opinion polling' that has arisen in recent years is 'push-polling', which is not opinion polling strictly speaking because the purpose of the inquiry is not to seek existing opinions but to give people information to ascertain how their opinions would be affected by such information. Push-polling does not seek to measure public opinion but to 'push' or manipulate it, and push-polls often give out false or misleading information under the guise of a legitimate public opinion poll. In the 2001 federal election, the Coalition accused the Labor Party of push-polling on the GST, claiming that the government would raise the tax rate if it won the election, a charge denied by Labor.

Opinion polls can be used quite accurately to ascertain public opinion, but a number of features of the opinion poll must be known before the findings can be used with confidence. The sample size and sample error are vital factors in interpreting the opinion poll results. Probability theory dictates that a relatively small sample can accurately predict the opinions of a national population, if the random sample has been correctly compiled. The sample size does influence, however, the sample error. Sample error does not refer to any mistakes by the pollster but to the amount of chance variation expected in a series of samples. With a sample size of 200, for example, there is a 95 per cent chance that the result will fall within 6.9 per cent of the poll outcome. This means the result could be as much as 6.9 per cent higher or 6.9 per cent lower than the poll outcome. The sample error falls to 4.4 per cent with a sample of 500, 3.1 per cent with a sample of 1000, and 2.2 per cent with a sample of 2000 people. Most of the established polling companies will compile opinion polls with sample sizes of between 1000 and 2000. Too small a sample raises the sample error to unsatisfactory levels, and larger sample sizes are costly for the polling companies with relatively small declines in the sample error. Such figures indicate that opinion poll findings need to be interpreted with caution. In a close political contest, an opinion poll may find that support for a candidate has risen 2 per cent but the sample error is such that the level of support could be actually static or could even have dipped slightly.

Pollsters have a number of techniques to ensure sampling quality. They must ensure a randomisation of the sample within households. To overcome the possible bias from constantly polling the person most likely to answer the telephone, pollsters will ask to speak to the person in the family who most recently had a birthday. Pollsters will also make a number of calls back to unanswered telephone calls to overcome the possible bias from oversampling those people more likely to be at home. One of the biggest difficulties facing pollsters is the rising number of refusals. In a bid to reduce the number of refusals, pollsters may make appointments with people if they are unable to answer questions from an initial call.

The wording of the questions is another factor that may influence the findings of a public opinion poll. Unlike the questions of journalists, which may be framed to provoke an individual response, the language of opinion poll questions must be neutral. The questions in a public opinion poll must also be free of technical terms, easily understood and specific. It is vital that the wording of the questions be balanced: a question such as 'Do you think it is fair that taxpayers bear the burden of funding the ABC?' is obviously loaded, and framed to elicit a particular response. The ordering of questions is important in a survey: a question about the popularity of a candidate will be influenced by preceding questions about issues on which the candidate is perceived to be 'weak'. In a public opinion poll it is also vital that interviewers read the question the same way for each respondent. The timing of an opinion poll is another factor in the interpretation of its results. Particularly during election campaigns, it is necessary to know when the opinion poll was conducted in order to judge what news and information were available to the public when they were questioned.

Media uses of opinion polls

The media have always been inextricably involved in modern forms of public opinion polling. Ever since the introduction of public opinion polling into Australia in 1941, opinion polls have not been independent products subsequently reported by the media: newspapers themselves commissioned and published the opinion polls (Mills 1999, p. 205). The first Australian opinion poll using modern principles of random sampling occurred after Sir Keith Murdoch approved a young finance journalist named Roy Morgan to travel to the United States to study the new work of pollster George Gallup. The first poll, published in the Melbourne *Herald*, found that 59 per cent favoured equal pay for women (Mills 1999, p. 205).

The introduction of public opinion polling was considered a major advance for the media because it ostensibly solved the difficult problem for journalists of how to ascertain public opinion. It was perceived that the democratic health of a society could be improved by providing the public with better means to express their views; journalism, in turn, could serve the public with more relevant information. The embrace of public opinion polls, however, was also prompted by more practical journalistic concerns. Public opinion polls were attractive to journalists because they were a valuable source of news stories: they offered new and topical information. The formulation of poll questions was motivated less by any public service ideals and more by the dictates of the news: Roy Morgan actually involved editors and journalists in the selection of poll questions (Mills 1999,

p. 206). Public opinion polls commissioned by newspapers not only generated news stories but provided newspapers with exclusive news stories. Opinion polls became a vital means by which newspapers could gain a competitive advantage over other publications. The commissioning of public opinion polls also gave the media greater autonomy in the production of news. This greatly enhanced the political power of the media: newspapers relied less on political sources for news, and the opinion polls played an important role in setting the public agenda to which politicians had to respond. Public opinion polls were further attractive to journalists because they quantified public opinion and were based on a scientific and statistically based methodology. As with other areas of public life, such as the stock market and parliament, numbers rendered complex issues and processes more manageable and provided journalists with information that was definite, impartial and easily understood.

These historical factors are still relevant in explanations of the prevalent use of public opinion polls by the contemporary news media. The findings of public opinion polls continue to generate front-page news stories, and the commissioning of public opinion polls are used to give news outlets an edge over their competitors. More so than ever, the public opinion poll used regularly by a news outlet is an integral part of the outlet's promotional strategies. The reporting by other media of the news outlet's public opinion poll gives valuable publicity to the news service. The news media also continue to use the findings of public opinion polls in their encounters with politicians and other public figures. The considerable power of journalists to challenge politicians is often legitimised by references to public opinion poll findings. In the 2001 Australian federal election, it was difficult to articulate alternative viewpoints to the government's response to incoming refugees because public opinion was perceived to be supportive of the government's actions.

The news media use of public opinion polls intensifies during election campaigns. During the 1998 Australian federal election campaign, there was collectively an average of almost one public opinion poll a day conducted by the various polling agencies (Goot 2000, p. 37). It becomes particularly evident during the hothouse environment of an election campaign that public opinion polls do not

167

just reflect public opinion but that they have a major influence on the campaign content and the conduct of the election participants. The public opinion polls highlight issues for the news agenda, and politicians adjust their behaviour and their focus on issues as they receive feedback from opinion polls. One of the major criticisms of media use of public opinion polls has been that it results in undue focus on the campaign contest at the expense of qualitative reportage of relevant issues. The election campaign becomes less a dialogue about political policies, values and future directions and more a focus on individual leaders and their performances during the campaign. Some critics argue that this kind of political reportage, where the election is reduced to a 'horse race', permits lazy journalism. Such a form of reportage is also in accordance with the journalistic professional ideology (Mills 1999, p. 213):

> While policy reporting is regarded as 'boring, abstract, complex and static', a contest is 'tangible, personal, fluid and simple'. It is also value-free. Covering a contest—with its focus on winners and losers, expectations, predictions, name recognition and campaign strategies—'neutralises the risks of appearing partisan, or the charge of imposing (journalists') own priorities and preferences'.

The uses of public opinion polls by the news media have given rise to important political effects. Although debate continues about any definitive theory of the political effects of public opinion polls, it does seem that in some instances opinion polls can play a vital role in the election outcome. Public opinion polls sometimes even create an 'underdog' effect, where expectations of a comfortable victory by one political party prompt people to vote for another party, resulting in a surprise election result. It was speculated that the defeat of the Victorian Liberal government led by Jeff Kennett in 1999 was partly a result of public opinion poll results that suggested a comfortable victory for the government. Alternatively, public opinion polls will sometimes cause a 'bandwagon' effect, where perceptions of an imminent victory help boost the standing of the campaign frontrunner. It is popularly believed that the Labor win in the Australian federal elections of 1972 and 1983 were assisted by the bandwagon effect. However, public opinion polls may fail to capture public opinion adequately because a significant section of the public refuse to declare their voting intentions. The surprising persistence of support for Pauline Hanson's One Nation party over several elections was sometimes attributed to the reluctance of her supporters to publicly announce their political preference.

The uses of public opinion polls by the media, and the influence of opinion polls on the political process more generally, will continue to provoke consternation and subsequent calls for change. One option would be to not publish public opinion polls in the last few days of an election campaign, similar to the political advertising black-out. It is unlikely that such measures will be implemented in Australia, given the implications for freedom of speech and the practical reality that public opinion polls are firmly entrenched as part of the political process. While many of the criticisms about the effects of public opinion polls are legitimate, particularly the decline of issues-based reportage, it also needs to be noted that public opinion polls have contributed to a better-informed public domain. Journalists, politicians, public figures and the public themselves have a much more accurate understanding of public opinion than in earlier times when judgements were sometimes dubious extrapolations from individual and group associations. While the idea and nature of public opinion measurement may be variously problematic, such information is not only necessary in a mass society but it also contributes to the democratic wellbeing of that society.

Conclusion

Modern expressions of public opinion are profoundly different in many ways from the expressions of public opinion that occurred in ancient Greece, but the ideals of earlier times persist: public opinion is privileged to the extent that it represents the free and rational evaluation of arguments, that it is the expression of a majority in a society, and that it is a means by which people can participate in the society. The history of techniques of public opinion expression, however, charts a progressively more structured and privatised form of public opinion. Now, public opinion is more often expressed through 'top-down' processes, where governments, media and commercial organisations seek opinions from the public rather than public opinion arising independently from the populace. Modern public opinion polls have been criticised as instruments of social control and have been subject to charges of having transformed public opinion from a behavioural to an attitudinal phenomenon and from the property of groups in society to a collective attribute of individuals. But modern public opinion also has a fundamentally indeterminate character, and it continues to be expressed through a variety of means other than public opinion polls, from demonstrations to talkback calls. Public opinion polls remain a necessary feature in any mass, democratic society and, assuming a sound methodological basis can contribute accurate and beneficial information. Opinion polls can be used by the media to gain an accurate sense of public sentiment but they have also become an important commodity for the news media, giving them a promotional tool and providing them with greater autonomy in the production of news. The increasing use of public opinion polls by the media has changed political coverage, putting greater emphasis on the 'contest' between parties and candidates and less emphasis on qualitative reportage of issues. Opinion polls are not 'detached' or 'independent' from the public but feed back into the social production of opinion. Finally, opinion polls can themselves shape public opinion, variously creating 'underdog' and 'bandwagon' effects.

9

The nation and national identity

'The nation' continues to be the most important site on which mediated public life is played out, despite the rise of a more globalised culture and the ongoing importance of state and local communities. As noted in chapter 3, our membership of 'the public' is not limited by a particular geographical boundary: we can variously participate in local community activities and engage with global occurrences. The meanings and values of the public are, however, very importantly defined at the level of the 'national public'. The nation in many ways seems a solid and permanent collection of political structures, institutions and culture, all confirmed through the weight of history, but it is also a mediated phenomenon, continually made and remade through media discourse, narratives and representations. Much of the ongoing life of a nation resides in struggles to mobilise the national public to support particular practices and values as embodiments of the nation. In this chapter I analyse these struggles through discussion of such events such as the referendum on an Australian republic and the Sydney 2000 Olympic Games.

The historical rise of 'the nation'

The concept of 'the nation' may seem unproblematic initially, but nations are not naturally occurring entities: they arose out of historical contexts due to particular factors, and an understanding of these historical conditions assists us in our analysis of contemporary nations. Republics of antiquity, such as Athens, were not 'nations' but city-states. In medieval Europe there were a large number of political units, ranging from cities to regional administrations and some more powerful states; around the end of the 15th century there were about 500 state-like entities in Europe (Thompson 1995, p. 49). Modern nation-states are fewer in number and much more established and formidable entities than many of those medieval administrations although, as we have seen in the past decade in Eastern Europe, the process of nation formation is ongoing, along with political change. The formation of what we recognise as the modern nation-state unfolded over several centuries, a result of many complex factors, although several primary factors have been identified. First, rulers developed more comprehensive military powers. Large-scale, permanent and disciplined armies enabled rulers to overcome smaller and less powerful administrations and subsequently to be able to establish more regularised borders, rather than ill-defined frontiers. Second, nation-states arose out of the establishment of more sophisticated systems of administration. These increasingly effective systems of administration, such as taxation and census systems, were means by which populations could be rendered more disciplined and were necessary to fund the expansions of military power (Giddens 1985).

The rise of the modern nation-state is also fundamentally linked to the rise and expansion of capitalism. During the 15th century the feudal system, based on a subsistence-style economy, began to give way to an economic system of commodity production and exchange, where individuals with capital employed people for the generation of profit by selling goods at a price in excess of the production costs. Throughout the 16th and 17th centuries this economic system expanded due to a proliferation of trading, both within Europe and by the formation of trade routes throughout the rest of the newly discovered world. The modern nation-state was further consolidated through the Industrial Revolution of the late 18th and early 19th centuries, which was based on new mechanised methods of production, together with the mobilisation of populations and the division of labour of the factory system.

The rise of the modern nation-state was also the result of profound cultural changes, which involved new processes of communication.

The invention of the printing press was an integral component of the newly burgeoning capitalist economy and the formation of early nation-states. Johann Gutenberg invented the printing press around the middle of the 15th century and a flourishing printing and book trade soon developed. By 1480 presses had been established in more than a hundred towns and cities throughout Europe; it has been estimated that by the end of the century at least 35 000 editions had been produced (Thompson 1995, pp. 54–5).

The process of printing and the publication of texts in languages other than Latin were vital factors in the development of social relations and a national collective consciousness or, in Benedict Anderson's phrase, 'imagined communities'. Anderson's work (introduced briefly in chapter 1) argues that the rise of 'imagined communities' were the product of what he calls 'print-capitalism'—the convergence of early capitalism economies and the technology of printing. Anderson argues that an essential feature of these new imagined communities was the consolidation of 'print languages', which 'created unified fields of exchange and communication below Latin and above the spoken vernaculars' (1991, p. 44). The communities were 'imagined' because the common communicative domain created through print languages enabled people to realise they were part of a virtual community, linked to people they might never meet through the technology of print. The rise of imagined communities challenged the authority of the Church, giving prominence to the secular realm and a humanist world view. In effect, a new kind of person was created: Anderson argues that early forms of journalism, along with the later development of the novel, enabled a regularising of time and a development of simultaneity that was quite foreign to the medieval mind. It was these developments, 'the idea of a sociological organism moving calendrically through homogeneous, empty time' (Anderson 1991, p. 26), which facilitated a greater understanding of a collective shared identity and triggered not only the development of the nation-state but also modern democratic impulses.

Early forms of print publication and journalism were central to both the freedoms and the disciplinary structures of the early nation-states. The early publishing houses were businesses but they were also important social centres, where clerics, intellectuals and scholars congregated to discuss ideas (Thompson 1995, p. 56). The publication of pamphlets and other forms of early journalism gave rise to the reading publics of the imagined communities. Of course, the social composition of those early reading publics was largely limited to elites due to low literacy levels, but the distribution of knowledge through forms of media nonetheless produced tremendous social freedoms. The early forms of journalism not only gave rise to a collective consciousness but elevated topical social issues and cultivated a sense of public agency, whereby people were themselves encouraged to act to bring about social improvement. At the same time, early forms of media facilitated the development of the market system of capitalism and the disciplinary grids of modernity. The commodity form of journalism and its mechanical production brought into being both large-scale reading publics and consuming subjects. Journalism also operated as a technology that managed and controlled the heterogeneity of the emerging nation-states, helping to establish, publicise and confirm value systems and lived patterns of human behaviour.

These social effects were initiated with the early printing presses and the publication of books and pamphlets, but they assumed greater relevance during the 17th and 18th centuries with the more regular publication of newspapers. The development of a daily press in the 18th century more closely approximates our understanding of modern journalism. The newspaper as a communicative form was, and remains, ideally suited to represent and contribute to the production of the nation (Mercer 1992). The newspaper, more so than other early types of publication, was able to reproduce a *sense of place*, not only through its representations of particular locales but through providing for its readers specific knowledges and a sense of belonging. The newspaper was also able to capture the temporal rhythms of a nation because of its status as a *daily* publication. This feature allowed the newspaper to quickly capture changes in national life and to consolidate features of national life through their ongoing and repetitive reportage. The newspaper was pre-eminently concerned with features of *everyday life*. The idea of the nation was produced to a large degree through the reportage of mundane matters, such as what was available at shops and markets, weather, and current entertainment. And the form of the newspaper was able, more so than other more singularly focused texts, to represent and manage the *heterogeneity* of a nation.

Different groupings in society and their respective concerns, important and trivial issues, were all able to be captured in the one text.

Broadcasting played a prominent role in building a sense of the nation in Britain during the early part of the 20th century, not only through the widespread distribution of information but also through the organisation of the events and institutions of public life and through changes to the very understanding of publicness. Paddy Scannell notes how the British Broadcasting Corporation (BBC) worked to restore and promote a plethora of occasions—comprising national cultural and religious traditions, key public and sporting events—and inserted them into a national consciousness. Before they were broadcast, sporting events like the FA Cup final and the Grand National horse race existed for specific sporting publics, but once they were broadcast they became 'punctual moments in shared national life' (Scannell 1989, p. 141). The monarchy contributed much to this process through events such as the Royal Christmas Broadcast. The myth of a unified nation was expressed through the idea of the 'nation as family' and was communicated through the monarch as head of the royal family interpellating the mass audience as a collection of families.

Broadcasting, more so than earlier print forms of media, expanded the boundaries of the public by bringing the concerns of private life into public life as well as public life into the domain of private life. It did this through forms of programming that were as much for entertainment and pleasure as for educative purposes. As broadcasting developed in the first couple of decades, the public 'mode of address' changed from the formal style of oration to the more personalised, conversational mode of address we now experience on radio and television. Over time, too, a greater spectrum of people gained access to the public domain: working-class people were actually heard on the radio. Scannell notes that the very idea of the 'public' changed with the introduction of radio broadcasting. Earlier ideas of what was constituted as public emphasised particular kinds of buildings, spaces and events; with the advent of broadcasting the notion of the public became more generalised (in terms of the population), broader (in terms of content) and generally more democratic (Scannell 1989, p. 140):

The fundamentally democratic thrust of broadcasting lay in the new kind of access to virtually the whole spectrum of public life that radio first, and later television, made available to all. By placing political, religious, civic, cultural events and entertainments in a common domain, public life was equalized in a way that had never before been possible.

The contemporary nation and national identity

Such a historical account of the rise of the nation underlines its immense importance in the processes of public life, yet that importance has now been questioned with the increasing impact of globalisation. It is true that the powers of individual nation-states have been challenged by a more pervasive globalised economic system, more global cultural product, values and forms of behaviour, together with supranational political structures such as the EU. These forces of globalisation have not resulted in the death of the nation-state: rather, 'the nation' has persisted, complicating the terrain of the 21st century. The nation-state has always developed in the contexts of global trade and information exchange. Stuart Hall has declared that the tension within capitalism to promote both transnational development and the formation of specific nation-states is 'at the heart of modernity' (1993, p. 353). This tension has, however, assumed a more distinctive focus in contemporary times and has become a central political issue—how to manage national sovereignty in an increasingly globalised environment. This tension has caused a plethora of nationalist movements to arise throughout the world in recent years.

This more globalised environment has also had profound ramifications for manifestations of national political identity. The concept of citizenship (introduced in chapter 2) has undergone stress and revision as it negotiates expressions of national unity and difference. Citizenship, in the contemporary political environment, may seem an almost old-fashioned form of identity. Manifestations of civic duty do not form a prominent part in the behaviour of the average Australian, who is often portrayed as more concerned with a lifestyle centred on leisure-based activities. Such a portrayal is a long way from traditional ideas of the ideal citizen, who takes an active role in the workings of the polis. But it would be a mistake to establish a binary between a civic tradition and a contemporary environment marked by the loss of that tradition. As David Burchell has noted, the classical civic tradition also acknowledged that the public-spiritedness of good citizens was not a natural human attribute but the product of training and discipline (1993, p. 18). Citizenship has always operated, and continues to operate, as a technology of governance. As modern Australia wrestles with issues of national identity there is a tremendous amount of political and discursive activity, which works to produce loyal, efficient and disciplined national subjects.

The nation-state may be demarcated by specific boundaries and protected by various uses of coercive power, but a contemporary nation is increasingly perpetuated through the use of symbols, narratives and myths that inform a *national identity* or *nationalism*. These two terms represent a type of symbolic power which binds people together through a sense of belonging to a specific place and culture. While the two terms are often conflated, they have also been distinguished by scholars. Giddens defines nationalism as a psychological phenomenon, where individuals identify with 'a set of symbols and beliefs emphasising communality' (1985, p. 116), which usually coincide with the actual distribution of populations within states, although there is not always a clear correspondence, as with emigré populations. Philip Schlesinger, however, is critical of the way Giddens conflates the concepts of nationalism and national identity and instead argues for the maintenance of a distinction in meaning between the two terms. Schlesinger posits nationalism as a less progressive force, arguing that nationalism carries with it the sense of 'a community mobilised (in part at least) in the pursuit of a collective interest' (1991, p. 168), while national identity captures more of the potential variability of cultural sensibility within a nation-state.

It should not be surprising that there have been both past and present calls for the dismantling of the very notion of 'the nation' and 'nationalism', given that over the past century we have seen many examples of nations being denied cultural and political differences, often with catastrophic effectiveness. Alternatively, there has been a range of work which, while acknowledging the potential negative effects of nationalism, argue for the maintenance of the concept. As already noted, Schlesinger emphasises national identity as a site of contestation. In a more local context, Graeme Turner has argued for a critical investigation of the uses of Australian nationalism and the maintenance of the concept of the nation, given that 'certain formations of the nation may be strategically useful in a postcolonial society such as ours' (Turner 1994, p. 122).

The meanings of the contemporary nation and modern citizenship are played out through a binary of unity and difference. As the very term suggests, a 'national identity' is conceptualised as a singular entity, although it may be informed by a series of national types, a range of historical events, and even a number of contradictory principles and values. Similarly, citizenship, as a form of political identity, is defined through its unifying force, even though 'we' citizens exhibit a remarkable array of differences. Of course, historically, despite the fact that Australia was a 'new' nation, it was easier to present a singular national identity because of the greater degree of homogeneity in the ethnic and cultural mix of the population. In more contemporary times the very idea of the nation is less 'ontologically secure', and the changing composition of the Australian population has prompted a need for 'a new paradigm of national representation' (Cochrane & Goodman 1992, p. 175). The project of incorporating ideas of difference within the singular identity of the nation and the national identity has best been encapsulated in the concept of multiculturalism, although under the Howard government multiculturalism has come under attack for its supposed emphasis of difference at the expense of the unity of the nation. The binary of unity/difference is not, however, a 'problem' that must be 'solved': contemporary societies cannot exist through the obliteration of difference, nor can they operate through the unrelational proliferation of differences. Rather, the unity/difference binary is an important and necessary basis on which meanings are generated in contemporary public life.

The mediated nation

It follows from one of the main arguments of this book that 'the nation' is a mediated phenomenon: the meanings of modern Australia, while played out in real institutions, cultural practices and everyday lives, are primarily constructed through media discourse. This needs to be proclaimed in opposition to some theorisations of nationalism and national identity. For example, Turner notes that, while there is a justifiable resistance to the conservatism and commercial features of national identity, there also exists resistance to the very construction of the public through the mass media as though there is a more authentic public existing autonomously of the media representations (1994, pp. 88-91).

The meanings of 'the nation' are mobilised through a wide variety of events and institutions, issues and people. The Australian national identity is perhaps most famously represented and performed through 'national days', such as Australia Day and Anzac Day. National days can be very effective occasions for consolidating national unity: Australia Day promotes national identity both through historical reference to the 'founding' of the nation and through the contemporary celebration of an Australian lifestyle. Australia Day activities, such as picnics and fireworks displays, work to mobilise family and community values and affiliations with the natural and urban environments. The meanings of nations, however, are always constructed and open to contestation, and this is particularly so for newer nations without such depths of tradition or culturally 'pure' identity. Australia Day also marks an occasion when the Aboriginal peoples were invaded and subjected to a violent overthrow. Similarly, Anzac Day, while commemorating the sacrifices of Australian soldiers in their defence of the nation, its political values and way of life, is also challenged by criticisms of its celebration of war and promotion of a particular kind of masculinity.

The meanings of the nation can be generated through the arts and sporting events and achievements. Particularly because they explicitly deal with representations and images, the arts are integral means through which national identity is produced, whether it be the art of Sidney Nolan or Men at Work singing 'Down Under'. And Australia has drawn heavily on its sporting traditions and achievements to construct a national identity. The Sydney Olympic Games was an excellent site for displaying expressions of Australian national identity to a global audience (see later in this chapter).

A sense of national identity is often produced through prominent news topics. In the lead-up to the 2001 Australian federal election, the federal government's refusal to allow the Norwegian vessel, the *Tampa*, to unload refugees it had rescued from the ocean initiated a more wide-spread debate about Australia's treatment of refugees. The debate ranged over a number of events, including the initial *Tampa* incident, the subsequent transporting of refugees to Pacific islands, the protests at detention centres and debates about the centres' conditions, together with accusations that the Howard government used national security information for political purposes and misled the Australian people over claims of refugees throwing their children overboard. These events and debates dominated national media and attracted considerable international news attention, and they generated much discussion about Australia's national identity. John Howard's election campaign declaration that 'We decide who comes to this country', while ostensibly about immigration policy, was also a particular way of mobilising and representing the unity of the nation, not only around issues of national sovereignty but through conservative fears about immigration. As with most constructions of national identity, the unity of 'we' as a nation was defined through opposition to an 'other', who was represented as of less value or as providing a threat to that national unity. The issues also prompted discussion about the values that constitute the Australian national identity: the country was often charged with being 'hard-hearted' and demonstrating a lack of compassion towards the refugees. The politicians and policy supporters engaged in much discursive work through the media and public forums to represent the stance on refugees as 'firm but fair'.

As noted earlier (see chapter 3), celebrities are important vehicles in contemporary society for the expression of a vocabulary of values and style. These values and sense of style contribute to the meanings of the celebrities themselves, but they also allow for the general cultural circulation of those values and style and often become relevant to the national identity. In film and entertainment, Nicole Kidman and Baz Luhrmann are represented as embodying both a sophistication and a practical, genuine, down-to-earth manner which is portrayed as encapsulating something of how Australians like to see themselves, in contrast to previous incarnations of the national Australian type in, say, Paul Hogan. We see something of this historical shift in representations of the national type in the public images of sport stars such as cricketer

Shane Warne and swimmer Ian Thorpe. Warne has something of a 'larrikin' image and has attracted publicity over his attempts to control his weight and to give up smoking, as well as being involved in several other controversies. Thorpe has a more sophisticated public image, is represented as polite, an elegant dresser and a figure on the international celebrity circuit. While Kidman, Luhrmann and Thorpe may represent more contemporary embodiments of an ideal national type, both 'types' of people continue to have popular support and currency. There is always a plurality of such ideal national types, but it is through the public negotiations of these types and the values they embody that an ongoing sense of national identity is produced.

An Australian republic

The question of Australia's national identity is profoundly expressed in the debate about whether the country should sever its links with the British monarchy and become a republic. The republic is a formal political issue with constitutional ramifications which would involve changes to the structure of political institutions. It also directly impinges on the cultural identity of the nation: becoming a republic would be an expression of national independence and would diminish the primary importance of the nation's British heritage. The referendum on the Australian republic in November 1999 and the constitutional convention in the preceding year were extraordinary political and cultural events, which mobilised a national debate about national identity and ideas of citizenship (Craig 2000a). The failure of the 'yes' campaign in the referendum has since sidelined the issue but Australia's future political identity will remain an important question for the nation.

The referendum on the republic considered two questions: whether the country should become a republic with a President elected by a parliamentary majority; and whether a new preamble to the Constitution should be adopted. Both questions were defeated: 55 per cent nationwide voted no to the change to a republic and 45 per cent voted yes; and 61 per cent voted no to the new proposed preamble with 39 per cent assenting to the change. Five states and the Northern Territory rejected the republic, only Victoria and the Australian Capital Territory voting to end the constitutional monarchy. As reflected in the vote, the referendum split the nation. Prime Minister John Howard, who had campaigned to retain the links with the monarchy, declared that the people had spoken and that the issue would not be revisited in the fore-seeable future. A disappointed Australian Republican Movement (ARM) leader Malcolm Turnbull condemned Howard, labelling him 'the Prime Minister who broke this nation's heart'. The referendum campaigns were vigorous: the 'yes' camp attempted to highlight the role of the Queen and the British monarchy in the country's constitutional structures and the 'no' camp highlighted public dissatisfaction with the parliamentary election of a President. The 'no' campaign was bolstered by the support of republicans who favoured direct election of a President.

The media coverage of the constitutional convention and the referendum was integral to both events. The issue of an Australian republic not only centres on constitutional matters but is a central site of struggle over the *meaning* of the nation and the worth of national symbols and values. The republic is largely a symbolic issue: the question of Australia becoming a republic is centrally concerned with the national identity—with the events, stories, myths and emblems that together constitute the nation's image of itself. Debate about the republic has focused on national symbols such as the Australian flag, which retains the British Union Jack in the top left corner. In response to charges that the republic will result in no practical change to the country's circumstances, comedian, lawyer and convention delegate Steve Vizard (1998; p. 13) declared:

> It's simply not good enough to argue that the Queen doesn't do us any harm . . . That's not the point. Symbols are supposed to get in the way, to be powerful, living and relevant. Symbols need to be tripped over, to unite, bond and draw together people, whether as a family, a team, a culture or a nation.

The media reportage of the constitutional convention and the referen-dum provided representations of the symbols associated with the republic while also offering a panorama of different types of Australian people, together with their views on the republic. The journalistic coverage demonstrated how the media perform the vital function of 'realising' the nation: they picture the diversity of daily practices, rituals and customs that constitute national life, they provide a sense of the temporal and spatial coordinates of everyday and institutional life. Newspaper coverage of the republican referendum did represent these different aspects of national life. *The Australian*, for example, ran a series of stories about 'average' Australians and their views on the republic. In the series, some young surfers profess ignorance about the details of the referendum but dismiss the republic as peripheral to their 'real-life worries' (Rothwell 1999a, p. 4); boat repairers in a 'sleepy, slow-paced fishing community' declare that the monarchy is 'hardly something to look up to' and that it is a 'natural progression' for Australia to become a republic (Rothwell 1999b, p. 5). It would be a mistake to dismiss such journalism as mere 'colour' stories, peripheral to the 'real' importance of the republic. The stories perform the important task of positioning the republic in the very 'Australian way of life' that is said to inform the need for a new, independent national identity. Such stories and photographs are significant because they visualise and individualise public opinion, grounding the republican issue in the exigencies of particular everyday lives, in specific life-narratives. The regular and mundane reportage of everyday life provides a vocabulary of ways of living and doing that help fashion the solidity of modern Australian life.

The issue of an Australian republic, more than other dominant news issues, was characterised not only by the active involvement of the public but also by the fact that 'the public' was *the* site of struggle in the debate. Arguably, no other contemporary Australian issue has subjected the identity and nature of the public to a greater degree of scrutiny and problematisation. The central struggle in the republican debate was over the degree of public involvement in the election of a head of state. The refusal of the ARM and many leading politicians to grant the public a greater say in the process was a dominant theme of the media coverage at the constitutional convention and became a decisive factor in the referendum on the republic. The 'no' campaigners directed their strategy away from support for the monarchy when they adopted the slogan 'This republic—vote no', playing on the popular support for the direct election of the President.

The debate about a future republic revealed and exacerbated divisions within the Australian public. These divisions centred on constructions of 'real' or 'ordinary' Australians in contrast to 'elites' and celebrities. The referendum vote starkly revealed national divisions along income, education and social class lines. *The Australian*, which campaigned strongly for a yes vote, ran the referendum result under the headline of 'One Queen, two nations' (Steketee 1999b, p. 1). The newspaper reported that: 'The defeat of the republic exposes Australia as two different societies—a confident, educated, city-based middle class and a pessimistic, urban and rural battler constituency hostile to the 1990s change agenda' (Kelly 1999, p. 1). The 'no' campaign referred to the referendum model as the 'politicians' republic', exploiting the alienation many people feel from their political representatives. While celebrities often work as focal points for the mobilisation of popular support, they can also be represented as disconnected from the general public and as symbols of elitism. The 'yes' campaign suffered from perceptions that it was controlled by high-profile celebrities and not supported sufficiently at the grassroots level, although some commentators noted the widespread, public support for the 'yes' campaign and called on the media to focus more on the general public (McKenna 1999, p. 17).

The issue of the republic was interesting because of the way formal notions of citizenship were counterposed against the private pursuit of happiness and luxury that marks the 'good life' of ordinary (and not so ordinary) Australians. The idea of the republic may have mobilised ideas of citizenship but it did little to problematise the everyday lives of Australians, constituted by family life and such leisure activities as watching the cricket. This was highlighted by the *novelty* of the republic: it was presented as an *interruption* to the regular flow of public life. Indeed, an argument against the republic that was sometimes articulated was that Australians were already independent in the ways they led their lives so there was no need to initiate structural change, however irrelevant those structures might be. The public's status as citizenry, then, was foregrounded explicitly in the debate about a republic, but the issue did not trigger a large-scale mobilisation of an active citizenry. Instead, the Australian people were given the task of voting on a preferred republican model. Calls for the people to have a greater say in the election of a President were denied. The

modern citizenship of the Australian people was marked less by autonomy and more by a process of management that facilitated the provision
of a range of options. As James Donald (1992, p. 135) has written:

> . . . citizenship in modern democracies may be understood as a reper-
> toire of attributes realized through disciplinary and pastoral
> technologies . . . Rights and responsibilities cease to be metaphysical
> attributes of the person, and appear instead as socially conferred
> capacities and capabilities: governmental techniques produce the indi-
> vidual *as* citizen. Men and women participate in democracy, one
> might say, but they do not participate under circumstances chosen by
> themselves nor in the terms defined by the formal rights of citizenship.
> [Author's emphasis.]

Modern citizenship may offer a circumscribed role for citizens but
it is still very much informed by a logic of equivalence, and the issue of
a republic did unite the nation in a limited but important manner. An
important feature of the journalistic reportage of the constitutional
convention was the organisation of readerships into full membership of
the Australian society. The media coverage of the issue of Australia
becoming a republic aptly demonstrated how journalism facilitates both
social controls and freedoms. On the one hand, the media coverage
provided a form of governance where the nation, its peoples, values and
ways of life could be both imagined or conceptualised and subsequently
managed. The convention and the referendum were presented as
pedagogical exercises where Australians were informed about their
citizenship status and the constitutional basis of their nation. On the
other hand, the convention and the referendum, more so than many
other public events, were characterised by their *indeterminate* status.
The novelty of the events, together with the process of debate leading to
conclusions that were not predetermined, meant that there was a high
degree of public deliberation. The republic media coverage was striking
because the meanings of the nation were so explicitly *problematised*. Of
course, media coverage provided structured access to people, and the
nature of the debate was circumscribed within particular parameters,
but the coverage nonetheless provided a context for a national response
to the question of whether Australia should become a republic.

The Sydney 2000 Olympic Games

Around the turn of the 21st century Australia had several occasions and issues on which the country's national identity was celebrated, critiqued and reworked. The centenary of Federation, although politically and nationally important, failed to arouse significant public response. However, the centenary of Federation advertising slogan, 'Australia. It's what we make it', did foreground that a national identity, while grounded in a particular history, is never a static entity but always the result of an ongoing production. The debate over Australia becoming a republic provoked a greater public response, but the more overt political nature of the issue highlighted divisions as much as national unity. In contrast, the spectacular staging of the Sydney 2000 Olympic Games portrayed a unified national identity, both for the nation itself and for the rest of the world. The Olympic Games is a sporting and cultural event, but it is also an overdetermined site of meaning involving the media, politics and business, where discourses of globalisation, national identity, race, gender, class, celebrity and individualism circulate.

The hosting of the Olympic Games gives a nation an ideal opportunity to generate meanings about itself and mobilise its population around a particular national identity. A narrative of the nation is produced through reference to historical events, rituals, stories, and the character of the people and the environment. This narrative provides a particular interpretation of the past, highlighting some events and ignoring others. The performance of this narrative animates the past, giving it a contemporary relevance and harmonising it with the current times and projected future directions. The Olympic Games is an ideal vehicle for the production of particular representations of a nation because the Games themselves are sites of ceremony and symbolism. The meanings of the Olympic Games also emanate from their mediated status. While the hosting of the Games is a huge physical undertaking, involving massive infrastructure and civic planning, the Olympic Games is a global event and its meaning is bound up in its televised coverage and media representations.

The sporting basis of the Olympic Games make it an ideal vehicle for the production of national identity. Sport is always informed by politics, in that it involves negotiations and judgements about social relations and practices. While this is so, sport is valuable in national identity formation, and cultural formation more generally, because of its perceived independence from politics. As Tara Magdalinski has written: 'the political "neutrality" that pervades hegemonic Western concepts of sport allows it to become a powerful site of socialization' (Magdalinski 2000, p. 311). In this sense, the 'non-political' nature of the Olympic Games made it a much more amenable entity for expressions of a unified nation, overshadowing politically divisive issues such as the republic and reconciliation (even if some people, such as Midnight Oil band members at the closing ceremony, attempted to politicise the event). Cathy Greenfield and Peter Williams also note several features about sport, and specifically media representations of sport, which make it conducive to national identity formation. First, they observe that drama is intrinsic to sporting events, and that media coverage of sport only exacerbates its dramatic basis and the emotional investment made by spectators in the events (2000, p. 49):

> Television sport in particular is styled to encourage us to invest emotionally in the competitors and the events. But all forms of media presentation amplify the event with the addition of players' biographies, personality profiles, scene-setting (comment, traditions, statistics, music), predictions and retellings of the game or fixture as a sequence of events with a beginning, middle and end. In short, they add character, narrative and setting to make the sporting occasion an entertainment.

Second, Greenfield and Williams note how media coverage of sport mobilises social myths, such as 'the myth of natural justice' and 'the myth of a transparent and perfectly intelligible reality' (2000, p. 49). The rule-governed basis of sport, its finite duration and its demonstrable outcomes facilitates ideas that moral virtue, physical strength and individual effort are rightly rewarded, ideas that support Australian notions of the 'fair go' and the 'gutsy underdog'.

The hosting of an Olympic Games is an excellent opportunity for the expression of national identity, even though the Games are a global event and there is an emphasis on the host *city*. In this global event, universal values are declared and enacted but there is a necessary interconnectedness between globalising forms and specific local involvement in those forms. Alan Tomlinson has noted that: 'As globalizing processes and regional and cultural traditions meet, the local has the capacity to absorb the global in an *arrogating* process of remoulding' (1996, p. 590, author's emphasis). By 'arrogating', Tomlinson means the 'process whereby values are inevitably reshaped while being claimed as preserved' (1996, p. 590). Similarly, the host city performs different functions: it assumes an international perspective as a 'global city', able to offer 'world-class' facilities and services and connected to transnational flows and networks, but at the same time it must represent the nation, providing a specific example of the national identity, character and values (Wilson 1996).

The Sydney 2000 Olympic Games, and particularly the opening ceremony, provided an excellent example of the kind of spectacle we have discussed in earlier chapters. The expression of a national identity was facilitated through the visual imagery and dramatic performance of the ceremony. The spectacle of the opening ceremony was not just a glitzy extravaganza but an important communicative form in a mediated culture. As a communicative form, spectacle is not just about the dramatic imagery—it is also necessarily about the spectators: the event is given shape and meaning through the process of observation. As extraordinary as the event itself was, the opening ceremony demonstrated how the meanings of contemporary public events are implicated in complex ways by their media representation. This is not just to note that the event was televised to a national and international audience: it extends to the ways in which television coverage was fed back into the direct experience of the event in the stadium through the huge screens showing close-ups of action and replays. The 'direct' and 'mediated' experience of *the event* is further complicated by the growing presence of huge screens in public spaces, often adjoining the location of the event (Rowe 2000).

In some ways, the opening ceremony embodied many of the criticisms of spectacle: the dramatic, emotive power of the event was used to portray the nation in a celebratory and unified manner, confirming dominant values and resisting oppositional viewpoints. The ceremony drew on a broad range of national icons, from bushmen on horses to lawnmowers, in a portrayal of an Australia that was in accord with, and reconfirmed, popular perceptions of the country. Alternatively, the meaning of the event was not closed but open to contestation and public debate. This occurred in the more general process of highlighting Aboriginal culture but also more explicitly in the closing ceremony through the actions of performers like Midnight Oil, whose clothes were covered with the word 'Sorry' (referring to the debate about the issuing of a national apology for the treatment of Aboriginal people). The representations of Aboriginal culture in the opening ceremony might have been expected at such an event, but it assumed a particular political significance because of the Howard government's controversial record on Aboriginal relations, on the back of an already turbulent national history of race relations. The negotiation of the meaning of the event also occurred in the organisation of the opening ceremony, after it was revealed that marching bands from the United States would be used instead of Australian ones. The constructed nature of the representation of national identity was further highlighted through contrasts with other events. The celebratory nature of the opening ceremony was juxtaposed with the preceding Melbourne World Economic Forum meeting, where the actions of protesters were dubbed 'un-Australian' by some public figures.

The Olympic Games provided an excellent example of the integral connections between expressions of public life and party or parliamentary politics. This was partly due to their size and scope: the Games had a major impact on the economy and the infrastructure of Sydney. Organisation of the Games became a major political issue – also raising concern about environmental issues, given initial claims that these would be the 'Green Games' and that toxic waste from the Games site had to be treated. There were many other worries about, for example, the capability and upgrading of the transport system. The Olympic Games were even connected to the politics of the debate about the republic, through the question of who would open the Games – the Prime Minister, the Queen or the Governor-General. On top of this, much media attention focused on the constant presence of the Prime Minister at the site of winning Australian performances.

Celebrities became focal points through which expressions of national identity could be produced and negotiated, and this was no more apparent than in the figure of Cathy Freeman. Her collapse on the track after winning the women's 400 metres was perhaps not due only to the joy and relief of winning the race but also from the pressure of shouldering so many meanings and values. Freeman was chosen to light the torch at the opening ceremony because she was a woman who had completed the relay of famous Australian women athletes and because she was an Aboriginal person. Freeman is a political subject since her famous and controversial victory lap at the 1994 Common-wealth Games, where she paraded the Aboriginal flag, and since her criticisms of the Howard government's stand on stolen generations. Freeman, however, is also a vehicle through which Australians can feel united: her cheerful and 'ordinary' nature together with her steely determination to succeed works to overwhelm racial and political dif-ferences, to the extent that she can be embraced by all Australians as 'our' Cathy. Freeman's 'iconicity' extends to processes of commodi-fication through her links with the transnational company Nike. Advertisements featuring Freeman at various stages of her career, together with the famous Nike slogan of 'Just do it', have worked to highlight ideologies of individualism.

The Sydney 2000 Olympic Games may have been an extraordinary global event, marked by a spectacular opening ceremony and dazzling display of sporting celebrities, but it also enabled more localised and 'everyday' expressions of national identity through the Olympic torch relay. The Olympic torch ceremony encompasses the kindling of the flame at Olympia in Greece, the lighting of the flame at the opening ceremony and its extinguishment at the end of the closing ceremony, but our emphasis here is on the torch relay around Australia before the start of the Games. In contrast to the spectacle, elitism and commercial-ism of the Games, the torch relay through outback towns and suburban streets provided a free, personal and more spontaneous form of contact with the Games. While it started in Australia in the highly symbolic heart of the country at Uluru, the torch relay was generally characterised by 'ordinary' Australians as torch carriers and the active participation of local communities—most notably through 'community celebrations', where a cauldron would be lit at the end of the day. In contrast to the focus on the host city during the Games, the torch relay was structured as a national event as it wound its way comprehensively throughout the country: the Organising Committee of the Games said its objective was to have the relay travel within one hour's drive of 85 per cent of the population. As with the media coverage of the referendum on the republic, the everyday reportage of the progress of the relay visualised the nation and worked to mobilise the nation in its support for the upcoming Games. The torch relay was also linked to other defining national events. In Tasmania, for example, the torch was carried by one woman who had been a guide at Port Arthur when Martin Bryant killed 35 people there in 1996. The media coverage not only linked the Port Arthur massacre to the torch relay but it also mobilised personal narratives, telling the story of the woman's recovery from the trauma of her earlier experience to the point where, after completing her leg of the relay, she 'ran into the welcoming arms of the children she was once too scared to get close to' (Montgomery 2000, p. 6).

Conclusion

Public life finds its dominant expression through the national public, and the nation retains a central importance to self and public formation. The nation also retains political importance despite the rise of an increasingly globalised society. Indeed, increasing trends towards globalisation result not only in greater interdependence between nations but in greater expressions of particularity, as nations define themselves in contexts of global scrutiny. The nation may seem to be a substantial and solid entity but it does not have a singular existence and it is always a contested entity, the product of much discursive work. A national identity is the product of a continual reworking of narratives and symbols as difference and historical change are negotiated. The media are integral to the production of national identity, but this has always been so: the historical rise of the nation was facilitated by the media and communication technologies, which enabled people to foster a collective consciousness that encompassed a nation. As our discussion of the Olympic Games and an Australian republic has demonstrated, the media have become even more central to the production of a national identity, not only through the representations of great spectacle but also through coverage of ordinary, everyday life.

10

The governance of everyday life

At first glance, everyday life is separate from the domain of public life. Everyday life occurs in the private sphere, removed from public scrutiny. It is constituted through our work, through our family life, through our leisure activities. Our work and our leisure activities can of course occur 'in public', but these activities are not deemed to be part of public life; our everyday individual practices and behaviours are not subject to a generalised scrutiny. Everyday life is difficult to define: it consists of a complex and often disparate array of relationships, practices and behaviours that are collected together only because they inform our everyday existence. In this sense, it is perhaps best defined through particular spatial and temporal contexts. Paradoxically, everyday life is highly individualised and amorphous, and as such is 'unknowable' in any total sense, and yet it also suggests activities that are shared and are uniformly recognised and understood by a large number of people. Understood in this latter sense, everyday life is a profoundly *social* phenomenon.

Theorisations of everyday life

The *value* of everyday life has been subject to extraordinarily diverse appraisals. In his well-known and influential study, Henri Lefebvre (1984) differentiates between the 'everyday', as the space and condition in which authentic and vital existence occurs, and 'everyday life', which is marked by the control and alienation of life in the contexts of developed capitalism and bureaucratic society. Everyday life has been considered more commonly from the latter viewpoint, which highlights the repetition and drudgery of work, the overwhelming focus on consumerism and the maintenance of the home, as well as an inordinate interest in personal relationships and romance and leisure activities such as sport. Everyday life is thus presented as a sphere that has been drained of politics but a sphere that nonetheless works to produce the disciplined subjects necessary for the ongoing growth of capitalism. In a range of work, from the development of the Marxist tradition in the Frankfurt School theorists to American cultural critics such as Lasch, everyday life is caught up in a binary logic which sets the public sphere against the private sphere, politics against leisure, citizens against consumers. (We saw this binary operating in chapter 9, where the referendum on an Australian republic was defeated because it was often presented as a 'political' issue without any bearing on the everyday lives of Australians.)

Alternatively, everyday life has been lauded as the sphere with greater freedom from the dictates of powerful interests in society. Everyday life is celebrated because it is where we can most authentically 'be ourselves', it is the place where ideas and attitudes are more 'naturally' generated from more concrete and practical contexts. Paradoxically, everyday life is said to provide greater opportunity for political action precisely because of its autonomy from the public realm. Everyday life is a democratic concept. It is constituted by those practices and behaviours, such as eating, sleeping and defecating, in which all humans (even celebrities) engage. As Rita Felski (1999/2000, p. 16) notes:

> Everyday life . . . does not only describe the lives of ordinary people, but recognises that every life contains an element of the ordinary. We are all ultimately anchored in the mundane.

The work of Michel de Certeau examines the dynamic and creative practices and uses of time in which individuals engage within the disciplined constraints and compulsions of everyday life. De Certeau charts this terrain by distinguishing between strategies and tactics. Strategies are actions which, thanks to the establishment of a place both physical and theoretical, enable those within that territory to exercise power over others. Tactics, conversely, are the art of the weak: they involve 'a clever *utilization of time*, of the opportunities it presents and also of the play that it introduces into the foundations of power' (de Certeau 1984, pp. 38–9, author's emphasis). Tactical behaviour occurs through many everyday practices, such as shopping, travelling, talking and reading. The personal use of office stationery or personal use of the Internet at work, the individual choices made when shopping or walking across town, constitute tactical behaviour.

De Certeau emphasises the productive capacities of acts of consumption in everyday life. These acts of consumption—reading, buying, using—are productive in that they bring about change in the objects consumed, but they are also activities which remain invisible because they do not manifest themselves through their own products. As de Certeau (1984, p. 31) states:

> In reality, a rationalized, expansionist, centralized, spectacular and clamorous production is confronted by an entirely different kind of production, called 'consumption' and characterized by its ruses, its fragmentation . . . its poaching, its clandestine nature, its tireless but quiet activity, in short by its quasi-invisibility, since it shows itself not in its own products . . . but in an art of using those imposed on it.

Throughout this book the involvement of the media in the production of public life has been discussed, but the media are also an integral feature of everyday life. Our experiences of public life are primarily mediated and encountered in the contexts of everyday life. In addition, the temporality, the spaces, the experiences of everyday life are diffused by the presence of the media, whether through reading the newspaper in the morning while munching on toast, or listening to the radio in a traffic jam, or spending the evening in front of the television. The *daily form* of the media is an important structuring device of everyday life. The *contents* of the media, while often dealing with extraordinary events and issues, also regularly present an ordinary, or at least a familiar world. Through the presentation of both extraordinary and ordinary stories, the contents of the media work to confirm the patterns, concerns and values of everyday life.

The media have had to learn to adopt the speech forms of everyday life (Scannell 1989, p. 148–9). Workers at the BBC in the early days of radio realised over time that the voice and rhetorics of various forms of public speaking such as lectures, sermons and political orations were unsuited to the new medium of the wireless. Instead, the individualised contexts of reception required a more personalised form of address. The communication contexts of radio, and later television, promoted not only everyday ways of talking but the subject matter of everyday life as media content.

Such a production of everyday life is a fundamental device by which we secure a sense of normality, which in turn enables us to counter the anxieties and stresses of contemporary existence. Everyday life has often been devalued because of its repetition. In such contexts everyday life is considered to generate alienation and an unthinking approach to the people, experiences and events we encounter. By contrast, modern life privileges the development of the self in its escape from the strictures of everyday life, through innovation and variation. Lefebvre employs linear and cyclical concepts of time to distinguish between modern life's valorisation of progress and accumulation and the more traditional and regularised patterns of everyday existence that are perceived to hinder such developments. This kind of categorisation, however, overlooks the value of everyday life in enabling us to remain 'grounded', facilitating not just the ability to cope with modern life but the resources by which we can act in modern life. As Felski (1999/2000, p. 21) writes:

> Within the maelstrom of contemporary life, change is often imposed on individuals against their will; conversely everyday rituals may help to safeguard a sense of personal autonomy and dignity, or to preserve the distinctive qualities of a threatened way of life. In other words, repetition is not simply a sign of human subordination to external forces but also one of the ways in which individuals engage with and respond to their environment.

Often, then, the classic theorisations of everyday life, usually informed by a Marxist perspective, emphasise the *alienation* of everyday life. From such a perspective, the sphere of everyday life is a bourgeois domain, with its domestic contexts, its focus on the family and the individual, and its remove from political realities. It has been argued that the growing prominence of the sphere of everyday life corresponds with the declining efficacy of people as political subjects. While such an argument is not without merit, it fails to appreciate the exercises of *agency* that occur in everyday life. The multitudinous activities of the mundane, such as eating and drinking, driving and even lazing in the sun, constitute activities where the agency of individuals is exercised, and are inscribed with cultural and political value. To highlight these exercises of agency is not to uniformly celebrate everyday life. Everyday life is too much of a heterogeneous sphere of life to be captured in either an overarching positive or a negative appraisal. Rather, following Silverstone, the agency of everyday life is bound up in its *ordinariness*, by which is meant 'the more or less secure normality of everyday life, and our capacity to manage it on a daily basis' (Silverstone 1994, p. 166). This exercise of agency, however, is not autonomous but represents choices that are to some degree structured through available options. Our decisions in everyday life—about how we treat our loved ones, how much we drink at dinner and even how long we might spend lazing in the sun—are subject to variously explicit and implicit forms of governance. As we will see below in our discussions of self-help media, lifestyle journalism and public information campaigns, this governance is not an oppressive form of control but a process that *enables* subject formation. As such, everyday life is best encapsulated not as a site of bourgeois alienation nor as a site where we can escape political and social strictures: rather, it is best understood as a complex site where the agency of individuals is exercised through the engagement with regulatory regimes.

Self-help media and lifestyle journalism

Much of the media we consume on an everyday basis is not concerned with strictly political content but instead deals with issues that have traditionally pertained to the private sphere. We read lifestyle magazines which report on everything from how to be a better parent to how to re-cover our loungeroom cushions. We watch television current affairs programs which conduct safety tests on consumer products and we watch talk show and reality television programs on self-help, health and body care. Part of the difficulty of commenting on such media resides in the proliferation of such genres, which take everyday life as a subject of discussion. Tabloid or popular journalism, discussed in chapter 4, is a broad term that captures much of this media (Lumby 1999, p. 17):

> The media formats we think of as tabloid, including popular newspapers, weekly women's magazines, talk shows and some commercial current affairs programs, tend to base stories around individuals, particularly celebrities, and to emphasise the personal and emotive impact of a given issue, at the expense of examining the broader structural context. They also tend to be image-dominated, favour shorter stories and rapid edits, and borrow techniques from entertainment-based media—tabloid current affairs programs, for instance, often use dramatic music, lighting and voice-overs.

Tabloid journalism's attention to celebrities may seem at odds with the domain of everyday life—although, as noted in chapter 3, stories about celebrities often are grounded in the concerns of everyday life, such as financial difficulties and the juggling of career and relationships. Reality television is an equally problematic genre, which features the surveillance and recording of everyday life. Sometimes 'reality' television portrays highly constructed and artificial scenarios, but sometimes it is more akin to cinema verité documentary and captures everyday private and working life. Following its phenomenal growth in book publishing, self-help media is another genre that explores everyday life. One of the best examples of this has been Oprah Winfrey's embrace of the concept for her talk show television program (see below). Lifestyle or 'infotainment' journalism is yet another media genre that focuses on everyday life. This genre includes gardening, cooking, and home care advice and information, but it extends to treatments of such political issues as household waste generation and land care.

Theoretical distinctions between the public and private spheres have little relevance to our everyday media consumption: within the same television news bulletin we can move from a story on the Middle

East conflict to another on how to manage your credit card debt. Much academic concern has been expressed at the explosion in popular or lifestyle media at the expense of more traditional political journalism as well as the increasingly blurred boundary between the two forms of media. While any erosion of political news media outlets and content are legitimate concerns, anxiety about a clearcut division between the two forms of media is misplaced. This is not to argue that distinctions between the public and private are insignificant: judgements about the content of such domains and their boundaries are informed by an always shifting set of political and social values.

The production and care of the self in everyday life has become a major source of mass media attention. This media attention highlights how the maintenance of physical and mental wellbeing is a major project for the modern subject, especially given the ever-increasing pressures of work and family life. The creation and maintenance of the self is often presented through a link with the care and attention to the body. Our ability to take care of our bodies through exercise and dietary regimens is an important marker of our status as 'normal' subjects. While our identities are often manifested in the care and pres-entation of our bodies, it is also the case that the production and care of the self in everyday life occurs increasingly through our attention to our emotional, mental and spiritual wellbeing. We see this in the rise of the 'men's movement', which has promoted the importance of men recognising and acting on their emotional needs.

Oprah Winfrey's self-titled television talk show is the best-known media example of this interest in the everyday spiritual needs of people. In the 1998/99 season *Oprah*, already an enormously popular talk show watched each day by 33 million viewers, adopted a new focus known as 'Change Your Life TV' (Parkins 2001). The new format of the program involved the regular appearances of five self-help experts to enhance viewers' spiritual awareness and personal growth. 'Change Your Life TV' also featured a segment at the end of each program called 'Remem-bering Your Spirit', which Winfrey described as intending to help viewers 'connect with the importance of listening to what their souls' desires are and remembering to incorporate those desires into their lives' (Winfrey, in Parkins 2001, p. 149). The shift in focus in Winfrey's program, while popular, generated criticism from some viewers and commentators. Conflicting opinions about the politics of self-help media is also found in academic studies. Epstein and Steinberg, for example, declare that self-help is limited because it is always 'divorced from the social' (1998, p. 85). Parkins, conversely, argues that 'Change Your Life TV' has an 'intersubjective dimension' (2001, p. 151), and that its process of self-transformation is 'always linked with relations with others and with a broader community' (2001, p. 148).

More generally, 'lifestyle' or 'infotainment' journalism has become one of the most prevalent media genres. Lifestyle journalism is ubiquitous on television in Australia and has covered a very broad range of topics, including gardening and home improvement (*Better Homes and Gardens*), finance (*Money*), sexuality (*Sex/Life*), and holidays (*The Great Outdoors*). Lifestyle programs are successful because they are concerned with the pleasures and exigencies of everyday life, but they are also characterised by a lively pacing and an informal and involving mode of direct address. And lifestyle television is attractive to the networks because it is usually cheap to produce and can easily be linked to product promotion. Often television lifestyle programs are linked to a magazine via cross-promotion, although there are many independent lifestyle magazines and lifestyle segments are a growing feature of daily newspapers. Lifestyle journalism directly involves the reader/viewer in user-friendly formats, although the genre is also characterised by expert instruction in knowledges, ethical conduct and practices to improve one's life. As Gay Hawkins states, writing with regard to gardening programs, announcers occupy 'an ambiguous space between amateur and expert' (2001, p. 187). Hawkins draws on the work of Nikolas Rose in order to explain how the rise of the expert in lifestyle journalism is an excellent example of 'neo-liberal forms of governing' (Hawkins 2001, pp. 187–8):

> [Rose] argues that the guidance of selves is no longer a matter of large scale authorities: religion, morality, 'the state' but rather the province of experts of subjectivity: 'who transfigure existential questions about the purpose of life . . . into technical questions about the most effective ways of managing malfunction and improving "quality of life"'.

In Australia, no program has been a more successful manifestation of the lifestyle or infotainment televisual genre than *Burke's Backyard*. Although the origins of this genre are debated, *Burke's Backyard*, which started in 1987, has been described as the founding Australian lifestyle program (McKee 2001, pp. 256–7). As the title suggests, the program is primarily concerned with the private and domestic spaces of Australian suburbia. It covers stories on gardening, home maintenance and improvement, as well as other domestic activities such as pet care and cooking. The program is a celebration of everyday life, and much of its success revolves around its production of the 'ordinary' Australian way of life. This is captured in Burke himself—in his casual dress, his manner and colloquial language, such as his sign-off of 'Hooroo'. *Burke's Backyard*, like other infotainment programs, negotiates a careful balance between the giving of expert advice and associating with the audience as 'an equal'. The program also works hard to construct a consensual community (McKee 2001, p. 262) through its invocation of the great diversity of ordinary Australian life. Celebrity gardeners, such as politicians, are presented in an intimate, non-professional manner which underlines the connections they have with their fellow Australians. While the program presents a predominantly suburban and middle-class Australia, it commonly features a range of other people who exhibit differences of geography, class, religion and sexual orientation. Burke sometimes runs politically oriented stories on the environment and on issues such as cat control, but the program ultimately is able to unify the Australian community through its non-political content. It is precisely the domain of the everyday—home, family and garden—which is presented as the domain that 'we' all share.

Public information campaigns

We regularly receive media messages about our conduct in everyday life through public information campaigns. Whether through an advertisement reminding us to put on some sunscreen or a warning about the evils of alcohol consumption and driving, we are constantly being exhorted about correct behaviour. Public information campaigns are usually funded and devised by government agencies. They are usually long-term projects with several different media and research phases, and they are distinguished here from more singular promotional material. Public information campaigns have been conducted for myriad purposes: they have been influential in the developing world in the areas of health, family planning and agriculture but they are also prevalent in industrialised countries; they seek to create a range of effects, from the changing of nutritional intake to the casting of a vote. Public information campaigns rely heavily on mass media campaigns, although they also distribute information in relevant places such as schools and workplaces. Many public information campaigns focus on the care, health and safety of individuals and emanate from a health department or a transport department, as with road safety issues. Alternatively, campaigns sometimes focus on relating individuals to the broader society. In Australia, the Federation campaign promoted the centenary of Federation and encouraged national pride. Neighbourhood Watch has been another campaign that has encouraged us to know our neighbours in order to prevent break-ins and other crimes. In other contexts, public information campaigns have focused on such issues as racial harmony (Taylor & Botan 1997).

Defining such a diverse range of communication campaigns is difficult but they can be captured under some general characteristics (Rogers & Storey 1987). First, a public information campaign must have a clearly defined purpose, with specific, measurable outcomes. The campaign may seek to bring about cognitive, attitudinal or behavioural change, and the campaign effects may benefit the sender or receiver. Second, public information campaigns occur within specified time limits so that evaluations can be conducted: they may run over a week or could extend over a decade. Third, public information campaigns involve an organised set of communication activities, from sophisticated mass media campaigns to the stall at the local shopping centre. Finally, a public information campaign is a *public* campaign: it is thus differentiated from interpersonal and private communication processes and is targeted at a large audience, although this may be limited to particular groups within a local community.

Public information campaigns involve the production of disciplined subjects. In this sense, everyday life is not disconnected from the public domain but is rather an object of great public scrutiny.

As with the above comments on lifestyle journalism, public information campaigns are manifestations of 'neo-liberal forms of governing', where the knowledges, attitudes and behaviour necessary for the efficient functioning of a society are conveyed to members of the public and responses to these messages are monitored and policed. Public information campaigns are more explicitly pedagogical exercises than lifestyle journalism: they involve direct instructions about correct conduct and often outline punishments and other consequences for those people who do not respond appropriately to the imparted information. The pedagogical feature of public information campaigns arises partly from their status as advertisements. Unlike most mass media texts (although like much lifestyle journalism) and like advertisements generally, public information campaigns usually employ direct forms of address. Public information campaigns can, however, sit oddly in conjunction with advertisements: in the same advertisement break we can be encouraged to buy a fast car and be warned about the dangers of speeding. As an example of a neo-liberal form of governance, the production of disciplined subjects by public information campaigns does not occur primarily through overt threats of punishment but through more 'productive' means, which involve the subject in their own 'production' and surveillance. The issues of governance in public information campaigns are also significant: the health and safety of the individual and their obligations to others are presented as practical and technical issues of 'managing' everyday life successfully. More fundamental moral, aesthetic and spiritual components of disciplined subjects are not usually considered by public information campaigns but are the domain of other social institutions, such as schools.

In Australia there have been a number of public information campaigns that have achieved high levels of public awareness and, in some instances, notoriety. The Health Department has been running anti-smoking campaigns for several decades, from the original QUIT campaign through to more recent campaigns such as 'Every Cigarette Is Doing You Damage'. Arguably, the most (in)famous campaign involved the 'Grim Reaper' television advertisements about HIV-AIDS. The advertisements featured 'Death' as the Grim Reaper, amid swirling smoke, rolling a bowling ball towards a group of people and knocking them over. The 'Grim Reaper' certainly did create a public consciousness about HIV-AIDS, sparking public outrage and concern and making a celebrity out of Siimon Reynolds, the young creator of the advertisements. The Grim Reaper advertisements and those from the QUIT campaign, such as the one showing the diseased lungs of a smoker, are deliberately constructed as 'shock' advertisements and are designed primarily to create public awareness of an issue. In the usual narrative of a public information campaign, subsequent advertisements will challenge attitudes and finally behaviour with emphasis on the provision of facts and information.

'Freedom From Fear'

The Freedom From Fear Campaign Against Domestic Violence was launched in August 1998. This campaign, an initiative of the Western Australian government, differed from other campaigns on domestic violence because it focuses on the perpetrators and men at risk of commiting acts of domestic violence. The campaign calls on these men to accept responsibility for their behaviour and to take action to stop the occurrences of abuse. Freedom From Fear is a multifaceted media and information campaign, employing television, press, radio and outdoor advertising. The campaign distributes information resources at various workplaces, involves community consultation, and places information products in recreational sites, such as on beer coasters in pubs. The campaign is linked to the policy developments of relevant institutional authorities, such as the police. It has also established a 24-hour telephone information helpline and counselling programs, for perpetrators and 'at-risk' men as well as for victims and children (Freedom From Fear 2002).

The first phase of the mass media advertising campaign highlighted acts of physical violence and focused on the suffering of children in the families in which domestic violence is happening. The advertisements usually cut between the act of physical violence against the partner and the fearful reactions of the children. They featured texts such as 'Every time you hurt her . . . he feels it too'. The advertisements urged the perpetrators of domestic violence to act to stop the occurrences of abuse with the message 'Do something about it', chosen partly because it was a 'positive' message that appealed to the agency of the men. Later stages of the campaign will focus on other types of domestic violence, including sexual and emotional abuse.

Public information campaigns, such as Freedom From Fear, face the arduous task of disciplining the everyday lives of people who engage in acts of deviant behaviour. Such campaigns work hard to overcome many psychological barriers: perpetrators may engage in selective perception and not acknowledge their engagement in domestic violence or they may manufacture excuses or 'rationales' for such behaviour. Subsequently, the campaign managers have to correctly identify the target audience, formulate an effective message, and accurately deliver that message to the target audience. Preliminary research employed focus groups of males aged 15–40 and focus groups comprising perpetrators of domestic violence. The research indicated that the campaign messages should avoid an accusatory or blaming tone if perpetrators were to be reached by the campaign, that there was a need for a prevention focus, and that 'potential perpetrators' should be targeted as well as current perpetrators. The strategy of emphasising the suffering of children and the need for the perpetrator to take action to stop the abuse was chosen over other possible messages, emphasising criminal sanctions, community intervention, social disapproval and the damage to the partner. Measuring the specific 'effects' of public information campaigns is difficult given the impossibility of isolating media effect from other political, social and cultural factors, but Freedom From Fear researchers found that overall campaign recall was high, that there was significant improvement in awareness of support services, and that a promising attitudinal trend had emerged over the course of the first stage of the campaign regarding how people viewed domestic violence and its effects on the whole of the family (Freedom From Fear 2002).

Domestic violence is an appropriate topic of discussion here because it illustrates how the social meanings of actions are determined through the ways they are located on the public/private spectrum. The very term 'domestic violence' distinguishes it from other, more public forms of violence. The assignation of violence against one's family as 'domestic' has located it in the private sphere, and historically this meant it was not always the subject of great scrutiny by public authorities, such as welfare organisations, the police and the legal system. Arguably, the assignation of the violence as 'domestic' has also worked historically if not to condone the violence then at least to classify the violence as less criminal than other, more public forms of violence. However, as we have noted throughout this book, the value system that differentiates and informs public and private activities is historical and subject to change as a result of political struggle. Largely as a result of the work of the feminist movement, domestic violence has over several decades come to be better acknowledged as a matter of public concern, and there has been subsequently greater news reportage of incidents of domestic violence. This is not to argue that the public/private boundary as a marker of social value has been dissolved because traditional private sphere activities have been 'politicised', but it is to argue that the boundary has assumed an even greater significance because the political values that always inform such distinctions have been made more explicit. The boundaries between the public and the private sphere continue to carry significance: public officials, such as police, are well aware of how issues of privacy must be respected and negotiated in any investigation.

Public information campaigns always involve processes of public formation, and are always informed by particular value positions. Freedom From Fear has the laudable aim of preventing and reducing the prevalence of domestic violence, and in order to do so it must make choices about which social values to mobilise and how to represent public life and types of people. Generally, the campaign works to unify the public through representations of concern about the welfare of children. As the public sphere becomes increasingly heterogeneous it becomes harder to conceptualise a common unity, and increasingly such constructions of unity work through the need to protect children. 'The public' is represented as a 'protecting public' (Brennan 2001, p. 94) and, while this may seem like a successful strategy to 'depoliticise' the public and bring together a plethora of differences, it nonetheless has political effects. I would not go so far as to say that the Freedom From Fear campaign suggests that the 'primary responsibility in a household facing domestic violence' is 'the preservation of childhood innocence'

(Brennan 2001, p. 97), but the advertisements do work to construct a unified public through representations of the powerlessness of children. As Marc Brennan (2001, p. 95) states:

> ... without agency children continue to be a site of powerlessness, constructing those with agency as a universalised site united by its concerns in responsibility and protection. This construction is central to the public service advertisement and its use is one of the ways in which the discursive space of the public may be organised. Through the discourse of childhood, individual differences within the public can be masked through the connotations of responsibility and the protection of the powerless ...

Conclusion

Everyday life has an unusual status: it is contrasted with public life but it is also the subject of much media attention. Everyday life is contrasted with formal politics, but so much of politics is about the structures, contents and values of everyday life. It is highly individualised, private and 'unknowable' in any complete sense, but everyday life is also a mundane, highly regularised existence, many of the features of which are shared or recognised by a large number of people in the society. Everyday life has also been valued in very different ways by theorists. On the one hand, everyday life has often been criticised as a site of repetitive and alienating activities, where people are cast as non-political subjects, primarily concerned with consumption, personal relationships and leisure activities. These criticisms maintain that such subject formation is nonetheless a highly political process and is vital to the ongoing viability of capitalism. On the other hand, everyday life has been praised as a site where people can exercise a greater degree of freedom from such disciplinary structures. It is argued that the repetitive basis of everyday life and its production of a sense of 'normality' is a mechanism that helps people cope with the pressures, stresses and upheavals of much modern life. Ultimately, it is argued, everyday life is a democratic phenomenon. The increasing media focus on everyday life is witnessed in the rise of lifestyle journalism and self-help media. These kinds of media encompass a disparate range of programs and texts, but they often take features of everyday life in order to engage in processes of commodification and they can divert people from other more explicitly political interests and activities. Different kinds of self-help media and lifestyle journalism can also be highly informative and helpful, performing an important role in the production of contemporary culture and assisting people in the maintenance of physical, emotional and spiritual wellbeing. Many forms of media that deal with the contents of everyday life, particularly public information campaigns, are engaged in the governance of the conduct of individuals and groups in society. This governance functions less through overt threats of punishment and more in 'productive' and 'educative' ways which involve people in their own subject formation.

References

Adams, P. and Burton, L. 1997, *Talkback: Emperors of Air*, Allen & Unwin, Sydney.

Ahmed, K. 2000, 'Bringing up baby in public and private' *Guardian Unlimited*, 21 May, www.guardianunlimited.co.uk/blairbabe/article/0,2763,223416,00. html [24 May 2000].

Albury, K. 1999, 'Spaceship Triple J: Making the national youth network' *Media International Australia*, no. 91, May, pp. 55–66.

Allen, R.C. 1992, 'Audience-Oriented Criticism and Television' in *Channels of Discourse, Reassembled*, ed. R.C. Allen, Routledge, London.

Anderson, B. 1991, *Imagined Communities: Reflections on the origin and spread of nationalism*, rev edn, Routledge, London.

Andrews, G. (ed.) 1991, *Citizenship*, Lawrence & Wishart, London.

Appleton, G. 1999, 'The lure of Laws: An analysis of the audience appeal of the John Laws program' *Media International Australia*, no. 91, May, pp. 83–95.

Arendt, H. 1958, *The Human Condition*, Chicago University Press, Chicago.

Aristotle 1981, *The Politics*, rev edn, trans T.A. Sinclair, revised and re-presented, T.J. Saunders, Penguin, Harmondsworth.

Audit Bureau of Circulations (UK) 2002, Six monthly report for the period December 2001 to May 2002, www.abc.org.uk/cgibin/gen...news pdata|nationalnews|sixmonthly [3 July 2002].

Bailey, J.W. 1999, 'To play the trump cards' *The Australian*, Media Supplement, 10–16 June, pp. 14–15.

Bakvis, H. 1997, 'Advising the executive: think tanks, consultants, political staff and kitchen cabinets' in *The Hollow Crown: Countervailing trends in core executives*, eds P. Weller, H. Bakvis and R.A.W. Rhodes, Macmillan, London.

Barker, C. 1997, *Global Television*, Blackwell, Oxford.

Barnes, B. 1988, *The Nature of Power*, Polity, Cambridge.

Bell, P. and van Leeuwen, T. 1994, *The Media Interview: Confession, contest, conversation*, University of New South Wales Press, Sydney.

Bita, N. 2001, 'Marked mags' *The Australian*, Media Supplement, 17–23 May, pp. 6–7.

Blumer, H. 1948, 'Public opinion and public opinion polling' *American Sociological Review*, vol. 13, pp. 542–54.

Boorstin, D. 1963, *The Image*, Pelican, Harmondsworth.

Bouma, G. 2000, *The Research Process*, 4th edn, Oxford University Press, Melbourne.

Bourdieu, P. 1979, 'Public Opinion does not exist' in *Communication and Class Struggle*, eds A. Mattelart and S. Sielgelaub, International General, New York.

Boyce, G. 1978, 'The Fourth Estate: the reappraisal of a concept' in *Newspaper History: From the seventeenth century to the present day*, eds G. Boyce et al., Constable, London.

Brantlinger, P. 1983, *Bread and Circuses: Theories of mass culture as social decay*, Cornell University Press, Ithaca, NY.

Brenchley, F. 1999, 'Ministry of Propaganda' *The Bulletin*, 16 February, pp. 30–2.

Brennan, M. 2001, 'Child(hood) abuse: Constructing the Australian public in public service announcements' *Media International Australia*, no. 99, May, pp. 91–104.

Brewster, D. 1996, 'Newspapers find it's the quality that counts' *The Australian*, 23 January, p. 63.

Brook, S. 2003, 'Now you can't even escape TV ads on the bus to work' *The Australian*, 30 January, p. 3.

Brunt, R. 1992, 'A "divine gift to inspire"? Popular cultural representation, nationhood and the British monarchy' in *Popular Media Culture in Post-War Britain*, eds D. Strinati and S. Wagg, Routledge, London.

Buck-Morss, S. 2002, 'A global public sphere' *Radical Philosophy*, no. 111, Jan/Feb, pp. 2–10.

Burchell, D. 1993, 'The virtuous citizen and the commercial spirit: the unhappy prehistory of citizenship and modernity' *Communal/Plural*, vol. 2, pp. 17–45.

Cadzow, J. 2001, 'The sultans of spin' *The West Australian*, Big Weekend Supplement, 16 June, pp. 1–2.

Chaney, D. 1993, *Fictions of Collective Life: Public drama in late modern culture*, Routledge, London.

Cochrane, P. and Goodman, D. 1992, 'The great Australian journey: cultural logic and nationalism in the postmodern era' in *Celebrating the Nation: A critical study of Australia's Bicentenary*, eds T. Bennett et al., Allen & Unwin, Sydney.

Collingwood, P. 1999, 'Commercial radio 1999: new networks, new technologies' *Media International Australia*, no. 91, May, pp. 11–21.

Conley, D. 1997, *The Daily Miracle*, Oxford University Press, Melbourne.

———2002, *The Daily Miracle*, 2nd edn, Oxford University Press, Melbourne.

Considine, M. 1994, *Public Policy: A critical approach*, Macmillan, Melbourne.

Corner, J. 1992, 'Presumption as theory: "realism" in television studies' *Screen*, vol. 33, no. 1, pp. 97–102.

———1995, *Television Form and Public Address*, Edward Arnold, London.

Cowlett, M. 2001, 'Learn how to avoid media stage fright' *Marketing*, 15 February [Online, Proquest, 3 September 2001].

Craig, G. 1993, 'Picturing the statement: visual representations of the Prime Minister's Economic Statement, February 1992' *Continuum: The Australian journal of media and culture*, vol. 6, no. 2, pp. 235–56.

———1997, 'Princess Diana, journalism and the construction of a public: an analysis of the *Panorama* interview' *Continuum: Journal of media and cultural studies*, vol. 11, no. 3, pp. 12–22.

———2000a, 'The Australian way of life: journalism, citizenship and the constitutional convention' *Journalism Studies*, vol. 1, no. 3, pp. 485–97.

———2000b, 'Perpetual crisis: the politics of saving the ABC' *Media International Australia*, no. 94, February, pp. 105–16.

———2002, 'The Spectacle of the Street: an analysis of media coverage of protests at the 2000 Melbourne World Economic Forum (WEF)' *Australian Journal of Communication*, vol. 29, no. 1, pp. 39–52.

Crossley, N. 1995, 'Merleau-Ponty, the elusive body and carnal sociology' *Body and Society*, vol. 1, no. 1, pp. 43–63.

Cunningham, S. and Flew, T. 2002, 'Policy' in *The Media and Communications in Australia*, eds S. Cunningham and G. Turner, Allen & Unwin, Sydney.

Curran, J. 1977, 'Capitalism and control of the press, 1800–1975' in *Mass Communication and Society*, eds J. Curran, M. Gurevitch and J. Woollacott, Edward Arnold, London.

———1991, 'Mass Media and Democracy: A reappraisal' in *Mass Media and Society*, eds J. Curran and M. Gurevitch, Edward Arnold, London.

Dahl, R.A. 1970, *Modern Political Analysis*, 2nd edn, Prentice-Hall, Englewood Cliffs, NJ.

Dàhlgren, P. 1995, *Television and the Public Sphere: Citizenship, democracy and the media*, Sage, London.

Day, J. 2002, 'Blair doubles cost of spin' *Guardian Unlimited*, 25 July, http://media.guardian.co.uk/marketingandpr/story/0,7494,762999,00.html [26 July 2002].

Dayan, D. and Katz, E. 1994, *Media Events: The live broadcasting of history*, Harvard University Press, Cambridge, MA.

de Certeau, M. 1984, *The Practice of Everyday Life*, trans S. Rendall, University of California Press, Berkeley.

DeFleur, M.L. and Ball-Rokeach, S.J. 1989, *Theories of Mass Communication*, 5th edn, Longman, New York.

Department of Culture, Media and Sport (UK) 2002, Press release, quoted in

Guardian Unlimited, 7 May. http://media.guardian.co.uk/whitepaper/story/0,7521,711449,00.html [9 May 2002].

Dermott, B. and Associates 1998, 'The status of media usage in Australia' *Quarter Q3 1997*, 27 January, Melbourne.

Diamond, E. and Bates, S. 1992, *The Spot*, MIT Press, Cambridge, MA.

Donald, J. 1992, *Sentimental Education: Schooling, popular culture and the regulation of liberty*, Verso, London.

Dow Jones 2002, 'The Wall Street Journal online at WSJ.com announces new design, new features, new content' www.businesswire.com/webbox/bw.012902/220292501.htm [3 July, 2002].

Eagleton, T. 1985, *The Function of Criticism*, Verso, London.

Eley, G. 1992, 'Nations, publics, and political cultures: placing Habermas in the nineteenth century' in *Habermas and the Public Sphere*, ed. C. Calhoun, MIT Press, Cambridge, MA.

Elster, J. (ed.) 1998, *Deliberative Democracy*, Cambridge University Press, Cambridge.

Epstein, D. and Steinberg, D.L. 1998, 'American dreamin': discoursing liberally on the Oprah Winfrey Show' *Women's Studies International Forum*, vol. 21, no. 1, pp. 77–94.

Fairclough, N. 2000, *New Labour, New Language?* Routledge, London.

Falk, P. 1994, *The Consuming Body*, Sage, London.

Felski, R. 1999/2000, 'The invention of everyday life' *New Formations*, vol. 39, pp. 15–31.

Fiske, J. 1992, 'Popularity and the politics of information' in *Journalism and Popular Culture*, eds P. Dahlgren and C. Sparks, Sage, London.

Flew, T. 2002, 'Television and pay TV' in *The Media and Communications in Australia*, eds S. Cunningham and G. Turner, Allen & Unwin, Sydney.

Foucault, M. 1991, 'Governmentality' in *The Foucault Effect: Studies in governmentality*, eds G. Burchell, C. Gordon and P. Miller, University of Chicago Press, Chicago.

——1995, *Discipline and Punish: The birth of the prison*, trans A. Sheridan, Vintage, New York.

Franklin, B. 1997, *Newszak and News Media*, Arnold, London.

Fraser, N. 1989, 'Rethinking the public sphere: a contribution to the critique of actually existing democracy' *Social Text*, vol. 25/26, pp. 56–80.

Freedom From Fear 2002 Freedom From Fear Campaign Against Domestic Violence, http://www.freedomfromfear.wa.gov.au/ [March 2002].

Galtung, J. and Ruge, M. 1981, 'Structuring and selecting news' in *The Manufacture of News*, eds S. Cohen and J. Young, Constable, London.

Gatens, M. 1996, *Imaginary Bodies: Ethics, power and corporeality*, Routledge, London.

Gawiser, S.R. and Evans Witt, G. 1994, *A Journalist's Guide to Public Opinion Polls*, Praeger, Westport, CT.

Giddens, A. 1985, *The Nation-State and Violence, Vol. 2: A Contemporary Critique of Historical Materialism*, Polity, Cambridge.

Ginsberg, B. 1986, *The Captive Public: How mass opinion promotes state power*, Basic Books, New York.

Goffman, E. 1969, *The Presentation of Self in Everyday Life*, Penguin, Harmondsworth.

Goot, M. 2000, 'The performance of the polls' in *Howard's Agenda: The 1998 Australian federal election*, eds M. Simms and J. Warhurst, University of Queensland Press, Brisbane.

Gordon, C. 1991, 'Governmental rationality: an introduction' in *The Foucault Effect: Studies in governmentality*, eds G. Burchell, C. Gordon and P. Miller, University of Chicago Press, Chicago.

Gordon-Smith, M. 2002, 'Media ethics after "Cash for Comment"' in *The Media and Communications in Australia*, eds S. Cunningham and G. Turner, Allen & Unwin, Sydney.

Gramsci, A. 1971, *Selections from Prison Notebooks*, eds and trans Q. Hoare and G. Nowell Smith, Lawrence & Wishart, London.

Grattan, M. 1998, 'The politics of spin' *Australian Studies in Journalism*, vol. 7, pp. 32–45.

Gray, J. 1995, *Liberalism*, 2nd edn, Open University Press, Buckingham.

Green, P. (ed.) 1993, *Democracy*, Humanities Press, NJ.

Greenfield, C. and Williams, P. 2000, 'The sporting gamble: media sport, drama and politics' *Media International Australia*, no. 97, November, pp. 47–58.

Grosz, E. 1994, *Volatile Bodies: Towards a corporeal feminism*, Allen & Unwin, Sydney.

Habermas, J. 1984, *The Theory of Communicative Action, Vol. 1: Reason and the Rationalization of Society*, trans T. Docherty, Beacon, Boston.

——1989, *The Structural Transformation of the Public Sphere: An inquiry into a category of bourgeois society*, trans T. Burger with F. Lawrence, Polity, Cambridge.

——1992, 'Further Reflections on the Public Sphere' in *Habermas and the Public Sphere*, ed. C. Calhoun, MIT Press, Cambridge, MA.

Hall, S. 1977, 'Culture, the media and the "ideological effect"' in *Mass Communication and Society*, eds J. Curran et al., Edward Arnold, London.

——1981, 'The determinations of news photographs' in *The Manufacture of News*, eds S. Cohen and J. Young, Constable, London.

——1993, 'Culture, community, nation' *Cultural Studies*, vol. 7, no. 3, pp. 349–63.

Hall, S. et al. 1978, *Policing the Crisis: Mugging, the state, and law and order*, Macmillan, London.

Hallin, D.C. 1994, *We Keep America on Top of the World: Television journalism and the public sphere*, Routledge, London.

Harris, M. 1987, *London Newspapers in the Age of Walpole: A study of the origins of the modern English press*, Associated University Presses, London.

Hartley, J. 1992, *The Politics of Pictures: The creation of the public in the age of popular media*, Routledge, London.

——1996, *Popular Reality: Journalism, modernity, popular culture*, Arnold, London.

——1999, *Uses of Television*, Routledge, London.

Hawkins, G. 1997, 'The ABC and the mystic writing pad' *Media International Australia*, no. 83, February, pp. 11–17.

——2001, 'The ABC and rhetorics of choice' in *Culture in Australia: Policies, publics and programs*, eds T. Bennett and D. Carter, Cambridge University Press, Cambridge.

Heater, D. 1990, *Citizenship: The civic ideal in world history, politics and education*, Longman, London.

Henningham, J. 1995, 'Media' in *Institutions in Australian Society*, ed. J. Henningham, Oxford University Press, Melbourne.

Herbst, S. 1991, 'Classical democracy, polls, and public opinion: theoretical frameworks for studying the development of public sentiment' *Communication Theory*, vol. 1, pp. 225–38.

Herbst, S. and Beniger, J.R. 1994, 'The changing infrastructure of public opinion' *Audiencemaking: How the media create the audience*, Sage, Thousand Oaks, CA.

Heywood, A. 1998, *Political Ideologies: An introduction*, 2nd edn, Macmillan, London.

Hindess, B. 1996, *Discourses of Power: From Hobbes to Foucault*, Blackwell, Oxford.

Hughes, C. and Wintour, P. 1993, *Labour Rebuilt: The new model party*, Fourth Estate, London.

James, O. 2000, 'Basking in the son' *Guardian Unlimited*, 22 May, www.guardian unlimited.co.uk/blairbabe/article/0,2763,223565,00.html [24 May 2000].

Jamieson, K. 1986, 'The evolution of political advertising in America' in *New Perspectives in Political Advertising*, eds Keid et al., Southern Illinois University Press, Carbondale, IL.

Johnston, J. and Zawawi, C. (eds) 2000, *Public Relations: Theory and practice*, Allen & Unwin, Sydney.

Kelly, P. 1999, 'New political schism rooted in distrust' *The Australian*, 8 November, p. 1.

Kettle, M. 2000, 'Parties about to top $1bn on TV ads' *Guardian Unlimited*, 28 October, http://media.guardian.co.uk/news/story/0,7541,389243,00.html [August 2002].

Kershaw, B. 1999, *The Politics of Performance: Between Brecht and Baudrillard*, Routledge, London.

Kingston, M. 1999, *Off the Rails: The Pauline Hanson trip*, Allen & Unwin, Sydney.

Klein, N. 2001, 'Between McWorld and Jihad' *Guardian Unlimited*, 27 October, www.guardian.co.uk/Archive/Article/0,4273,42848884,00.html [November 2001].

Kress, G. and van Leeuwen, T. 1990, *Reading Images*, Deakin University Press, Geelong.

Kumar, K. 1977, 'Holding the middle ground: the BBC, the public and the professional broadcaster' in *Mass Communication and Society*, eds J. Curran, M. Gurevitch and J. Woollacott, Open University Press, London.

Kurtz, H. 1998, *Spin Cycle: Inside the Clinton propaganda machine*, Pan, New York.

Laclau, E. and Mouffe, C. 1985, *Hegemony and Socialist Strategy: Towards a radical democratic politics*, Verso, London.

Landes, J. 1988, *Women and the Public Sphere in the Age of the French Revolution*. Cornell University Press, Ithaca, NY.

Lefebvre, H. 1984, *Everyday Life in the Modern World*, Transaction Publishers, New Brunswick.

Lefort, C. 1986, *The Political Forms of Modern Society: Bureaucracy, democracy, totalitarianism*, ed. J. Thompson, Basil Blackwell, Oxford.

Little, G. 1999, *The Public Emotions: From mourning to hope*, ABC Books, Sydney.

Little, J. 1999, 'Damage control' *The Australian*, Media Supplement, 4–10 November, pp. 6–7.

Lloyd, C.J. 1988, *Parliament and the Press: The Federal Parliamentary press gallery 1901–88*, Melbourne University Press, Melbourne.

Lloyd, C. and Hippocrates, C. 1997, 'Public journalism, public participation and Australian citizenship' *Culture and Policy*, vol. 8, no. 2, pp. 9–21.

Lloyd, S. 2001, 'Big brother, big spender' *Business Review Weekly*, vol. 23, no. 9, pp. 76–81.

Lukes, S. 1974, *Power: A radical view*, Macmillan, London.

——(ed.) 1986, *Power*, Basil Blackwell, Oxford.

Lumby, C. 1999, *Gotcha: Life in a tabloid world*, Allen & Unwin, Sydney.

Maddox, G. 1996, *Australian Democracy in Theory and Practice*, 4th edn, Longman, Sydney.

Magdalinski, T. 2000, 'The reinvention of Australia for the Sydney 2000 Olympic Games' in *Sport in Australasian Society*, eds J.A. Mangan and J. Nauright, Frank Cass, London.

Marshall, T.H. 1964, 'Citizenship and social class' in *Class, Citizenship and Social Development: Essays by T.H. Marshall*, Doubleday, New York.

Mansfield, N. 2000, *Subjectivity: Theories of the self from Freud to Haraway*, Allen & Unwin, Sydney.

Mayer, H. 1994, 'The morality of political advertising' in *Mayer on the Media: Issues and arguments*, ed. R. Tiffen, Allen & Unwin and AFTRS, Sydney.

McCombs, M.E. 1993, 'The evolution of agenda-setting research: twenty-five years in the marketplace of ideas' *Journal of Communication*, vol. 43, no. 2, pp. 100–27.

McKay, J. 2000, *The Magazines Handbook*, Routledge, London.

McKee, A. 1997, 'Putting the "public" into "public toilets"' *Continuum: Journal of media and cultural studies*, vol. 11, no. 3, pp. 85–100.

——2001, *Australian Television: A genealogy of great moments*, Oxford University Press, Melbourne.

McKenna, M. 1999, 'We, the people, must be heard' *The Australian*, 22 September, p. 17.

McNair, B. 1998, *The Sociology of Journalism*, Arnold, London.

——1999, *An Introduction to Political Communication*, 2nd edn, Routledge, London.

McQuail, D. 1994, *Mass Communication Theory: An introduction*, 3rd edn, Sage, London.

—1997, *Audience Analysis*, Sage, Thousand Oaks, CA.

Mercer, C. 1992, 'Regular imaginings: the newspaper and the nation' in *Celebrating the Nation: A critical study of Australia's bicentenary*, eds T. Bennett et al., Allen & Unwin, Sydney.

Mickler, S. 1998, *The Myth of Privilege: Aboriginal status, media visions, public ideas*, Fremantle Arts Press, Fremantle.

Mills, S. 1999, 'Polling, politics and the press 1941–1996' in *Journalism: Print, politics and popular culture*, eds A. Curthoys and J. Schultz, University of Queensland Press, Brisbane.

Mitchell, B. 2000, 'S-11 thanks officers for "victory"' *The Australian*, 12 September, p. 3.

Montgomery, B. 2000, 'Torch puts tragedy site in new light' *The Australian*, 4 August, p. 6.

Mouffe, C. 1993, *The Return of the Political*, Verso, London.

'Murdoch gets his way' 2002, *Guardian Unlimited*, 8 May, http://politics.guardian.co.uk/labour/comment/0,9236,711593,00.html [9 May 2002].

Negrine, R. 1996, *The Communication of Politics*, Sage, London.

Negt, O. and Kluge, A. 1993, *Public Sphere and Experience: Toward an analysis of the bourgeois and proletarian public sphere*, trans P. Labanyi, J.O. Daniel and A. Oksiloff, University of Minnesota Press, Minneapolis.

Nimmo, D. and Combs, J.E. 1992, *Political Pundits*, Praeger, New York.

Noelle-Neumann, E. 1984, *The Spiral of Silence*, University of Chicago Press, Chicago.

O'Sullivan, T. et al. 1994, *Key Concepts in Communication and Cultural Studies*, 2nd edn, Routledge, London.

Parkins, W. 2001, 'Oprah Winfrey's change your life TV and the spiritual everyday' *Continuum: Journal of media and cultural studies*, vol. 15, no. 2, pp. 145–57.

Parsons, W. 1989, *The Power of the Financial Press: Journalism and economic opinion in Britain and America*, Edward Elgar, Aldershot.

Payne, T. 1999, *The Canberra Press Gallery and the Backbench of the 38th Parliament 1996–98*, Department of the Parliamentary Library, Canberra.

Peters, J.D. 1993, 'Distrust of representation: Habermas on the public sphere' *Media, Culture and Society*, vol. 15, pp. 541–71.

Pink, S. 2000, 'The voice of persuasion' *The Australian*, Media Supplement, 19–25 October, p. 5.

Ponton, G. and Gill, P. 1993, *Introduction to Politics*, 3rd edn, Blackwell, Oxford.

Productivity Commission 2000, *Broadcasting*, Report no. 11, Ausinfo, Canberra.

Rogers, E.M. and Storey, J.D. 1987, 'Communication campaigns' in *Handbook of Communication Science*, eds C.R. Berger and S.H. Chaffee, Sage, Newbury Park, CA.

Rosen, J. 1996, *Getting the Connections Right: Public journalism and the troubles in the press*, Twentieth Century Fund Press, New York.

Rothwell, N. 1999a, 'When surf's up, ain't no republic dropping in on this wave' *The Australian*, 7 October, p. 4.

——1999b, 'Tin Can's king tide turns against rusty monarchy' *The Australian*, 8 October, p. 5.

Rowe, D. 2000, 'Global media events and the positioning of presence' *Media International Australia*, no. 97, November, pp. 11–21.

Sampson, A. 1996, 'The crisis at the heart of our media' *British Journalism Review*, vol. 17, no. 3, pp. 42–51.

Scannell, P. 1989, 'Public service broadcasting and modern public life' *Media, Culture and Society*, vol. 11, pp. 135–66.

Schirato, T. and Yell, S. 1999, 'The "new" men's magazines and the performance of masculinity' *Media International Australia*, no. 92, pp. 81–90.

Schlesinger, P. 1991, *Media, State and Nation: Political violence and collective identities*, Sage, London.

Schultz, J. 1998, *Reviving the Fourth Estate: Democracy, accountability and the media*, Cambridge University Press, Melbourne.

Schulze, J. 2002, 'PBL dumps its unwanted' *The Australian*, 4 June, p. 17.

Sekuless, P. 1991, *Lobbying Canberra in the Nineties: The government relations game*, Allen & Unwin, Sydney.

Silverstone, R. 1994, *Television and Everyday Life*, Routledge, London.

Simons, M. 1999, *Fit to Print: Inside the Canberra Press Gallery*, UNSW Press, Sydney.

Sligo, F. and Williams, J. 1999, 'What does discussion do? Perspectives on public opinion and the formation of polarised viewpoints' *Australian Journal of Communication*, vol. 26, no. 3, pp. 37–48.

Smith, J. 2000, 'Enough already' *Guardian Unlimited*, 22 May, www.guardian unlimited.co.uk/blairbabe/article/0,2763,223551,0.html [24 May 2000].

Sparks, C. 1992, 'Popular journalism: theories and practice' in *Journalism and Popular Culture*, eds P. Dahlgren and C. Sparks, Sage, London.

——1999, 'The press' in *The Media in Britain: Current debates and developments*, eds J. Stokes and A. Reading, Houndmills, Basingstoke.

Steketee, M. 1999a, 'Felled by the polls' *The Australian*, Media Supplement, 2–8 December, pp. 6–7.

——1999b, 'One Queen, two nations' *The Australian*, 8 November, p. 1.

——2001, 'Canberra in control' *The Australian*, Media Supplement, 8–14 March, pp. 6–7.

Stewart, R.G. and Ward, I. 1996, *Politics one*, 2nd edn, Macmillan, Melbourne.

Tam, H. 1998, *Communitarianism: A new agenda for politics and citizenship*, Macmillan, London.

Taylor, M. and Botan, C. 1997, 'Public relations campaigns for national development in the Pacific Rim: the case of public education in Malaysia' *Australian Journal of Communication*, vol. 24, no. 2, pp. 115–130.

Thompson, J. 1995, *The Media and Modernity: A social theory of the media*, Polity, Cambridge.

——2000, *Political Scandal: Power and visibility in the media age*, Polity, Cambridge.

Thompson, M. 1999, 'Some issues for community radio at the turn of the century' *Media International Australia*, no. 91, May, pp. 23–31.

Tiffen, R. 1989, *News and Power*, Allen & Unwin, Sydney.

——1999, *Scandals: Media, politics and corruption in contemporary Australia*, UNSW Press, Sydney.

Tomlinson, A. 1996, 'Olympic spectacle: opening ceremonies and some paradoxes of globalization' *Media, Culture and Society*, vol. 18, pp. 583–602.

Toohey, P. 2001, 'Campaign that moved PM to act on petrol-sniffing' *The Australian*, 21 February, p. 1.

Turner, B. 1993, 'Contemporary Problems in the Theory of Citizenship' in *Citizenship and Social Theory*, ed. B. Turner, Sage, London.

Turner, G. 1994, *Making it National: Nationalism and Australian popular culture*, Allen & Unwin, Sydney.

Turner, G., Bonner, F. and Marshall, P.D. 2000, *Fame Games: The production of celebrity in Australia*, Cambridge University Press, Cambridge.

Utley, G. 1997, 'The shrinking of foreign news' *Foreign Affairs*, vol. 76, no. 2, pp. 2–10.

Vizard, S. 1998, 'Symbolism is more than window dressing' *The Australian*, 30 January, p. 13.

Walker, D. 2000, 'Pssst . . . I've got something to tell you' *Guardian Unlimited*, 20 July, www.guardian.co.uk/Labour/Story/0,2763,345221,00.html [26 July 2000].

Ward, I. 1995, *Politics of the Media*, Macmillan, Melbourne.

Ward, I. and Cook, I. 1992, 'Televised political advertising, media freedom, and democracy' *Social Alternatives*, vol. 11, no. 1, pp. 21–6.

Wark, M. 1994, *Virtual Geography: Living with global media events*, Indiana University Press, Bloomington.

——1999, *Celebrities, Culture and Cyberspace: The light on the hill in a postmodern world*, Pluto, Sydney.

Warner, M. 1992, 'The mass public and the mass subject' in *Habermas and the Public Sphere*, ed. C. Calhoun, MIT Press, Cambridge, MA.

Watt, N. 2001, 'Campbell to quit as PM's voice' *Guardian Unlimited*, 12 April, www.mediaguardian.co.uk/marketingandpr/story/0,7494,472226,00.html [15 April, 2000].

Weale, A. 1999, *Democracy*, Macmillan, London.

Wilson, H. 1989, 'Public Relations: Mobilising consent' in *Australian Communications and the Public Sphere*, ed. H. Wilson, Macmillan, Melbourne.

——1996, 'What is an Olympic city? Visions of Sydney 2000' *Media, Culture and Society*, vol. 18, pp. 603–618.

Wrong, D.H. 1979, *Power: Its forms, bases and uses*, Harper & Row, New York.

Wynhausen, E. 2000, 'Shock of the new Left' *The Australian*, 26 September, p. 31.

Young, I.M. 1987, 'Impartiality and the civic public: some implications of feminist critiques of moral and political theory' in *Feminism as Critique*, eds S. Benhabib and D. Cornell, Polity, Cambridge.

Index

Aboriginal
   communities, 77
   culture, 189
   flag, 190
   peoples, 179
   youth, 107
A Current Affair, 94
Adams, P & Burton, L, 103, 105
advertising, 76, 92, 93, 105, 202;
   see also politics: political
   advertising
Age, The, 11, 77
agency, 61, 114, 196
agenda-setting, 16, 81
agonistic pluralism, 32–3
Ahmed, K, 125
Albury, K, 109–10
alienation, 195–6
Allen, RC, 16
American Broadcasting
   Company (ABC), 13
ancient Greece, 28, 49, 172
Anderson, B, 5–6, 173
Andrews, G, 28
anti-globalisation, 54, 63–4,
   125–8; *see also* globalisation
Anzac Day, 179
apartheid, 36
Appleton, G, 106–7

Arendt, H, 48
Aristotle, 24
Associated Press, 14
audience research, 16
audiences, 59–61
Austereo, 11
Australia Day, 179
Australian, The, 10, 36, 76, 77, 84,
   127, 183–4
Australian Broadcasting
   Authority (ABA), 38–9
Australian Broadcasting
   Corporation (ABC), 9, 12,
   42, 62, 80, 94, 100, 108
Australian Competition and
   Consumer Commission
   (ACCC), 40
Australian Consumers
   Association, 138
Australian Council of Trade
   Unions (ACTU), 35, 138
Australian Financial Review, The,
   11, 73, 76
Australian Labor Party (ALP),
   35, 144
Australian Medical Association
   (AMA), 35, 138
Australian Press Council, 40–1
Australian Radio Network, 11

Australian Republican
    Movement (ARM), 182–3
Australian republican
    referendum, 36, 61, 62,
    181–5
Australian Women's Weekly, The,
    11, 86, 87,

B magazine, 86
background briefings, 144–6
Bailey, JW, 143–4
Bakvis, H, 139
Barker, C, 13
Barnes, B, 25
Beckham, D, 125
Bell, P & van Leeuwen, T, 99–101
Bita, N, 85
Blair, T, 13, 113, 118, 123–5, 141,
    146; *see also* British Labour
    Party; British government
Blumer, H, 157
body, the, 116–8
Boorstin, D, 118–9
Boston Globe, The, 13
Bouma, G, 163
Bourdieu, P, 157
Boyce, G, 19
Branson, R, 15, 57
Brantlinger, P, 21
Brenchley, F, 148
Brennan, M, 205–6
Brewster, D, 76
Britain
    magazines, 85–6
    media regulation, 41
    monarchy, 175, 181–2, 189
    newspapers, 12–13, 74
    political advertising, 132–3
    radio, 13, 175
    television, 13, 175
British Broadcasting
    Corporation (BBC), 9,
    12–13, 41–2, 62, 175, 195

British Labour Party, 13, 113,
    124–5, 141, 143; *see also*
    Blair, T; British government
British government, 41, 146–7,
    149; *see also* Blair, T; British
    Labour Party
broadcast media, 92–111; *see also*
    television; radio;
    journalism
    history, 175–6
Broadcasting Services Act, 38
Brook, S, 7
Brown, G, 146
Brunt, R, 57
Bryant, M, 191
BSkyB, 13
Buck-Morss, S, 64
Bulletin, The, 11, 84, 86
Burchell, D, 177
Burke's Backyard, 200
Burson-Marsteller, 139
Bush, G, 95
business, 54, 64, 126–7, 147; *see
    also* media: as business
Business Council of Australia,
    138

Cadzow, J, 135
Callaghan, J, 145
Cameron, R, 162
Campbell, A, 141
capitalism, 17, 36, 117, 172–4,
    176, 193
Carleton, R, 100
Carr, B, 106,
Carter, J, 164
cash for comment crisis, 39, 108
celebrities, 55, 56–8, 74, 87, 106,
    180, 184, 189–90, 197, 200
Centenary of Federation, 186,
    201
Chaney, D, 57–8
charisma, 57, 124

children, 205–6
citizenship, 28, 30–3, 56, 58, 61, 78, 176–8, 184–5
civil society, 49–50
class, 73, 75–6, 120–1
Cleo, 11, 86
Clinton, B, 10, 79, 124, 141
Cochrane, P & Goodman, D, 178
Coles Myer, 148
Collingwood, P, 12
Columbia Broadcasting System (CBS), 13
commodification, 60, 71, 190
communicative action, 54
communitarianism, 31–32
conflict, 26, 32, 51, 107, 127, 145
Conley, D, 40–1, 70, 80, 88, 147
consensus, 26, 37, 54, 63, 138, 200
Considine, M, 37
constitutional convention, 181–5
consumer groups, 34–5
consumption, 194
Corner, J, 94–6
Cowlett, M, 123
Craftsman, The, 72
Craig, G, 61–2, 98, 116, 126, 181
crisis management, 136–7
Crossley, N, 117, 120
cross-media ownership regulations, 11, 40
Crowe, R, 57
Cunningham, S & Flew, T, 38
Curran, J, 50, 72

Dahl, RA, 25
Dahlgren, P, 31, 53
Daily Courant, The, 72
Daily Express, The, 12
Daily Mail, The, 12
Daily Mirror, The, 12
Daily Telegraph, The, 10, 77

Daily Telegraph The (UK), 12–13, 116
Day, J, 149
Dayan, D & Katz, E, 119
death penalty, 35
De Certeau, M, 193–4,
De Fleur, ML & Ball-Rokeach, SJ, 70
defamation laws, 80
deliberative democracy, 32
democracy, 28–33, 40, 117, 154, 175–6,
and everyday life, 193
Dermott, B, 9
Despoja, NS, 117
Diamond, E & Bates, S, 134
Diana, Princess, 15, 116, 124
Disney, 13
Dolly, 87
domestic violence, 203–6
Donald, J, 185
Dow Jones, 88
DMG Radio Australia, 11
Drudge, M, 10
Dukakis, M, 131

Eagleton, T, 49
'economic rationalism', 121
editorials, 36, 81
elections, 56, 161
Eley, G, 51–2
Elster, J, 32
emotion, 120
entertainment, 3, 7, 107, 175
Epstein, D and Steinberg, DL, 199
Evans, G, 86–7, 101
Evatt Foundation, 139
everyday life, 58, 108, 174, 184, 192–207

Fairclough, N, 118, 124
Fairfax, *see* John Fairfax Holdings

Falk, P, 117
Felski, R, 193
feminist movement, 63, 87–8,
    205; *see also* women's rights
film, 6, 69
Financial Times, The, 12
Fiske, J, 74, 75
Flew, T, 38
FHM, 87
Fortune, 156
Foucault, M, 26, 33, 114
Four Corners, 80
fourth estate, 19
Fox Network, 13
Foxtel, 10,
Franklin, B, 74
Fraser government, 44
Fraser, N, 51, 63
Freedom From Fear campaign,
    203–6
Freedom of Information, 147–8
freedom of speech, 13, 30, 37, 40,
    133
Freeman, C, 54, 190
French revolution, 20, 30, 155
Freud, S, 114
Friends of the ABC, 161
Friends of the Earth, 126

gaffes 121–2
Gallup, G, 156, 166
Galtung, J and Ruge, M, 82
Gatens, M, 117
Gates, B, 127
Gawiser, SR & Evans Witt, G,
    156, 164
Gay and Lesbian Rights Lobby,
    138
gay rights, 20
gender, 86–8
General Electric, 13
genetically modified foods, 35
Giddens, A, 172, 177

Ginsberg, B, 157–8
Girlfriend, 87
Glanz, D, 127
globalisation, 17, 36, 176, 186–8;
    see also anti-globalisation
global public, 62–4
global warming, 63
Goebbels, J, 113
Goffman, E, 115
Goot, M, 162, 167
Gordon, C, 33
Gordon-Smith, M, 39
Gore, A, 95
governmentality, 33–4
government media offices, 44–5,
    146–8
Gould, P, 143
Gramsci, A, 25
Grattan, M, 140–2
Gray, J, 31
Green, P, 28
Greenfield, C & Williams, P, 187
Green movement, 34
Greenpeace, 21, 35, 138
Grosz, E, 117
Guardian, The, 12–13, 116
Gutenberg, J, 69, 173

Habermas, J, 48–55, 63, 71, 72,
    86, 154–5
Hall, S, 16, 62, 97
Hall, S, et al, 160
Hallin, DC, 49, 94
Hanson, P, 15, 84, 169
Harris, M, 72
Hartley, J, 5, 20, 31, 86
Hawke government, 44, 130, 133
Hawkins, G, 62, 199,
Heater, D, 28
hegemony, 25–6, 55
Henningham, J, 40
Herald Sun, The, 10, 77
Herbst, S, 155–6

Herbst, S & Beniger, J, 156, 159
Hewitt, L, 57
Heywood, A, 31
Hill & Knowlton, 139
Hindess, B, 25
HIV-AIDS, 202–3
Hogan, P, 180
Home Beautiful, 86
Horton, W, 131
Howard government, 11–12, 40, 148–9, 178–80 189–90; *see also* Howard, J
Howard, J, 77, 106, 142, 180, 182; *see also* Howard government
Hughes, C & Wintour, P, 143

ideological analysis, 16
ideology, 26, 82, 97
image, political, 112–129
imagined communities, 6, 173
Independent, The, 12, 116
Industrial Revolution, 172
Institute of Public Affairs, 139
International Monetary Fund (IMF), 64, 127
international news agencies, 14
Internet, 17, 39, 54, 64, 69–70, 88–90, 126, 128

James, O, 125
Jamieson, K, 132
John Fairfax Holdings, 11, 88, 91, 162
Johnston, J & Zawawi, C, 135
Jones, A, 39, 102, 105–6
journalism; *see also* media
   and democracy, 19–20
   and opinion polls, 166–7
   and public relations, 135
   autonomy and control, 16–17
   commentary, 36, 77, 80–1

computer-assisted reporting, 89
investigative reporting, 80
lifestyle, 196–200
public 77–8
relationship with politicians, 42–3, 140–2
reporting 73–74

Keating government, 130; *see also* Keating, P
Keating, P, 40, 105, 120, 141; *see also* Keating government
Kelly, P, 184
Kennedy, JF, 113
Kennett, J, 168
Kernot, C, 86–7, 101
Kershaw, B, 116–7
Kettle, M, 133
Kidman, N, 180–1
Kingston, M, 84
Kinnock, N, 113
kite flying, 145
Klein, N, 126
Kress, G & van Leeuwen, T, 98
Kumar, K, 101
Kurtz, H, 141–2

Laclau, E & Mouffe, C, 20; *see also* Mouffe, C
Landes, J, 51
Lateline, 94
Laws, J, 39, 102, 104–7
leaks, 144–6
Lebovic, S, 162
Lefebvre, H, 192, 195
Lefort, C, 20
Lewinsky, M, 10
liberalism, 31–3
Literary Digest, 156
Little, G, 120
Little, J, 136
Lloyd, C, 83

Lloyd, C and Hippocrates, C, 77
Lloyd, S, 148
lobbyists, 131, 137–40
Los Angeles Times, The, 13
Luhrmann, B, 180–1
Lukes, S, 25
Lumby, C, 75, 87, 197

McCombs, ME, 16
McCurry, M, 141–2
McDonalds, 148
McKay, J, 85
McKee, A, 48, 200
McKenna, M, 184
McNair, B, 17, 98, 132, 143
McQuail, D, 59–61, 72, 159
Maddox, G, 24, 25, 28–9
magazines, 70, 85–8
Magdalinski, T, 187
Major, J, 113
Mandelson, P, 130, 141, 143
Mansfield, N, 114
market research, 153–4, 163
Marshall, TH, 30–1
Marxism, 16, 38, 195–6
masculinity, 179
Mayer, H, 133
Mayne, S, 89
media; *see also* journalism
    and democracy, 19–20, 173–6
    as business, 17, 36–7, 39, 71
    as political organisation, 36
    coaching, 122–3, 136
    criticisms, 14–19
    events, 119, 121
    interviews, 43, 45
    merits, 19–22
    ownership, 10–14, 16–17,
        39–40
    policy, 37–8
    quality and tabloid, 7, 8–9,
        12–13, 73–75, 197–8
    regulatory frameworks, 37–42

    self-help, 196–200
Media, Entertainment and Arts
    Alliance, 41
media relations officers, 44–5,
    140–2
Melbourne Express, 91
Men at Work, 179
men's movement, 87, 198
Menzies Research Centre, 139
Mercer, C, 174
Mickler, S, 105, 107–8
Midnight Oil, 187, 189
Mills, S, 166–8
Milne, G, 84
Mitchell, B, 127
Montgomery, B, 191
Morgan, G, 162
Morgan, R, 162, 166
Mouffe, C, 32–3; *see also* Laclau,
    E & Mouffe, C
multiculturalism, 178
Murdoch, K, 166
Murdoch, R, 10, 11, 13, 17, 41;
    see also News Corporation
MX, 91

Napoleon, 83
National Broadcasting Company
    (NBC), 13
National Farmers' Federation
    (NFF), 138
national identity, 61–2, 171–191
national public, 61–2
national security, 147
nation-state, 6, 171–191
    contemporary, 176–8
    historical basis, 171–6
Nazi party, 22, 113
Negrine, R, 145, 147, 160
Negt, O & Kluge, A, 53
New Idea, 86, 87
new media technologies, 17,
    38–9, 69

news agenda, 79–82, 135
News Corporation, 10, 13, 91,
    162; *see also* Murdoch, R
newspapers, 8–9, 10–11, 12–13,
    60, 69–91, 92; *see also* print
    media
  community, 70
  commuter, 90–1
  history, 70 2, 174 5
  readerships, 75 9
Newspoll, 162
news values, 18–19, 81–2, 127
New York Sun, 70
New York Times, The, 13
Nielsen, AC, 162
Nike, 190
Nimmo, D and Combs, JE, 80–1
Nine Network, 10, 84, 100; *see
    also* Packer, K; Publishing
    and Broadcasting Ltd
Nixon, R, 113
Noelle-Neumann, F., 159
Nolan, S, 179
nuclear energy, 35

Oakes, L, 83, 100 1
Oasis, 125
objectivity, 36, 81, 97, 101, 105
O'Brien, K, 100
Ofcom, 41
O'Leary, T, 142
One Nation, 169; *see also*
    Hanson, P
One.Tel, 11
online media, 9–10, *see also*
    Internet
opinion polls, 36, 48, 56,
    153–170; *see also* public
    opinion
  criticisms, 157–9
  media uses, 166–9
  types 162–6
Oprah, 95, 198–9

O'Sullivan, T, et al., 3
outbursts, 121–2

Pacific Publications, 86
Packer, K, 9, 10, 11, 16, 86;
    see also Nine Network;
    Publishing and
    Broadcasting Ltd
Panel, The, 95
Parkins, W, 198–9
parliamentary reporting,
    82–5
Parliament House, 83–4
Parsons, W, 71
party conferences, 35, 43, 45
Payne, T, 83, 84, 85
Peters, JD, 48, 52
Pink, S, 102
Policing the Crisis, 160
politics, 24–46
  political advertising, 43,
    131–4, 148–9; *see also*
    advertising
  political communication, 27,
    34–5, 43–5, 77, 79, 98, 106,
    117, 143–4
  political image, 112–129
  political information
    management, 130–149
  political organisations, 34–7
  political parties, 34–5, 43, 138,
    140, 163
  politics of trust, 121
Ponton, G & Gill, P, 26
postmodern public sphere, 86
power, 25–6, 51, 55, 106
Prescott, J, 117, 122
press, *see* newspapers; print
    media
press conferences, 35, 43, 44, 122,
    141–2
press gallery, 83–5
press photography, 97

press secretaries, *see* media relations officers
pressure groups, 34–5, 137–40
Prime Ministerial address to the nation, 44
printing, 6, 69, 71, 159, 173
print media, 6, 40, 69–91; *see also* newspapers; journalism
privacy, 17–18, 99
Productivity Commission, 8, 40
pseudo-events, 118–9
public broadcasting, 12, 62, 161
public information campaigns, 148, 200–203
public life, 53–55; *see also* public sphere
  heterogeneous basis, 55
  mediated basis, 4–7, 14, 30, 55–9, 79, 94, 118, 121, 159–61, 173–6, 178–81
  performative basis, 20–1, 52, 112–129
  visual representations, 21–2, 52, 118–22
public opinion, 36, 48, 56, 63, 79, 104, 153–170; *see also* opinion polls
  history, 154–7
  in mediated society, 159–62
public relations, 52, 95, 130, 134–7,
public sphere, 48–55, 63, 86–7, 137, 154; *see also* public life
public subjectivity, 55–9, 103; *see also* subjectivity
public, the, 36, 47–65, 79, 101–3, 183–4
Publishing and Broadcasting Ltd, 9, 10, 11; *see also* Nine Network; Packer, K

racism, 106
radio, 9, 11–12; *see also* broadcast media

characteristics, 102–4
community, 12, 60
networking, 11–12
talkback, 9, 102, 104–8
Radio National, 12
Ralph, 11, 86, 87
ratings, 60
Reagan, R, 122, 133, 164
reconciliation, 21
refugees, 62, 167, 180
republic, *see* Australian republican referendum
Reuters, 14
Reynolds, S, 203
Richardson, G, 130
Rogers, EM & Storey, JD, 201
Roosevelt, FD, 113
Rose, N, 199
Rosen, J, 77
Rothwell, N, 183
Rowe, D, 188

60 Minutes, 100
Sampson, A, 89
Sattler, H, 107
scandals, 18–19, 122
Scannell, P, 175–6, 195
Schirato, T & Yell, S, 87–8
Schlesinger, P, 177–8
Schultz, J, 19
Schulze, J, 11
Sekuless, P, 139
Seven Network, 84, 86; *see also* Stokes, K
Silverstone, R, 196
Simons, M, 84–5
Simpsons, The, 93
Sligo, F & Williams, J, 159
Smith, J, 125
social movements, 35, 138
social, the, 47–8
soundbites, 94, 121, 133
Southern Cross Broadcasting, 11
Sparks, C, 12, 13, 74–5

Special Broadcasting Service (SBS), 12
spectacle, 188
spin, 35, 43, 95, 123, 140–2
spiral of silence, 159
sport and politics, 186–7
Star, The, 12
Steketee, M, 83, 146, 162, 184
Stewart, RG & Ward, I, 138–9
Stokes, K, 86; *see also* Seven Network
Structural Transformation of the Public Sphere, The, 49, 52
subaltern counter-publics, 54, 62–3
subjectivity, 114–6, 177, 196, 198–9, 201–2; *see also* public subjectivity
suffragettes, 36
Sun, The, 12–13, 76, 77
Sydney Morning Herald, The, 11, 77, 78
Sydney 2000 Olympic Games, 62, 119, 186–91

Tam, H, 31
Tarde, G, 159
Taylor, M & Botan, C, 201
technologies of the self, 33
television, 6–7, 7–8, 14–15, 60, 112; *see also* broadcast media
  characteristics, 93–6
  history, 175–6
  news, 94
  political interviews, 96, 98–102
  reality, 197
  talk shows, 94–5
  televisual realism, 15, 95–6
  visual representations, 96–8
Telstra, 10, 79, 148
terrorist groups, 35–7

Thatcher, M, 113, 124
thinktanks, 137–40
Thompson, J, 6, 20, 114, 121–2, 172–3
Thompson, M, 12
Thorpe, I, 181
Tiananmen Square, 119
Tiffen, R, 18, 82, 83, 137, 144–6
Time, 86
Times, The, 12, 76, 116
Tomlinson, A, 188
Toohey, P, 77
Trade Practices Act, 40
trade unions, 34–5, 72; *see also* Australian Council of Trade Unions
Triple J, 12, 63, 104, 108–111
Turnbull, M, 182
Turner, B, 31
Turner, G, 178–9
Turner, G, Bonner, F & Marshall, PD, 57

United States
  magazines, 86
  media regulation, 41–2
  newspapers, 13
  political advertising 131–4
  Presidential elections, 43, 54, 95, 131–4, 156, 164
  Presidential spokesperson, 141–2
  television, 13–14
USA Today, 13
Utley, G, 14

Viacom, 13
violence, 35–6, 93; *see also* domestic violence
visibility, management of, 118–22, 126, 136
Vizard, S, 182

Wall Street Journal, The, 13, 88
Ward, I, 44
Ward, I & Cook, I, 133
Wark, M, 119, 160–1
Warne, S, 181
Warner, M, 59
Washington Post, The, 13
Weale, A, 28, 29
Wendt, J, 100
whistle blowing, 145
Whitlam Institute, 139
Wilson, H, 137, 188
Woman's Day, 87

women's rights, 20, 36; *see also* feminist movement
World Bank, 127
World Economic Forum (WEF), 64, 127, 189
World Trade Center bombing, 7, 64, 126
World Trade Organisation (WTO) 126–7
Wrong, D, 25
Wynhausen, E, 128

Young, IM, 55
youth public, 63, 108–10